Exploring Interc
Communication

Routledge Introductions to Applied Linguistics is a series of introductory level textbooks covering the core topics in applied linguistics, primarily designed for those beginning postgraduate studies, or taking an introductory MA course, as well as advanced undergraduates. Titles in the series are also ideal for language professionals returning to academic study.

The books take an innovative 'practice to theory' approach, with a 'back to front' structure. This leads the reader from real-world problems and issues, through a discussion of intervention and how to engage with these concerns, before finally relating these practical issues to theoretical foundations. Additional features include tasks with commentaries, a glossary of key terms, and an annotated further reading section.

Exploring Intercultural Communication investigates the role of language in intercultural communication, paying particular attention to the interplay between cultural diversity and language practice.

This book brings together current or emerging strands and themes in the field by examining how intercultural communication permeates our everyday life, what we can do to achieve effective and appropriate intercultural communication, and why we study language, culture and identity together. The focus is on interactions between people from various cultural and linguistic backgrounds, and regards intercultural communication as a process of negotiating meaning, cultural identities, and – above all – differences between ourselves and others.

Including global examples from a range of genres, this book is an essential read for students taking language and intercultural communication modules within Applied Linguistics, TESOL, Education or Communication Studies courses.

Zhu Hua is Professor of Applied Linguistics and Communication at Birkbeck, University of London, UK. She is editor of *The Language and Intercultural Communication Reader* (2011, Routledge).

Routledge Introductions to Applied Linguistics

Series editors:

Ronald Carter, *Professor of Modern English Language, University of Nottingham, UK*

Guy Cook, *Chair of Language in Education, King's College London, UK*

Routledge Introductions to Applied Linguistics is a series of introductory level textbooks covering the core topics in Applied Linguistics, primarily designed for those entering postgraduate studies and language professionals returning to academic study.

The books take an innovative 'practice to theory' approach, with a 'back-to-front' structure. This leads the reader from real-world problems and issues, through a discussion of intervention and how to engage with these concerns, before finally relating these practical issues to theoretical foundations. Additional features include tasks with commentaries, a glossary of key terms and an annotated further reading section.

Exploring English Language Teaching
Language in Action
Graham Hall

Exploring Classroom Discourse
Language in Action
Steve Walsh

Exploring Corpus Linguistics
Language in Action
Winnie Cheng

Exploring World Englishes
Language in a Global Context
Philip Seargeant

Exploring Health Communication
Language in Action
Kevin Harvey and Nelya Koteyko

Exploring Professional Communication
Language in Action
Stephanie Schnurr

Exploring Language Pedagogy through Second Language Acquisition Research
Rod Ellis and Natsuko Shintani

Exploring Vocabulary
Language in Action
Dee Gardner

Exploring Intercultural Communication
Language in Action
Zhu Hua

'The innovative approach devised by the series editors will make this series very attractive to students, teacher educators, and even to a general readership, wanting to explore and understand the field of applied linguistics. The volumes in this series take as their starting point the everyday professional problems and issues that applied linguists seek to illuminate. The volumes are authoritatively written, using an engaging "back-to-front" structure that moves from practical interests to the conceptual bases and theories that underpin applications of practice.'

Anne Burns, *Aston University, UK,*
University of New South Wales, Australia

Exploring
Intercultural
Communication

Language in Action

Zhu Hua

Routledge
Taylor & Francis Group

LONDON AND NEW YORK

First published 2014
by Routledge
2 Park Square, Milton Park, Abingdon, Oxon OX14 4RN

Simultaneously published in the USA and Canada
by Routledge
711 Third Avenue, New York, NY 10017

Routledge is an imprint of the Taylor & Francis Group, an informa business

British Library Cataloguing in Publication Data
A catalogue record for this book is available from the British Library

Library of Congress Cataloging in Publication Data
Hua, Zhu, 1970-
Exploring intercultural communication : language in action / Zhu Hua.
pages cm. -- (Routledge Introductions to Applied Linguistics)
Includes bibliographical references and index.
1. Intercultural communication--Study and teaching. 2. Language and culture--Study
and teaching. 3. Multicultural education--Study and teaching. 4. Applied lingustics--
Study and teaching. I. Title.
P94.7.H83 2013
303.48'2--dc23
2013006476

ISBN: 978-0-415-58550-7 (hbk)
ISBN: 978-0-415-58551-4 (pbk)
ISBN: 978-0-203-79853-9 (ebk)

Typeset in Sabon
by Saxon Graphics Ltd, Derby

To Andrew (安祝) and Timothy (天祝)

Contents

Acknowledgements

My heartfelt thanks go to all the people who have helped me with the book in many different ways. In particular, I would like to thank the following individuals:

The two series editors for their comments and advice at various stages of the book, particularly, Guy, for reading through the drafts and nudging me gently along the way, and Ron, for reassuring me that they would support me to write the book in my way.

Louisa Semlyen and Sophie Jaques of Routledge for their assistance and guidance in all editorial matters. The working relationship we have built between us through this and other projects has certainly contributed to the smooth completion of the book. I am also grateful to the anonymous reviewers whose feedback is immensely valuable

Jennifer Watson for proof-reading my chapters timely and efficiently.

Many colleagues and friends from whom I have taken advice on various matters (you know who you are!). I have cited some of the collaborative work with colleagues. It has been a pleasure to be part of the team.

My students at Birkbeck College where I work and teach. I have tried out some of the examples and tasks on the students on my courses and am very grateful for the ideas and comments they have given me.

My extended family in Beijing. Thank you, 爸, 妈, 姐, 妹, 乐乐. Thank you for your unconditional love for an absent daughter/sister/auntie over the years.

And finally, my immediate family in London. They have lived through the book project with me. Thank you, Li Wei, for allowing me to raid your bookshelves from time to time, readily providing advice at odd hours and commenting on the drafts. Thank you, Andrew and Timothy, my two wonderful boys, for understanding why Mum disappeared into her study so often and for so long, and for asking, gently but from time to time, 'Have you finished the book yet?'

Permissions

The author and the publisher would like to thank the following copyright holders for permission to reprint material:

Figure 2.1 Sequential stages of a meeting. From Handford, M. (2010) *The Language of Business Meetings*. Cambridge: Cambridge University Press (copyright: Cambridge University Press)

Figure 2.2 Small talk continuum. From Holmes, J. (2000) Doing collegiality and keeping control at work: Small talk in government departments. In J. Coupland (ed.), *Small Talk* (pp. 32–61). Harlow, England: Longman (copyright: Pearson Education).

Table 3.1 My Tempus does that. From Hoeken, H., Brandt, van C., Crijins, R., Dominguez, N., Hendriks, B., Planken, N. and Starren, M. (2003) International advertising in Western Europe: Should differences in uncertainty avoidance be considered when advertising in Belgium, France, the Netherlands and Spain? *The Journal of Business Communication*, 40(3), 195–218 (copyright: Association of Business Communication).

Figure 5.2 Diminishing stress-adaptation-growth fluctuation over time. From Kim, Y. Y. (2001) *Becoming Intercultural. An Integrative Theory of Communication and Cross-cultural Adaptation*. Thousand Oaks, CA: Sage (copyright: Sage).

Figure 9.1 Byram's ICC model. From Byram, M. (1997) *Teaching and Assessing Intercultural Communicative Competence*. Clevedon: Multilingual Matters (copyright: Channel View Publications).

Figure 10.1 Representations of development of arguments in second language learners' writing. From Kaplan, R. B. (1966) Cultural thought patterns in intercultural education. *Language Learning*, 16, 1–20 (copyright: John Wiley and Sons).

Transcription conventions

Conversation examples are re-transcribed where possible, using the following conventions in the interests of consistency. Some less relevant details are omitted. Additional transcription conventions are explained immediately after each example.

(.)	a micropause of less than one second;
(2.0)	pause of indicated length in seconds
[laughter]	paralinguistic features or comments
[ ]	Across two or several overlapping turns by different speakers. The brackets indicate beginning and end points of overlap
] [	Across two turns by different speakers, indicating 2nd turn latched onto the 1st turn without perceptible pause.
:	lengthened sound
<u>Stress</u>	underlining indicating emphasised syllable or word
?	question or rising intonation
(( ))	unclear utterance, transcriber's best guess
...	Section of transcript omitted

Series editors' introduction

The Introductions to Applied Linguistics series

This series provides clear, authoritative, up-to-date overviews of the major areas of applied linguistics. The books are designed particularly for students embarking on masters-level or teacher-education courses, as well as students in the closing stages of undergraduate study. The practical focus will make the books particularly useful and relevant to those returning to academic study after a period of professional practice, and also to those about to leave the academic world for the challenges of language-related work. For students who have not previously studied applied linguistics, including those who are unfamiliar with current academic study in English speaking universities, the books can act as one-step introductions. For those with more academic experience, they can also provide a way of surveying, updating and organising existing knowledge.

The view of applied linguistics in this series follows a famous definition of the field by Christopher Brumfit as:

> The theoretical and empirical investigation of real-world problems in which language is a central issue.

> (Brumfit 1995: 27)

In keeping with this broad problem-oriented view, the series will cover a range of topics of relevance to a variety of language-related professions. While language teaching and learning rightly remain prominent and will be the central preoccupation of many readers, our conception of the discipline is by no means limited to these areas. Our view is that while each reader of the series will have their own needs, specialities and interests, there is also much to be gained from a broader view of the discipline as a whole. We believe there is much in common between all enquiries into language-related problems in the real world, and much to be gained from a comparison of the insights from one area of applied linguistics with another. Our hope therefore is that readers and course designers will not choose only those volumes relating to their own particular interests, but use this series to construct a wider knowledge and understanding of the field, and the many crossovers and resonances between its various areas. Thus the topics to be covered are wide in range, embracing an exciting mixture of established and new areas of applied linguistic enquiry.

The perspective on applied linguistics in this series

In line with this problem-oriented definition of the field, and to address the concerns of readers who are interested in how academic study can inform their own professional practice, each book follows a structure in marked contrast to the usual movement *from* theory *to* practice. In this series, this usual progression is presented back to front. The argument moves *from* Problems, *through* Intervention, and *only* finally to Theory. Thus each topic begins with a survey of everyday professional problems in the area under consideration, ones which the reader is likely to have encountered. From there it proceeds to a discussion of intervention and engagement with these problems. Only in a final section (either of the chapter or the book as a whole) does the author reflect upon the implications of this engagement for a general understanding of language, drawing out the theoretical implications. We believe this to be a truly *applied* linguistics perspective, in line with the definition given above, and one in which engagement with real-world problems is the distinctive feature, and in which professional practice can both inform and draw upon academic understanding.

Support to the Reader

Although it is not the intention that the text should be in any way activity-driven, the pedagogic process is supported by measured guidance to the reader in the form of suggested activities and tasks that raise questions, prompt reflection and seek to integrate theory and practice. Each book also contains a helpful glossary of key terms.

The series complements and reflects the *Routledge Handbook of Applied Linguistics*, edited by James Simpson, which conceives and categorises the scope of applied linguistics in a broadly similar way.

Ronald Carter
Guy Cook

Reference

Brumfit, C. J. (1995). 'Teacher Professionalism and Research', in G. Cook and B. Seidlhofer (eds) *Principle and Practice in Applied Linguistics*. Oxford, UK: Oxford University Press, pp 27–42

Note

There is a section of commentaries on a number of the tasks, at the back of the book. The (**TC**) symbol in the margin indicates that there is a commentary on that task.

Part I

Intercultural communication in everyday life

What are the practical concerns?

This part focuses on five sites (i.e. language classroom, workplace, business, family and studying/travelling aboard) in everyday life where people from different cultural backgrounds come into contact with each other. It aims to explore how intercultural communication permeates our everyday life and what the practical issues concerning intercultural communication are in these five sites.

To start exploring what the practical concerns are, we need a working definition of intercultural communication so that we know what the scope is. Conventionally, intercultural communication studies refer to studies of both interaction between people of different cultures and comparative studies of communication patterns across cultures. There is a caveat: the notion of culture is a matter under constant debate and has a cascading effect on the concerns of the field. We will further explore the term 'culture' and the definition of the field of intercultural communication in Part III (Chapter 11). But for now, we will take 'culture' as a system of values and practices of a group or community of people.

1 Language classrooms

Language learning has been a long-standing practice throughout human history. In today's globalising world, there are increased motivations, purposes, opportunities and means to learn languages in addition to one's first language(s). The language to be learned can be the language used as the primary language of communication in their host community for minority or immigrant language speakers, a foreign language to which the learner has little direct access in daily communication, or a heritage language which younger generations in immigrant families learn from their parents or grandparents. It can also be a classical language, like Latin, or an artificial language like Esperanto, for scholarly pursuit. Whilst one can learn a new language by living amongst its speakers or studying alone using resources and technology, the most common means is attending language classes.

In this chapter, we will look at language classrooms as sites of intercultural communication. The central question we will focus and reflect on is: What are the *cultural* and *intercultural communication* issues in learning and teaching languages in the classroom? We will explore this question in three sections.

1.1 Culture and language learning and teaching (Does learning a language mean learning a culture?)

Reality link: a suitcase of stereotypes

It has been interesting to observe both as a parent and a researcher how my 12-year-old son, Andrew, is taught French in his school in London. One day he came home with a piece of homework called 'A suitcase of stereotypes'. The teacher had asked him to prepare a list of things he would bring in a suitcase if he were to visit a French pen-friend and likewise things his French pen-friend would bring for him. For the first suitcase, Andrew wrote: 'roast beef, Yorkshire pudding, fish and chips, a model of Big Ben, a model of the London Eye, a model of a black cab, PG Tips, and a jar of Marmite'. For the second suitcase, Andrew wrote 'baguette, croissant, a model of the Eiffel

Tower, frogs' legs and snails, a copy of the Mona Lisa, a model of Concorde, a model of the TGV, a model of Euro Star, hot chocolate, champagne, red wine, cheese, a French flag, and a souvenir of the Tour de France'. Clearly, Andrew's French teacher is trying to encourage her students to think about the differences between the English and French cultures. At the same time, she is very aware that there are many stereotypes associated with them.

Learning another language inevitably exposes the learner to facts and practices of a society or community where the target language is used. For many language learners, learning about the cultural traditions and practices of other people is the primary motivation for learning their language. For others, language learning provides an opportunity to interact with the people whose language they are learning and to understand their culture and traditions. Language and culture, then, become intrinsically linked to each other in this specific context. Nevertheless, issues such as what cultural and intercultural knowledge is useful in language learning and how that knowledge should be incorporated into language teaching and learning are a matter of debate, and very often shaped by motivations and purposes of language teaching or learning at an individual level, and by pedagogy, policy and politics at the macro level. We will look at several different ways in which culture is 'handled' in language teaching and learning.

Teaching culture as content

The culture-as-content approach to language teaching focuses on getting to know the language community and developing cultural awareness through fact finding. While listening, speaking, reading and writing are the core skills the language teacher aims to transmit, culture is used as a pedagogic device to capture the learner's interest or to contextualise language teaching. In the early days, culture-as-content language teaching was very much limited to literature, history and geography, which were often simplified and reduced to what Kramsch (1991) called the four Fs, i.e. food, fairs, folklore and statistical facts.

With the influence of anthropology on the study of culture since the early 1960s, it has become clear that culture does not exist merely in facts and statistical information. Instead, it is a form of sharing among a group of people. While it may be 'invisible', it exists wherever human beings conduct their social life. Here, it is particularly worth mentioning two scholars' work in describing and analysing what culture is with reference to language teaching and learning. Brooks (1960) distinguished 'Culture with a Capital C' and 'culture with a small c' in language learning. While the former refers to art, music, literature, politics, etc., the latter refers to the 'behavioural patterns and lifestyles of everyday people' which is less visible, but equally significant, if not more so. To illustrate his point, Brooks listed sixty-four cultural topics ranging from patterns of politeness to verbal taboos, from cafes and restaurants to medicine and doctors, from contrasts between city and country life to careers, etc. Nostrand (1967, 1974), on the other hand, believed that a culture is characterised by certain core elements such as values, traits and worldviews. He proposed an inventory of themes under the categories of culture, society, ecology, and the individual personality as a way of discovering emergent patterns in 'feelings, beliefs, and thought processes' of members of the target culture. For example, Nostrand (1974) defined the twelve themes of French culture as the art of living; intellectuality; individualism and civil liberty; realism and good sense; law and order; distributive justice; friendship; love; family; religion; the quest for community and loyalty to a province or region; and patriotism. Following such broader views of culture, theme-based language teaching, which explored various aspects of culture, became popular and non-fiction texts of various kinds representing everyday life such as menus, travel guides, instructions, newspaper and magazine clips, are used as teaching materials.

In addition, a range of practical teaching techniques have been developed to raise the learner's cultural awareness as part of language teaching and learning. Summaries of these techniques can be found in Hughes (1986) and Risager (2007). To give some examples:

Culture capsule   This technique encourages explicit discussion of the difference between one's own culture and the target language culture, facilitated by visual illustrations of the differences. The visual illustrations and a summary of the discussion will be put into a capsule for later use.

Culture assimilators   This technique takes the form of scenario-based questions and answers. In each scenario, a critical incident of intercultural communication (i.e. events in which there is communication breakdown or misunderstanding) is described and a number of possible explanations are given. The students would be asked to select the correct explanation.

Culture island   This technique aims to raise one's awareness about cultural differences through decorating the classroom with posters, pictures, or anything else that remind students of the target language culture, and encouraging students to think and talk about them.

Drama   This technique provides an opportunity for students to act out intercultural interactions in which misunderstandings take place, and then to explore possible explanations and solutions in the classroom.

Teaching language-and-culture: an integrated approach

The 'teaching culture-as-content' approach assumes that culture is another dimension of language learning in addition to pronunciation, vocabulary and grammar, and therefore separable from language. Since the 1980s, many language teaching professionals have called for an integrated approach to language and culture in language teaching and learning. There is a range of perspectives on what is to be integrated and how to integrate it, as well as different teaching methods and techniques. For example:

The need to integrate the learner's native culture and language into language and culture learning   Work from this perspective has moved away from a theme-oriented approach to one that gives more attention to the learner's background, such as their native culture and their motivations in learning a second or foreign language. Crawford-Lange and Lange (1984), in their attempt to define stages of an integrated approach, include a needs analysis and dialogue between what they call target and native cultures.

The need to integrate culture at all levels of language teaching   Work from this perspective is very much influenced by the notion of 'communicative competence' (Hymes, 1972), i.e. the idea that the knowledge of how to use and interpret a language in a context-sensitive and culturally appropriate way is essential to successful communication (more in Chapter 9). Crozet and Liddicoat (1997) analysed the way culture influences the spoken and the written language and demonstrated how culture, despite being invisible and not being easily accessible, is embedded in all aspects of language use, ranging from formulaic languages and rituals (such as greetings) to literacy development, and from content to structure. They also proposed a number of practical solutions regarding the integration of language and culture, including teaching culture in conjunction with language, not as something supplementary; developing new materials to expose the learner to the target culture while encouraging them to reflect on their own; revising teacher training pedagogies in light of the integrated language and culture teaching approach. Others called for authentic teaching materials to place the teaching content in 'real-world' situations or a greater emphasis on notional-functional aspects of language use.

The need to make cultural awareness an essential and integrated component of communicative competence   Byram, together with his colleagues, played an instrumental role in the so-called 'cultural turn' in language teaching in the 1990s, placing culture at centre stage in language and culture pedagogy. In his early model for foreign language teaching, Byram (1989) included cultural awareness, cultural experience and language awareness in addition to language learning. This last perspective serves as a precursor to an intercultural approach to be discussed in the next section.

Teaching culture through language: an intercultural approach

Both the teaching-culture-as-content and the integrated language-and-culture approaches have as one of their objectives to teach language learners to such a level that they can ultimately 'pass as native speakers'. From these two perspectives, the learner is either expected to accumulate knowledge about the target culture, or to familiarise herself with the cultural codes embedded in language use so that she can behave in a way similar to that of a native speaker in specific communicative contexts. The relevance of the learner's own linguistic and cultural background is often downplayed if not entirely neglected. In contrast, 'intercultural' language and culture pedagogy (e.g. Corbett, 2003) believes that the goal of language learning is not simply to develop perfect linguistic skills or amass cultural information, but to become an 'intercultural speaker' who can mediate between different cultures and different viewpoints. The objective of language and cultural learning, then, is not to replace one's native language and culture with a different language and culture, but to define for learners themselves a 'third culture' or 'third place', a term used by scholars such as Kramsch (1993, 2009b), following Peirce (e.g. 1898/1955) and Bhabha (e.g. 1994), to refer to a symbolic space where one's own and the target culture interact with each other. The idea is later captured in the notion of 'symbolic competence' by Kramsch (2009a) and will be further discussed in Chapter 9.

The intercultural perspective calls for teaching methods and techniques that de-emphasise 'norms' and favour learner-oriented approaches. The following case studies by Menard-Warwick (2008) illustrate how two English language teachers brought their transnational life experiences and consequently the intercultural approach into their teaching.

Case studies: Ruby and Paloma (Menard-Warwick, 2008)

Ruby is an English instructor in California. She was born in Brazil to bilingual English–Portuguese-speaking parents. She went to America at the age of 17, got a degree in agronomy and later a master's degree in TESOL. She now teaches English in an adult school.

In her class, the researcher, Julia Menard-Warwick, observed that Ruby largely adopted a 'cultural comparison' approach in discussion of potentially culturally sensitive topics. She asked students to talk in groups about how an issue is regarded in their own countries before reporting back to the class. When students from the same country disagreed, she encouraged them to share their ideas, thereby drawing attention to the heterogeneous nature of cultural practices. She shared her personal experiences with her students. One example is that when discussing 'eating contests' in connection with the issue of affluence and waste, she recalled her shock as a child when her 'American cousins' started a 'food fight' during their visit to her family in Brazil.

Paloma is a Chilean teacher of English as a foreign language who has worked for many years in the United States before settling back in Chile. Born in Chile, she learned English as a foreign language. She lived in America for two considerable periods of time: the first time as an MA student between 1970 and 1973 and then as a coordinator of teaching assistants in a Spanish department in a university between 1985 and 2003. She now teaches English at a university in Chile.

In her teaching, Paloma very much focused on cultural change and transformation in Chile, a perspective she believed that she gained through being away from Chile for 18 years. For example, when discussing public speaking skills and the value of fake smiling as a way of encouraging an audience, she asked the students how they felt about that. When the students began to critically evaluate the practice in the context of the relationship between professors and students, Paloma responded by drawing on her own changing identity as a teacher:

> I come from that model, in the past, that in education you do not have 'clients'. And today, that's *all* there is to it! Everything is selling a good product, selling a good education, with a methodology. And also, we become clients. I become a client of [textbook publisher] if I am a good professor, and you are my students. It's interesting that in our mind we have no concept for that. A client is only – for business.

Moving towards a critical understanding of the notion of culture in global cultural flows

In the last two decades, a growing number of scholarly works have called for a critical understanding of the notion of culture. We will examine theories of culture in depth in Chapter 11. In this section, we refer to several representative arguments specifically regarding language and culture learning and teaching. As an example, Atkinson (1999) reviewed different practices regarding the notion of culture in the field of TESOL (Teachers of English to Speakers of Other Languages). One was a 'received' view of culture which regards cultures 'in their most typical form as geographically (and quite often nationally) distinct entities, as relatively unchanging and homogeneous and as all-encompassing systems of rules or norms that substantially determine personal behaviour' (p. 626). This view often surfaces through an uncritical use of terms such as Japanese culture, Hispanic culture, American culture, etc. (criticism of the construction of Japanese culture can be found in Kubota, 1999). The second practice is the 'received-but-critical' view, which is critical of the essentialist tendency in the way the term is used, but still sees cultures in some sense as a collection of shared, possibly normative, values. The third recognises culture as a problematic concept and turns to terms such as identity as a postmodernist alternative to traditional approaches to culture. Interestingly, Atkinson called for a middle-ground approach to culture, arguing that these different views are not necessarily oppositional or mutually exclusive.

Some recent studies take account of the impact of globalisation on the relationship between language and culture. For example, Risager (2006, 2007) articulated the view that languages spread across cultures and cultures spread across languages. Among many implications of this argument on language and cultural pedagogy are: learning a language is no longer just getting to know 'the language area' in a geographical sense but the worldwide network of the target language; the target language exists not only as first language, but also second and foreign language. In a similar vein, Pennycook (2007) examined how global Englishes and transcultural flows (which are 'the ways in which cultural forms move, change and are reused to fashion new identities in diverse contexts', p. 6) form a circular process of local adaptation, transcending local boundaries and influencing other linguistic varieties, and then returning with new forms and meanings. Reflecting on the growing role of English as a lingua franca, Baker (2009) challenged the conventional way of linking one language with one culture and revealed that cultural forms, practices and frames of reference should not be viewed as pre-defined categories. Users of English were able to make use of their global, national, local and individual orientations to construct dynamic, hybrid cultural identities. The process is further explained in interculturality, which we will turn to in Chapter 12.

Task 1.1 'It will be just a bunch of facts to memorize'   (TC)

In Chavez's study (2002), she investigated how students of German at the University of Wisconsin wished to see culture embedded in their language classrooms. When asked whether foreign language culture could be taught in class and why, a student commented:

> I don't really care. It's just not that big a deal – don't you think grammar's more important? There are people in my class who have

> trouble recognizing a predicate nominative in English. [...] Don't you think that's where you should be spending your time? I know that if you start forcing German teachers to teach German culture, they won't spend enough time on it to make it part of real study like History. It will be just a bunch of facts to memorize. [...] Don't you think that learning how to think straight is more important than learning how to spit back information the way a parrot does?
>
> What concerns do you think the student raised through his comments? What do you think of these concerns in light of the discussion in this section?

To summarise and to answer the question we asked at the beginning of this section – Does learning a language mean learning a culture? – we have reviewed four approaches to language and culture pedagogy and related teaching methods. It is clear that culture has an important role in language learning, and learning a language inevitably involves learning a culture. However, the approaches differ in the degree of importance attached to culture, the ultimate goal of language learning and how language and culture relate to each other in language teaching and learning. We will further discuss the relationship between language and culture at a more theoretical level in Chapter 10.

1.2 Culture of learning (how many times do I need to practise?)

There are many stereotypes and myths regarding cross-cultural differences in learning and teaching approaches, especially concerning the dichotomy of East vs. West. Kember (2000), for example, described his initial experience of teaching in Hong Kong. He was given a list of characteristics often associated with the Chinese students there. The list included:

- rely on rote-learning
- passive
- resist teaching innovations
- largely extrinsically motivated
- have high levels of achievement motivation
- high achievers
- good at project work
- willing to invest in education.

Other common perceptions associated with Asian students generally include 'lack of criticality', 'rely on guidance and lack of independence', 'reluctance to participate in classroom discussion', etc. Whilst such stereotypical perceptions are often criticised for their inherent essentialism, they highlight an important issue, that is, learning and teaching are culturally bound and culturally meaningful activities. In other words, how people learn may depend on how members of their cultural group view learning as a social activity.

Studies of learning styles (i.e. general approaches that students use in learning a new language or any other subject) and learning strategies (i.e. the specific behaviours or techniques learners use to enhance their learning) have identified a number of contributing variables. Culture and language background is one of them, along with other factors such as language proficiency, motivation, age, gender, length of time living in the target culture and studying in the target culture. In synthesising the different factors that influence cultural variation in learning styles and strategies, Jin and Cortazzi (1998, p. 100) propose the notion of 'culture of learning', which they define as culturally based ideas about teaching and learning, including appropriate ways of learning and participating in class, relationship and communication between teachers and students, etc. In a traditional Chinese cultural model of learning, for example, language learning is more concerned with mastery of knowledge of grammar and vocabulary from two primary sources, the teacher and the textbook; the process of learning is likely to be compared to an apprenticeship whereby students and teachers have not only academic but also moral duties and responsibilities towards each other. In contrast, in a so-called 'Western' cultural model of foreign language learning, the learner often has a specific motivation for learning a language. A learner-centred pedagogy (e.g. learner autonomy and the role of the teacher as facilitator) is preferred to a teacher-centred one. The differences between these two cultural models, as Jin and Cortazzi (1998) and Scollon (2000) argued, are due to different cultural values and beliefs that are dominant in the respective societies; for example, traditional cultural beliefs and values embodied in Confucianism and Taoism in the Chinese context.

In addition to cultural beliefs, socio-economic and geopolitical factors and national and regional policies on foreign language education also impact on the learner's motivation and goals in language learning and subsequently on their learning styles and strategies. For example, the need to improve national security and defence and economic competitiveness in an era of globalisation has been an important consideration for national language policy makers. Pavlenko (2003) compared how policies on 'languages of enemies', e.g. German in the US after World War I, German and English in the Soviet Union, Russian in Hungary after World War II, were managed and adjusted in the context of a country's current allegiances and oppositions. Kramsch (2005) reviewed foreign language policies in the US after 9/11. Likewise, Charalambous and Rampton (2012), using the case of Turkish in the

Greek-Cypriot language curriculum, explored the challenges of learning languages of (past) enemies in contexts of conflict. In China, where there are an estimated 300 million learners of English, there has been growing unease about the spread of English and its impact on the Chinese language and culture (Lo Bianco et al., 2009). The Chinese government is campaigning to strengthen the status of the Chinese language nationally and internationally through a greater emphasis on the teaching of classical Chinese in schools and universities inside China and through a chain of Confucius Institutes and classrooms around the world. These language policies and initiatives from governments have important implications for learners' attitudes towards specific languages and the cultures associated with those languages.

Cross-cultural differences in learning styles, which reflect shared practices among members of a community, have sometimes been interpreted as something that applies to every individual in the community concerned. It is not an uncommon practice to use what is known about the 'typical' practice of an ethnic group to predict and explain the behaviour of all the individuals in that group. The risk of over-generalisation and over-labelling in such a practice is well demonstrated in Gutiérrez and Rogoff's study (2003). It is often observed that due to 'learning style differences', American children from newly immigrated, rural Mexican families tend to watch ongoing events attentively, while children from European-American families tend to ask for explanation. Gutiérrez and Rogoff (2003) argued that these learning behaviours need to be examined in the context of culturally mediated, historically developing practical activities rather than simply labelling Mexican children as visual learners and European-American children as aural learners. The learning behaviour in fact results from how children participate in adults' activities in these communities: while the Mexican children are encouraged to observe and take part in their families' work and activities, the European-American families tend to exclude children from adult activities.

Another challenge facing researchers into learning styles is the risk of imposing values and educational practices of Western societies or dominant cultural groups and the related 'deficit' model (i.e. treating anything that differs from dominant practices as less adequate and in need of improvement). Some myths or common misperceptions associated with a particular group of students may, in fact, be due to a lack of understanding of the nature of learning and teaching practices concerned. The assumption that Chinese students rely on rote-learning, mentioned at the beginning of this section, may well be a misinterpretation out of context of the memorising strategy used by Chinese students. Both Kember (2000) and Watkins and Biggs (1996) argue that there is some evidence that memorisation occurs in conjunction with attempts to reach understanding and therefore memorisation in Chinese culture should be understood as an effective learning strategy that helps students to excel in many subjects. Studies on learner autonomy (reviewed in Holliday, 2003) also found that despite frequently reported lack of autonomy, students of all types and from all sorts of places demonstrate considerable autonomy in classroom interaction and organising their learning through a variety of means, ranging from active engagement in different kinds of study outside the classroom to taking opportunities to clarify confusion with their teachers in the classroom. The challenge for practitioners is to recognise and encourage autonomous behaviours which often disappear or remain undetected beneath the radar of Western educational pedagogy.

Task 1.2 A little boy   (TC)

Read the following story, adapted from a poem by Helen Buckley, and discuss what the story tells you about the role of teachers in learning.

Once a little boy went to a school. He was quite a little boy and it was quite a big school. But when the little boy found that he could go to his room by walking right in from the door outside, he was happy; and the school did not seem quite so big any more.

One morning, when the little boy had been in school a while, the teacher said, 'Today we are going to make a picture.' 'Good!' thought the little boy. He liked to make all kinds: Lions and tigers, chickens and cows, trains and boats. He took out his box of crayons and began to draw.

But the teacher said, 'Wait! It is not time to begin!' She waited until everyone looked ready.

'Now,' said the teacher, 'We are going to make flowers.' 'Good!' thought the little boy, he liked to make beautiful ones with his pink and orange and blue crayons. But the teacher said, 'Wait! I will show you how.' And it was red, with a green stem. 'There,' said the teacher, 'Now you may begin.'

The little boy looked at his teacher's flower and then he looked at his own flower. He liked his flower better than the teacher's, but he did not say this. He just turned his paper over, and made a flower like the teacher's. It was red, with a green stem.

And pretty soon the little boy learned to wait, and to watch, and to make things just like the teacher. And pretty soon he didn't make things of his own any more.

Then it happened that the little boy and his family moved to another house, in another city.

And the little boy had to go to another school. This school was even bigger than the other one. And there was no door from the outside into his room. He had to go up some big steps and walk down a long hall to get to his room.

> And the very first day he was there, the teacher said, 'Today we are going to make a picture.' 'Good!' thought the little boy. And he waited for the teacher to tell what to do. But the teacher didn't say anything. She just walked around the room. When she came to the little boy, she asked, 'Don't you want to make a picture?'
>
> 'Yes,' said the little boy, 'What are we going to make?' 'I don't know until you make it,' said the teacher. 'How shall I make it?' asked the little boy. 'Why, any way you like,' said the teacher. 'And any colour?' asked the little boy. 'Any colour,' said the teacher. 'If everyone made the same picture, and used the same colours, how would I know who made what and which was which?' 'I don't know,' said the little boy. And he began to make a red flower with a green stem.

Insight into learners' preferred learning styles and strategies has important implications for how to improve learning and teaching, as witnessed in the internationalisation initiative in UK higher education in recent years. In this section, we have discussed some areas where cross-cultural differences in learning and teaching may arise. It is important to recognise that different cultural, ethnic and national groups may have different preferences towards learning and teaching practices as the result of different cultural values and beliefs, socio-economic and geopolitical factors, and related national and regional policies, among other things. At the same time, it is also equally important to avoid any 'imposed' interpretation and to recognise that these cross-cultural differences in teaching and learning styles need to be critically examined in their cultural and historical contexts.

1.3 Multicultural classrooms (Why is she so quiet in the classroom?)

Multicultural classrooms, where students from diverse linguistic, ethnic and cultural backgrounds are taught and work together, are increasingly common in schools and universities across the world. In one class in a Canadian secondary school in Duff's study (2002), half of the group are 'local' and 'NES' (native English speaker) students and the other half are immigrants and 'NNESs' (non-native English speakers). The so-called local and NES students are those who were born in Canada but of a diverse range of ethnic backgrounds, including First Nations, Punjabi, Chinese, and mixed-European Anglo-Saxon. Among the immigrants, some are old-timers who have stayed in Canada for more than 8 years and some newcomers who have newly arrived in Canada and stayed in the country no longer than 3 years. Heterogeneity of this kind can be found frequently in a language classroom or academic course and poses challenges both for communication between students and teachers and for participation in the classroom.

Classroom participation

There was a very strong feeling at the time that 'passive students' (i.e. not speaking, only listening) lacked the autonomy to learn effectively. I always felt that the best classes were the ones where the students were orally 'active', and that the less successful classes were the ones where the students were quieter and 'less active'.

(Holliday, 2003, p. 112)

'Active' participation from all the students in a classroom has very often been regarded as an optimal learning condition in teachers' professional development manuals. Although it is unclear how this teaching ideal has evolved and developed into the contemporary philosophy of teaching and learning, the consensus seems to be that active participation, strongly linked with learner autonomy, maximises learning opportunities and thus contributes to learners' success. In contrast, 'quietness', 'reticence' and 'passivity' are seen as problematic and deficient and frequently attributed to a lack of willingness to take part on the learners' behalf. Behind the facade of non-participation, there is a variety of facts and factors that lead to tension in classroom participation.

Facts first:

There is unequal distribution of turns, and differences in quality of contribution between native speakers and L2 learners (second language learners) in classroom discussion. Non-native speakers' turns tend to be brief, less forthcoming, often inaccessible to others, and provide only minimal responses (Duff, 2002, p. 305).

Despite the observed differences, the validity of often-cited binary contrast between native speakers of English and L2 learners in their participation patterns in classroom discussion is questionable. For one thing, there is significant within-group variation: each group is internally heterogeneous and includes members who are outspoken and those who are reluctant to participate (Duff, 2002); for another, one individual student's non-participation may have different causes or meanings across classroom contexts or in the same classroom context over time, and therefore needs to be examined in a specific context. When Morita (2004) compared the participation by one of her subjects, Nanako, in a number of courses, she found that Nanako reported different reasons behind her silence in various contexts. For one course, Nanako felt that she knew little about the topics of discussion which were too fast-paced for her anyway. For another course which was jointly attended by PhD and master's students, Nanako felt that she, along with other master's students who happened to be international students, was largely ignored and marginalised.

L2 learners as newcomers to second language academic communities employ various strategies and exercise their agency in negotiating their participation and membership with various degrees of success. In some cases, they may even choose to remain at the margin. Socialisation into a community is a process which involves finding out and learning new practices and negotiation with other members of the community. At the same time, learners also actively choose their strategies and influence how members of other communities interact with them. Some examples of interactional strategies that could be used by learners include speaking in earlier stages of a discussion, introducing new perspectives, or seeking support from teachers. In contrast, students who either choose or are made to remain silent also exercise their agency by various forms such as showing little interest in the topics under discussion, withdrawing completely from class discussion, or avoiding speaking when the teacher who ignores their presence is around (Morita, 2004).

Factors

A variety of factors have been reported to explain the observed lack of participation among learners. Some frequently cited ones are:

'Culture of learning' in L2 learners' first language and native culture   This may include social and cultural orientations towards speaking and disagreeing in public, making one's mind known, purpose of learning, concerns for face and group harmony, expectations towards teachers (authority vs. facilitator), etc. The culture of learning may have a cascading effect on other factors.

Language learning anxiety   Fear of not being understood or being laughed at because of accent or making language mistakes is often reported by learners. The dilemma is that the very anxiety also occurs or is exacerbated when learners are talking to people in whom they have a particular symbolic or material investment (Norton, 2001).

Linguistic proficiency   While a certain level of listening proficiency makes it easier for newcomers to become integrated into mainstream society, what counts as linguistic proficiency and its relationship with communicative competence is under constant debate in the field of second language learning and teaching.

Interactional patterns   Turn-taking behaviours, ways of articulating one's opinions, agreement, disagreement, repairs, negotiation, context-ualisation signals, silence and its significance, topic management, discourse structure, etc., can be different for L2 learners.

Content-related issues   Non-participation in some cases could be the result of limited content knowledge and, related to it, lack of content or subject-specific linguistic expressions. In other cases, learners may refrain from or resist engaging with topics with which they either feel uncomfortable or they do not want to associate publicly. The practice of drawing on students' background knowledge, cultures, experiences and opinions, found in many classrooms, needs to be examined closely.

Language ideology   Language ideology is one's beliefs about the socio-cultural values of language and its use. While for some people, learning a language used by the mainstream community is a way of opening doors and gaining better job prospects, for others, learning such a language is imposed by the society and imbued with imperialism and colonialism. This is the case with Sri Lankan students learning English in a study by Canagarajah (1993) and Guatemalan refugee informants in an ESL classroom reported by Giltrow and Calhoun (1992).

Teachers' classroom discourse style   A typical episode of classroom exchanges consists of three parts: the teacher's initiation (I), the learner's response (R) and the teacher's evaluation of the learner's response (E). In responding to the student's response, whether the teacher makes a narrow evaluation or follows up and extends the student's response makes a significant difference to the degree of participation. More participation occurs when the teacher follows up the student's response with questions for further clarification, requests for elaboration from other students, validation and acknowledgement of the student's contribution, paraphrasing and rearticulating the student's contribution, and connections with other topics.

Personalities   At an individual level, one's personality often interacts with other factors contributing to non-participation. For example, shyness or nervousness has often been reported by students who are reluctant to participate.

An act and outcome of co-construction and negotiation   One important factor which has been identified in recent years is the role of social interaction in construction of learner identity and competence. There is a reciprocal relationship between learners' perceived competence (either by themselves or by others) and participation.

Students who struggle to participate actively in discussions are seen as less competent members, which in turn makes their participation even more difficult. There might be tension between the identities learners want to construct through their language learning, consciously or subconsciously, and identities their teachers or other members of groups assign to them (Chapter 12). In some cases, learners may prefer not to be associated any more with the culture and communities they come from and wish to become members of the new community or imagined community, while in some other cases, learners may consider it more important to preserve the identity of their home culture in front of peers from the same culture and communities.

To sum up, second language learners' or speakers' participation in a multicultural classroom is subject to a number of interacting factors. While it is wrong to assume that active participation is the norm and an ideal, an inclusive and supportive environment is essential to reduce the incidence of marginalisation of L2 learners or newcomers. Some practical pedagogical advice can be found in the literature. Morita (2004) suggests the use of strategies such as explanation of the purpose of discussion, summary of the discussion from time to time, provision of background information, equitable turn-taking practices, and choice of topics appropriate and relevant to L2 learners, to help students to understand, follow and contribute to discussion. In addition, employing different types of classroom activities, such as small group work and class presentations, can also create opportunity for students with different styles of interaction and provide a chance for them to renegotiate their roles and perceived competence.

Student–teacher interaction

Interaction between the student and the teacher takes place in a variety of contexts and through different media. Contexts may differ in the degree of task- and goal-orientation: for example, both teachers and students may have specific agendas and tasks in mind in tutorials and advisory meetings, while the opposite can be said for informal occasions such as a chance encounter in the corridor or the lift, at welcome receptions, etc. Some interactions take place face-to-face while others are mediated through technologies such as email or on-line discussion forum.

Some insights into student–teacher interaction have been gained through research carried out in the traditions of cross-cultural pragmatics (the study of how the same speech act is realised in different languages) and interlanguage pragmatics (i.e. the study of the development of pragmatic knowledge and skills by non-native speakers). These studies look into how speech acts such as requests, apologies, refusals, complaints, etc., are achieved by learners of English and whether and how variables such as social distance, power status and degree of imposition make differences to the realisation of speech acts. The consensus is that there are some cross-cultural variations regarding how students as learners of English perceive the relationship between themselves and their teachers, which in turn impact on their ways of communication (also see culture of learning in the previous section). For example, a student coming from a culture which emphasises the status and authority of teaching professionals is likely to address the teacher in formal terms and initiate less in conversation. In the following, we are going to look at some of the recent research findings on email requests. In particular, we are interested in the question of whether there are differences in the way native speakers of English and learners of English make email requests, and if so, how these differences impact on the success of the communication.

Emails are one of the most frequently used ways of communication between students and teachers nowadays, especially in universities. Emails sent by students can be broadly categorised into different types in terms of their motives and topics (a review can be found in Chalak et al., 2010). Studies comparing native and non-native English speakers' email requests find that both groups of students use the same general request strategies and are aware of the need to adjust their request strategies according to the reader, i.e. authority vs. peers. However, L2 learners tend to realise the same strategies qualitatively differently. They tend to use a more restricted range of modifiers or under-use linguistic modifiers, i.e. words, phrases or sentence structures that mitigate the request such as past tense modal words (e.g. *could*), negation + tag questions (e.g. you *couldn't* help me, *could* you?), politeness marker (e.g. *please*), understaters and downtoners (e.g. *just*, *maybe*). These differences may partly reflect the developing nature of linguistic proficiency of learners of English, in particular, a lack of 'linguistic flexibility' (a term used by Biesenbach-Lucas, 2007) in selecting appropriate linguistic forms, and are partly to do with 'pragmatic mismatch', a topic we will look into further in Chapter 7.

Do these differences impact on how teachers perceive email requests from students? Some studies (e.g. Vignovic, 2010) found that although people tend to have negative perceptions of the senders of emails with language mistakes such as spelling and grammatical errors, these negative perceptions are significantly reduced when they know that the sender is a non-native speaker of the language. However, the knowledge of whether the sender is a non-native speaker of English does not make a difference in cases when there is breach of etiquette. In a study by Hartford and Bardovi-Harlig (1996), they found that teachers tend to think less favourably of those email requests that either assess staff obligations and duties inappropriately or incur greater cost than staff can afford in terms of time and commitment.

They suggest that in making requests, students should employ sufficient mitigation devices such as acknowledgement of the imposition, downgrading the request and allowing room for negotiation to address the issue of status difference and the balance between teachers' institutional role and teachers' own needs as (over-worked) fellow human beings.

In sum, research on email requests shows that in addition to differences in the range of linguistic means and degree of flexibility employed by native speakers and non-native speakers to make a request, the challenge facing students (including both native speakers and non-native speakers) is to discover 'unwritten' rules regarding what can be expected from staff and what may be over and above their duties. The challenge is even greater for those learners of English who do have adequate linguistic flexibility and are very often newcomers to an academic community. The importance of these unwritten rules or hidden knowledge about how the system or institution works in communication is also confirmed in studies that investigate student–teacher interaction in a more goal-oriented context such as tutorials, meetings with international officers and orientation sessions for new students (reviewed in Boxer, 2002). Boxer (2002) found that, compared with native speakers or local students, students who are non-native speakers or from a different culture very often miss some contextualisation cues (verbal or non-verbal signals or indicators that allow participants to evoke relevant background knowledge and social-cultural or institutional expectations that are necessary to interpret interaction) which would help them to achieve their goals in these interactions, due to lack of shared schema. The shared schema range from ways of managing small talk (i.e. informal and less goal-oriented conversations) to knowledge of how the system works, such as who should be the point of contact on what matters, the roles of different teams and units such as student centre, international office, career adviser, registry, administrator vs. academic staff, etc., in an academic institution.

1.4 Chapter summary

In this chapter, we have explored the role of culture in language classrooms. In particular, we have looked at:

- approaches in using culture to facilitate language learning;
- culture of learning;
- intercultural issues in multicultural classroom.

A final note before we move on to the next chapter. In the process of writing this chapter, in particular the last section, I have come across a range of labels in the literature describing the groups and communities I have in mind: learners, L2 learners, L2 speakers, L2 users, non-native (English) speakers, international students, overseas students, newcomers and non-locals are some of examples. Some of the terms, such as 'overseas students', seem rather old-fashioned, while some, such as 'L2 learners' or 'non-native speakers' are controversial, given the debate on the notion of norms. In the end, I have decided to use 'L2 learners' to refer to those students in a language classroom who are, at the same time, very often newcomers to an academic community. However, the heterogeneity of the groups, both native/local groups and non-native/non-local, under discussion should not be under-estimated, as the example of a Canadian secondary school class discussed at the beginning of Section 1.3 shows.

2 The workplace

In recent years, workforce diversity in terms of age, gender, cultural and ethnic background, sexual orientation, disability, religion, and educational background has become an important issue in many sectors in society. The driving need for workforce diversity not only comes from ethical and legal requirements, but also arises from the potential benefits that a diverse workforce can bring to an organisation. In a workforce diversity guide for engineering businesses commissioned by the Royal Academy of Engineering, UK, it is argued that workforce diversity can increase productivity and effectiveness of the workplace, attract talent, develop wider appeal amongst customers and open up new business. In this chapter, we will consider the workplace as a site of intercultural communication and look into opportunities as well as the challenges for intercultural communication that come with workforce diversity. We will focus on general features of the workplace, irrespective of its business, professional or organisational nature, and leave features specific to business communication to the next chapter.

2.1 Meetings (Has anything been decided in the meeting?)

Reality link: my anecdotal observation on staff meetings

Having worked in both Chinese and British universities, I cannot help noticing differences in the function of staff meetings for decision-making and the way staff meetings are conducted. In the Chinese university where I worked briefly, staff meetings are held regularly at a fixed time slot. They are mainly used to pass down information. No agenda is given prior to the meeting. It is usually expected that the head of the department, the departmental party secretary, section heads, and the trade union head will give an update on things that matter. Staff will be asked whether they have any suggestions or issues to raise, but this is usually understood to be a 'procedure' rather than an opportunity to hold substantial discussion.

Staff meetings are altogether a different game in British universities, as I soon found out when I began my first academic job in a British university. Believe me, you do not want to miss staff meetings, not only because lots of essential information is passed on, but also because many things, ranging from student placements to staff recruitment, are discussed and decided in the meetings. The meeting also has a format that makes it look 'formal' and structured: an agenda is circulated before or at the start of the meeting; a chairperson opens and concludes the discussion and summarises action points; minutes are taken and circulated afterwards among the staff members. In my first meeting, I felt the tension between two members of staff when they put forward two opposite views on a matter under discussion. The language they used in the discussion was direct and confrontational. Yet it was nothing personal, and disagreement seemed to be contained just within the meeting. They remain on friendly terms: I saw them joking with each other in the corridor soon after the meeting.

The conclusion from my own anecdotal observation above is confirmed by a number of studies which noted differences in cultural norms on the role of meetings in decision-making and management practice. A good explanation of the Chinese style of meeting, as described above, is offered in Gu and Zhu (2002). They examined the notion of 'power' in relation to various stages of meetings and argued that in China 'power' is exercised most in pre-meeting and the conclusion of a formal meeting. A person in a leadership position, not a subordinate, can initiate a meeting and decide which items are ready to be ratified or legitimised during the meeting and which items need to be negotiated further before being put on the agenda. He also needs to decide who else shall be, either nominally or in real terms, invited to the meeting as a way of showing respect for one's superiors and seeking support from those higher up. Seating arrangements are also carefully managed, either beforehand or on the day, with the highest-ranking person guaranteed a central seat in the first row on a platform facing all other attendees. The highest-ranking person is usually expected to make either an opening or closing speech.

While the Chinese model of 'power' seems to create an invisible wall between leaders and subordinates and to place them in a hierarchy, paradoxically, the Chinese style of meetings is also known for its orientation towards interpersonal harmony and relationship-building. In an example provided by Spencer-Oatey (2005a), both British and Chinese counterparts on E-China–UK e-learning programmes produced a draft agenda separately for a joint 3-day end-of-project meeting to be held in Beijing. The two draft agendas differ in the degree of formality, content, and practical arrangement. The proposed Chinese version begins with an 'opening ceremony', followed by four addresses by officials and representatives of various levels. The British version starts with a welcome speech by a Chinese representative followed by an introduction by the head of the International Division, HEFCE, UK (Higher Education Funding Council for England). In terms of content and activities, the Chinese version proposes three themes similar to the British version: e-learning policy and practice (Day 1), discussion of academic issues (Day 2), and discussion of academic issues and publication of results (Day 3). However, different from the British version, it includes three dinners, one entertainment party, and a visit to the Lao She Tea House which, named after a well-known writer, offers traditional Chinese entertainment. In terms of practicality, the Chinese version proposes an earlier start, at 9:00 a.m., than the British version which suggests 9:45 a.m. for Day 1 and 9:30 for Days 2 and 3; there is a longer lunch break in the Chinese version, 2 hours each day between 12:00 and 2 p.m., while the lunch break seems to be less 'protected' in the British version. It follows and fits between presentation slots and varies each day: 12:15–2:00 (Day 1); 12:00–1:30 (Day 2); 12:45–2:00 (Day 3). Amusingly, break time between presentations is put down as 'tea break' in the Chinese version while it is just a 'break' in the British version.

The reasons for the differences in the examples provided by Spencer-Oatey are manifold. The differences in start time and lunch break may be due to differences in traditional daily routines. In China, work usually starts at 8:00 and finishes at 6:00 with 2 hours lunch break. The long break allows people to go home if they live nearby, have a hot meal and a nap (and respite during the summer when it can be very hot). The differences in the formality and content reflect the paradoxical orientations towards *hierarchical* and *harmonious* relationship as well as the Chinese notion of hospitality. While it seems 'over the top' to outsiders, the appearance of government officials and the highest ranking official of the organisation, from the Chinese perspective, is not only an indicator of the importance and impact of the project, but also a way of showing respect and hospitality to their guests. Entertainments, meals and accompanied visits to tourist attractions are equally important, and in some cases more important than formal meetings, since they provide an opportunity for people to get to know each other and build trust and personal ties.

So far, we have looked at the function and organisation of meetings in the overall context of management and some cross-cultural variations. The question we would like to explore next is how conversation flow is structured and managed in meetings and whether there are cross-cultural variations.

Based on the Cambridge and Nottingham Business English Corpus, a business meeting usually has six sequential stages, as illustrated in Figure 2.1 (Handford, 2010). It begins with two

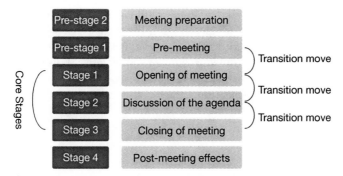

Figure 2.1 Sequential stages of a business meeting
Source: Adapted from Handford, 2010, p. 69.

optional stages: one is 'meeting preparation' including preparation and circulation of the agenda and relevant documents and follow-up from the previous meeting; and the other is 'pre-meeting' just before the meeting starts. During the pre-meeting, participants can do 'small talk', which we will discuss in the next section. Following the pre-meeting, the main meeting will be opened. There is some evidence suggesting that the pre-meeting stage can vary cross-culturally. Richard Lewis, a business communication expert, compares the beginning of meetings in several countries in terms of the length of time used to open a meeting and to get around to items on the agenda (Lewis, 2006). He observes that meetings in Germany get down to business in the shortest period of time, roughly within 2 or 3 minutes. In contrast, starting the business in meetings in Spain and Italy usually takes about 20 or 30 minutes.

Example 2.1 shows the transition from pre-meeting to the stage of opening the main meeting. Whether the issues to be discussed will be explicitly outlined and agreed upon depends on whether the meeting is external or internal, or how regularly the meeting is held. If it is a regular internal meeting, the transition stage can be short and perfunctory. If it is the first external meeting, an effort will be made to agree on the agenda and aims and objectives of the meeting. Stage 2, discussion of items on the agenda, is the core component of a meeting. It often takes the form of problem-solving, with issues put forward for discussion. Problem-solving patterns in the meeting vary in two ways: one is linear whereby each problem is solved before moving on to the next one, and the other is 'spiral' whereby issues related to a problem may occur several times at different points of the discussion (Holmes and Stubbe, 2003). Closing a meeting, similar to the opening of a meeting, can be short or 'circuitous' depending on the relationship between participants and the frequency of meetings. In Example 2.2, there is a pause of 4 seconds before the chair, S1, moves to make a meta-comment on the structure of the discussion ('facts and then decisions'). He then signals the change in the move with 'okay' and makes an evaluation. 'Thank you' at the end is used to acknowledge his/her colleagues' contribution to the meeting and the work as well as to draw the meeting to a close. The last stage, post-meeting effects, concerns the impact of the meeting on the subsequent chain of events.

Example 2.1

Internal meeting. Relationship of speakers: peer; purpose: planning; topic: strategy.

> S2:   Okay. We may as well, we may as well start. (2 seconds) So ...
>
> (Handford, 2010, p. 71)

Example 2.2

Internal meeting. Relationship of speakers: manager–subordinate; purpose: reviewing; topic: sales

> S4:   Well I've been told it is but +
> S1:   Yeah.
> S4:   +y, you never know.
>   (4 seconds)
> S1:   Very very ((inaudible)). Facts and then decisions. (1 second) Okay folks
>   (3 seconds) ((inaudible)) looking looking a bit more cheerful which is good.
>   (1 second) Thank you.
>   (13 seconds of various incoherent murmurings and rustle of papers)
>   [speakers separate]
>
> (Handford, 2010, p. 75; transcription altered slightly;
> +: speaker's turn breaks and continues)

Although some alternative models exist to the one proposed above (e.g. the opening, debating and closing phrases identified in Bargiela-Chiappini and Harris, 1997), the general consensus is that meetings constitute a distinct genre with many similar features across formal and informal meetings (Angouri and Marra, 2010). In addition to similarities in the overall structure, meetings share the following features:

- The role of the chair usually consists of opening and closing the meeting; introduction of items on the agenda; moving between agenda items; turn allocation; and sanctioning inappropriate conduct (for a review, see Angouri and Marra, 2010).

- Some significant linguistic features and key words are identifiable. These include the use of personal pronouns (such as exclusive or inclusive 'we'), back-channels (short verbal responses made by listeners such as 'yeah', 'oh'), hedges (such as 'kind of'), specialised lexis (such as abbreviations, technical terms), evaluation (such as 'it was not easy'), among others (for a review, see Handford, 2010; Poncini, 2002).
- Turn-taking dynamics are related to the status of the individuals and to their level of expertise. As Bargiela-Chiappini and Harris (1996) discovered in their study of multi-party talk in British and Italian management meetings, participants with higher status or expertise tend to have longer and more turns, and at the same time, they interrupt and are interrupted more frequently. Those with low status or less expertise rarely interrupt and are rarely interrupted.
- A number of factors appear to be significant in the participants' perceived expertise and status. The following four categories are adapted from Bunderson and Barton (2011).
  - generic social category (race, ethnicity, gender), appearance (attractiveness, height), age, education;
  - generic behaviours: language (accent, grammar), dress (wealth, style), bearing (poise, style, confidence), dominance (expressing anger, eye contact, posture expansion);
  - specific attributes: task experience (tenure, level), task qualification (certifications, specialised degree), task specialisation (job title), past task success (awards, cv);
  - specific behaviours: non-verbal task confidence (factual tone, fast/fluent speech, relaxed posture), verbal task confidence (claiming expertise), and task skill (citing facts, performing analyses, proposing solutions).

Studies on meetings involving participants with different levels of language proficiency have identified some of the challenges facing participants operating in languages other than their native languages. Cases are reported where, despite a high level of technical expertise, non-native speakers of English appeared to struggle to provide much input to meetings and fail to establish themselves as experts in meetings because of lack of familiarity with turn-taking strategies in English (Vickers, 2010). The following research summary illustrates some of the concerns facing non-native speakers in their participation and performance in meetings.

Research summary

Rogerson-Revell (2008) carried out a survey among employees of the Groupe Consultatif Actuariel Européen (GCAE), an organisation representing the actuarial profession across Europe and requiring regular face-to-face meetings with different actuarial associations they represent. The survey revealed a range of concerns and challenges facing those non-native English-speaking employees, as shown in the following sample of responses:

'Interrupting speakers spontaneously; communicating difficult messages politely; fine-tuning statements diplomatically' (German participant)

'Interrupting speakers sometimes difficult as is expressing small but important differences in opinion/feeling' (Dutch participant)

'This limitation [of vocabulary] does not prevent me from participating but I feel less efficacy in expressing my thoughts' (Italian participant)

'Difficulties in finding adequate words for immediate reaction in a discussion. Then it is easy to be quiet. This is in comparison with discussions in my mother tongue' (Swedish participant)

'Difficult to understand speakers who speak in low volume and/or too fast' (Greek participant).

Task 2.1 'OK just going back over the previous minutes'

Read the following transcription of a monthly meeting of the senior management team attended by department heads in a New Zealand production company. Answer the following questions:

1 What is the function of Lines 1–4?
2 What is the function of Line 5?
3 Who has the most turns in the conversation? Why?

Extract

Context: monthly meeting of the senior management team. Jaeson is the chair.

```
 1   Seamus:   is that now who are we waiting for
 2   Jaeson:   Just Harry
 3             (...)
 4   Seamus:   can't wait forever
 5   Jaeson:   OK (.) get into it (.) OK thanks everyone for coming
 6             along just like to welcome our newest
 7             member to the management team (.)
 8             Darryl (.) who's now serving as the er per production
 9             manager and um we have a new IS manager
10   Paul:     IS?
11   Jaeson:   yeah it's twenty first century now it's called IS
12   Harry:    IT comes after IS
13   Jaeson:   is it [laughs]
14   Paul:     [laughs]: yeah: [laughs] ism jism
15   Harry:    oh b s ism
16   Jaeson:   OK so um well (.) that's um going well anyway
17             What's what's your plan IVO as in um moving out and (.)
18             (oh) flying the coop
19   Ivo:      [laughs]: yeah: flying the coop I will be scheduling that
20             in pretty soon probably next week
...
28   Jaeson:   OK just going back over the previous um minutes
29             I there's nothing really to to cover off there was just
30             one question I had that came up last time that was
31             the um that extra shelving um
32             those last three bays
33   Harry:    they're sitting in the dock way
34   Jaeson:   okay cool (.) so they're all here
```
                                          (Angouri and Marra, 2011, p. 92)

In addition to the generic features listed above, small talk and humour both frequently occur in meetings. We will look at these two interactional activities in turn in the following sections, although our discussion is not limited to the context of meetings, but workplace discourse in general.

2.2 Small talk (Haven't seen you for ages!)

Example 2.3

Context: People are gathering for a meeting and chatting as they wait for others. Monica is the chair. Helen is to do a presentation.

1 L: I met your um friend Marie Cross last night
2 M: oh good (.) how is she
3 L: she is fine really lovely
4 M: what was that at
5 L: that was at that thing um ((the)) international institute thing (omitted)

6 M: [inhales] okay (.) this is everybody isn't it except Gavin when he comes (omitted)
7 H: just tell me Monica when you think you're ready for my bit
8 M: yeah really I just want to sort of (.) um sort of just use this opportunity
9   to get a bit of a review on where we're at with

(Holmes, 2000a, p. 40, transcription altered slightly)

In the above conversation, speakers L and M are chatting about someone L met the night before the meeting and then M moves to open the meeting with a non-verbal behaviour (i.e. inhaling) and a discourse marker 'Okay' in Line 6. Her transition move and her role as chair are acknowledged in Line 7 when speaker H responds by making a comment about the timing of her presentation which also serves as a reminder for what seems to be a previously agreed item for the meeting (i.e. her presentation). Speaker M then moves on to brief people about the aim of the meeting in Lines 8–9 and thereby opens the meeting.

Lines 1–5 show an example of small talk in the context of a structured workplace discourse. Small talk is originally defined as 'phatic communion', i.e. 'the language used in free, aimless social intercourse' (Malinowski, 1923/1999, p. 302 in 1999). Nowadays, small talk refers to non-task-oriented conversation in which speakers have no explicit transactional goals in comparison with 'core business talk'. Although small talk is often assumed to be a range of 'supposedly minor, informal, unimportant and non-serious modes of talk' (Coupland, 2000, p. 1), differences between small talk and work-related talk are a matter of degree rather than categorical. According to Holmes, small talk can occur on a continuum with 'core business talk' and 'phatic communion' at either end (Figure 2.2). Example 2.4 shows how a work-related topic can be embedded in small talk. The first couple of lines are typical social talk in which greetings are exchanged between speakers. In Line 3, in responding to Bob's reciprocal greeting, Mat brings in a work-related topic and therefore renders their social exchanges less context-free and more informative.

Figure 2.2 Small talk continuum
Source: Holmes, 2000a, p. 38.

Example 2.4

Context: Two male colleagues of equal status, Matt and Bob, in the lift.

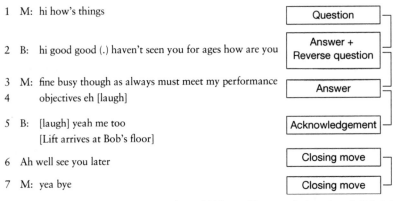

1 M: hi how's things
                                                          Question

2 B: hi good good (.) haven't seen you for ages how are you
        Answer +
        Reverse question

3 M: fine busy though as always must meet my performance
4   objectives eh [laugh]
    Answer

5 B: [laugh] yeah me too
      [Lift arrives at Bob's floor]
    Acknowledgement

6 Ah well see you later
    Closing move

7 M: yea bye
    Closing move

(Holmes, 2000a, p. 39, transcription altered slightly)

Example 2.4 also follows a typical structure of small talk, beginning with a question from the first speaker, followed by an answer along with a reverse question/acknowledgement/evaluation from the second speaker. The first speaker then responds to the second speaker's question with an evaluative comment, which the second speaker acknowledges by sharing the laughter and a comment. The conversation then closes in Lines 6–7. In small talk, the sequence of question → answer + reverse question → answer + further question/comments can go on over several turns or it can be brief or formulaic.

In terms of distribution, small talk between work colleagues usually occurs at the boundaries of working days as well as at boundaries of interaction, according to Holmes (2000a). Greetings such as 'Lovely day!', 'Great concert last night?', 'How's things?' are close to phatic communion on the continuum of small talk and obligatory for the first encounter of the day or prior to a structured meeting as in Example 2.3. It can be done in passing or in a more elaborated way, depending on the place and time of the encounter, the relationship between colleagues, or the presence of other colleagues, among other factors. Similarly, 'closing', such as 'see you later', 'give us a call', 'keep us posted', very often occurs at the end of the day or towards the end of task-oriented and structured conversation. Other types of small talk, such as office gossip, timeout chat, can occur during the break, in the corridor or in the lift where informal interaction is expected. On some occasions, small talk occurs in the middle of task-oriented talk, sometimes triggered by a topic in the talk. The shift towards small talk and back to task-oriented talk is often managed smoothly among the parties involved.

The occurrence of small talk prior to task-oriented interactions helps with consensus-building, since small talk 'warms people up socially, oils the interpersonal wheels and gets talk started on a positive note' (Holmes, 2000a, p. 49). Similarly, small talk towards the end of or during task-oriented interaction helps to tone down the transactional nature of the interaction and address addressee's positive face needs, i.e. the needs to be liked by others (Brown and Levinson, 1978; more discussion on face needs can be found in Chapter 6). While some task-related interactions may start without small talk of any kind, participants often seek to redress the lack of small talk later, a testimony to the role of small talk in 'doing collegiality', a term used by Holmes (2000a). In Example 2.5 provided by Holmes (2000a), although Kate gets down to business without any small talk at the beginning of the interaction, she apologies for being up-front at a later point by saying ' sorry I'm a bit mean doing this and when you are just walking in'. What is interesting is that Kate then goes on to make another request. This, according to Holmes, shows that small talk can also be used to 'legitimise' an extension of the interaction beyond the core business talk.

Example 2.5

Context: Kate, a relatively senior person in the organisation addresses Anne, the computer adviser, as Anne walks through the office.

1	K:	can I just talk to you
2	A:	yeah
3	K:	I got your message saying that you'd set up the Turner ID for me
4	A:	yep
5	K:	but I can't log on to it yet 'cause I don't have a (.) code number or anything

(Holmes, 2000a, p. 46, transcription altered slightly)

Task 2.2 Waiting for mother to tell me what to do!

We have discussed the various functions humour serves in this section. Re-examine Lines 11–13 in the extract in Task 2.1 and the following extract, and discuss what functions you think humour serves in the conversations.

Extract

Context: The patient is undergoing mammography and the technician is getting the patient ready.

D: medical provider; P: patient

1   D: Need your arm outta your right sleeve
2   P: Sorry. I'm just standin' here waitin' for mother to tell me what to
3   do! [both laugh]

(DuPré, 1998, cited in Ragan, 2000, p. 275)

Beyond 'doing collegiality', small talk plays no small part in the successful completion of the task in hand in settings such as healthcare contexts where it is preferable or obligatory to address social or psychological needs of patients, thus blurring and reconciling relational and transactional goals of the talk. In her review, Ragan (2000) found that small talk in the form of self-disclosure, empathic comment and humour during the interaction between female medical providers (a generic label to refer to doctors, nurses, technicians, etc., in healthcare) and female patients works effectively to get patients involved in treatment decisions and improve the possibility of patients' cooperation, thus achieving medical goals. In Example 2.6, the medical provider successfully negotiates the dosage of a prescription with her patient. Instead of explaining the pros and cons of different dosages directly, she discloses her own story of using a higher dosage with a transition move: 'I don't know if I should even be telling you this' in Line 8. She then adds to the argument with an empathic comment on the inconvenience that a low dosage but higher frequency can bring to a 'busy' college student. This leads to compliance from the patient in Line 17.

Example 2.6

D: medical provider; P: patient

1   D: Um, the typical dosage that they suggest for it is 200 milligrams
2   Five times a day. Now that's kind of a pain.
3   You can also get it in 800 milligrams that's really used
4   More for genital herpes]
5   P: [mm hmm
6   D: We just happened to have some of the 800 milligrams at home
7   From the drug rep sent us, so I took that for this, and I,
8   I don't know if I should even be telling you this
9   Because a typical dose is 200 five times a day, but I
10   Took that, I took one of those, and it just knocked it
11   out]
12   P: [really?
13   D: Yeah, and I just know for a busy college student it might

14		Be hard to take [something five times a day]
15	P:	[five times a day]
16	D:	So, if you want, we can try the 800]
17	P:	[that would be great because

(Beck et al., pp. 89–90, cited in Ragan, 2000, p. 278)

Small talk is also a site for displaying and negotiating power between superiors and subordinates in the workplace. While subordinates can negotiate the direction of conversation, it is very often the case that superiors decide the extent to which small talk can be elaborated upon and whether to include personal topics in small talk through their response or their control of turns. In Example 2.7, Tom tries to initiate small talk by commenting on the weather. However, Greg gives a minimal response. Tom then tries to bring in a personal topic. Again, Greg responds circumspectly. He then indicates his intention to proceed to business with 'now', a discourse marker often used to signal a change of topic.

Example 2.7

Context: Tom enters Greg's office to request a day's leave.

1	T:	can I just have a quick word
2	G:	yeah sure have a seat
3	T:	[sitting down] great weather eh
4	G:	mm
5	T:	yeah been a good week did you get away skiing at the weekend
6	G:	yeah we did (.) now how can I help you
7	T:	I was just wondering if I could take Friday off and make it
8		a long weekend?

(Holmes, 2000a, p. 56, transcription slightly altered)

In addition to its social functions, small talk can serve as a discourse strategy of time-filling to avoid undesirable silence while people are waiting, because it is flexible in its length, topic and degree of elaboration. This is one of the areas where considerable cross-cultural variation exists. For native English speakers, the threshold for allowable silence in conversation is about 1 second (Jefferson, 1989) and about 3 seconds in business meetings, as proposed by Handford (2010). However, the available literature suggests that for some cultures, the threshold for allowable silence in conversation seems to be considerably higher. These cultures include communities that prefer or can tolerate longer interactive pauses between turns, such as the Aboriginals in Australia who are comfortable with lengthy silences in their conversations (Eades, 2000; Mushin and Gardner,

2009); Athabaskan Indian people in North Canada whose maximum length of silence can be up to 1.5 seconds (Scollon and Scollon, 1981); the Amish in Pennsylvania (Enninger, 1987); Finns, who tend to engage in relatively less small talk (Lehtonen and Sajavaara, 1985); Japanese (Nakane, 2012); and Chinese (Giles et al., 1991, cited in Jaworski, 2000).

Cross-cultural differences also exist in the extent and weighting of small talk as well as appropriateness of topics to small talk. Lewis (2006) observed that in Spain and Italy pre-meeting small talk can be as long as 20–30 minutes, while in Germany meetings usually start without any small talk. While weather, recent activities (such as holidays, concerts, etc.) and general enquiries about things and well-being are safe topics for small talk among British English speakers, topics of a more personal nature may be acceptable in other cultures. One of the Taiwanese participants in Takaya's study (2011) gives some idea of the scope of safe topics in Chinese culture: 'When Chinese meet a new friend, they love to know "everything" about him. I mean "everything" like what his parents does, what kind of job he has, how much he earns, etc.' (Takaya, 2011, p. 21). Related to this, a study by Endrass et al. (2011) shows significant cross-cultural difference in choice of topics for small talk. Topics in small talk can be classified into three types: topics related to the immediate situation, topics related to external situations and topics about conversation partners such as their hobbies, family and career (Schneider, 1988). Using this classification, Endrass and her colleagues find that Japanese participants do not show any preference among the three types of topics in role play, while German participants talk about external and private topics more frequently than topics related to the immediate situation.

When people from different cultures interact with each other, misunderstanding can occur as the result of different norms and expectations in small talk. In the following example provided by House (2000), Brian and Andi evidently have different conceptions of what constitutes a dinner table conversation. After a brief greeting, Brian starts talking about his cooking and the food. However, instead of expanding the topic and carrying on with the small talk, Andi takes the opportunity to make a comment about the amount of the food prepared in Line 6 and then quickly extends the topic from immediate to external context in Line 8. He continues to dominate the rest of the conversation without giving in to Brian's attempt to take the floor. When asked later how they feel about the conversation, Brian is disappointed that 'his friend did not keep a real conversation going' and feels overrun by the monologue, while Andi thinks they have reflected well on the social problems although he suspects that Brian is not interested in the topic, since he says so little.

Example 2.8

Context: Brian, an American student spending a year in Germany, has cooked a meal for Andi, a German friend, who has recently helped with his German seminar paper. Andi has just arrived.

1	B:	hello Andi how are you?
2	A:	yeah fine oh fine really yeah;
3	B:	so (.) everything's ready now (.) I hope you like it (0.3) I
		have cooked it myself [so because]
4	A:	[yeah fine]
5	B:	that's what we eat in the South
6	A:	[in a loud voice] but that's so much that is <u>far too much</u> rice
7	B:	that doesn't <u>matter</u> (0.1) I have paid for it (.) and I
		have <u>invited</u> you (.) [you have]
8	A:	[no it] <u>does</u> matter it <u>does</u>
		it <u>does</u> think of the many poor people who go hungry
		and would like to eat something like that
		[well I]
9	B:	[I I] believe I (0.1) I [find]
10	A:	[I find] one should in this common
		world in which we do all live (0.2) the world in
		which we are all endowed with material goods so
		<u>un</u>equally we should at least on a small scale try to
		produce no waste no useless [waste]
11	B:	[well Andi] I am not I (0.2)
		[don't believe]
12	A:	produce [no waste] and always in our consciousness
		think that we in the rich western world…
		(monologue continues for 1.5 minutes)

(House, 2000, p. 155, transcription altered slightly)

To sum up, small talk is by no means small in its role in maintaining interpersonal relationships and facilitating social cohesion in the workplace. Understanding its cross-cultural variations and potential areas of cross-cultural differences would help to avoid unnecessary misunderstanding in culturally and linguistically diverse work teams.

2.3 Humour (I didn't get that!)

Along with small talk, humour also frequently occurs in workplace discourse, whether it is core business talk or casual talk. There are many ways of classifying different types of humour (e.g. Chiaro, 1992; Norrick and Chiaro, 2009). One way is to differentiate supportive humour from contestive humour on the basis of the pragmatic orientation of the content (Holmes and Marra, 2002). In supportive humour, participants add to, elaborate on, or strengthen the propositions or arguments of previous contributions. In Example 2.9, following Peg's comment, Clara gave a humorous example, in Line 3, to illustrate how people created hypothetical situations to 'test the water'. In Line 6, Peg showed her appreciation of the joke by elaborating on the appearance and resemblance of 'the friend of mine'. The collaborative nature of the humour is also reflected in the way the joke was constructed over a sequence of turns with contributions from several participants. In contrast, participants in contestive humour challenge the propositions of previous contributions. In Example 2.10, Eric disputed Callum's assertion by jokingly referring to Callum's failure in a computer training course and suggesting this as the reason behind the wrong document. Compared with the previous example, the humour is located in one turn only.

Example 2.9

Context: meeting of team in a commercial organisation. They are discussing how people find out about a job in which they might be interested. P: Peg; C: Clara; XF: Unidentified female voice.

1	P:	people quite often like to ask the hypothetical question just to
2		[test the water as well]
3	C:	[a friend of mine] wanted to know
4	XF:	[laughs] yeah
5		[general laughter]
6	P:	just like me in the mirror

(Holmes and Marra, 2002, p. 1687, transcription slightly altered)

Example 2.10

Context: regular meeting of a project team in a large commercial organisation. Callum has failed to update a header in a document, leading Barry to think he has got the wrong document. C: Callum; B: Barry; E: Eric.

1	C:	I definitely sent you the right one
2	B:	[laughs]
3	E:	yep Callum did fail his office management [laugh] word processing lesson
4	C:	I find it really hard being perfect at everything

(Schnurr and Holmes, 2009, p. 111)

These different types of humour serve different functions in the workplace. Similar to small talk, humour plays a range of roles in workplace discourse. The primary functions discussed below are based on Janet Holmes and her colleagues' work on language in the workplace (Holmes, 2000b; Holmes and Marra, 2002; Holmes, 2007; Holmes et al., 2009) and Rogerson-Revell (2007).

According to Holmes and her colleagues, humour contributes to social cohesion in the workplace by doing collegiality and promoting solidarity. The creative use of humour is conducive to effective workplace relationships and workplace creativity, and is very often associated with 'transformational' leadership, a type of leadership that encourages intellectual stimulation, among other factors. In Example 2.11, the speakers are discussing a recent presentation given by Yvonne. Yvonne is being modest about the presentation and humour is used subsequently as a collaborative discourse strategy responding to Yvonne's modest comments. Humour in this case helps to shift the focus of the talk from the quality of the presentation to a more personal topic.

Example 2.11

Context: monthly staff meeting of Maori organisation. Yvonne is the CEO.

```
1    Y:   I was with the um I felt the presentation wasn't that good
2         Because my briefing was about a two second phone [laughs] call
3         and so I ((didn't)) know who was going to be at the conferences
4         and (( )) what's it about I had no programme beforehand
5         so I was a bit um (( ))
6    S:                   [is this the one you had yesterday
7    Y:   yeah
8    S:   I loved it
9    Y:   oh did you
10        general laughter]
11   S:   I actually came home raving
12   Y:   [oh that's only because I had a photo of you
13   R:   [smoking
14        [general laughter]
```
(Marra and Holmes, 2009, p. 160, transcription altered slightly)

Moreover, humour can be used to defuse pressure and as a discourse strategy to 'cushion' difficult and embarrassing topics. As a face-saving strategy, humour can modify the force of undesirable acts such as disagreement, requests, or directives, either by subordinates when they challenge their superiors or by superiors when they give instructions. In Example 2.12, Sam responded to a face-threatening directive from his manager with a humorous comment which helped him and his co-workers to make light of the task. Holmes et al. (2009) point out that when directives and reprimands are used with humour, it can be harder for recipients to contest them and therefore humour can have an assertive side as well.

Example 2.12

Context: meeting of factory team. Manager is establishing objectives for the day's work. G: Ginette; S: Sam; L: Lesia.

1	G:	if you don't finish it by six o clock you're staying here until you do finish it.
2		that a good deal
3	S:	that's the good news give me the bad news now
4		[laughter]
5	L:	the er two kg is the er priority

(Holmes and Marra, 2002, p. 1690, transcription altered slightly)

In addition to these two functions, humour can be used strategically to 'include' and simultaneously 'exclude' participation in meetings and have subsequent consequences on relationships (Rogerson-Revell, 2007). Although humour is one of the interactional strategies frequently occurring in meetings, not everyone uses and responds to humour in the same way. People also use different types of humour in different workplaces and organisations with differing frequencies and styles. For those who share the same style of humour, its usage can mark group affiliation and solidarity. However, for those who do not, the use of humour can distance and exclude people from participation and divide people into 'in-group' vs. 'out-group'. This point is well articulated by Rogerson-Revell (2007), who commented that while the kind of humour shared by a group of 'male, high ranking, native English speakers' may be perceived by 'in-group' users as a bonding device, reinforcing the group's solidarity by mirroring each other's behaviour, it may be seen by people who do not use this kind of humour as signalling hierarchical superiority or exclusion.

Hay (2001) argued that understanding humour requires at least three steps: recognition, understanding and appreciation. Bell and Attardo (2010, p. 430) further identified seven levels at which a speaker may fail to engage in a humorous exchange. These are:

- failure to process language at the locutionary level (i.e. surface meaning)
- failure to understand the meaning of words (including connotations)
- failure to understand pragmatic force of utterances (including irony)
- failure to recognise the humorous frame, either missing a joke or seeing a joke where none was intended

- failure to understand the incongruity of the joke
- failure to appreciate the joke
- failure to join in the joking (humour support/mode adoption).

Since humour requires high levels of linguistic and contextual knowledge and failure can occur at various levels, expressing and appreciating humour often pose challenges when communicating with people from different linguistic and cultural backgrounds. Anecdotal evidence is abundant about how a well-intended joke can fall flat. An example was reported by Whitten (2012). During her visit to China, the head of public programmes from a well-known British art museum attempted to tell a joke in English at the start of a social event to lighten the atmosphere. She read out the following joke that she had found on the internet:

> Work rules and dress codes:
>
> If management see you are wearing expensive clothes it is assumed employees are paid too much so will not get a raise;
>
> If management see you are wearing old and worn out clothes it is assumed employees are bad at managing their money so will not get a raise;
>
> If management see you are well turned out and appropriately dressed for work it is assumed employees are paid the right amount and will not get a raise.

She was hoping that her Chinese counterparts would find the joke, which contains no word play, amusing. Instead, the group reacted to her joke with nods and positive acknowledgements while she spoke. She was left wondering about why the joke failed: was it because the group did not have the linguistic competency to fully follow her joke; was it because they did not get the stereotype of 'management' in the joke, or was it the way she delivered the joke? It turned out that because the joke was long, slow and told over a long turn, most of the people there were busy chatting with each other and had temporarily switched off attention.

Apart from the anecdotal evidence, some studies have attempted to identify and understand cross-cultural variation in humour. The edited volume by Ziv (1988) compared national styles of humour, in terms of historical development and contemporary trends, in eight countries: Australia, Belgium, France, Great Britain, Israel, Italy, the United States and Yugoslavia. It was found that sexual, aggressive, social, intellectual and defensive humour developed differently and were appreciated differently in different nations. Grindsted (1997) compared the use of humour in Danish and Spanish negotiation and found that although both groups resorted to humour to relieve tension, the strategies and patterns were different across the two groups, perhaps due to different face concerns. Some studies in psychology, using cross-cultural comparative study design, reported differences in the use of humour for coping and in the content of humour. For example, Nevo et al. (2001) found that when asked to supply a favourite joke, Singaporean students submitted a greater number of jokes with aggressive content and relatively fewer jokes with sexual content compared with their American counterparts.

2.4 Chapter summary

According to a Robert Half International survey cited in Sultanoff (1993), of all the employees fired, only 15 per cent are let go because of lack of competence. Eighty-five per cent are in fact fired because they cannot get along with others. In a diverse workplace environment, getting along with other employees requires understanding of the institutional, professional culture, of fellow employees' ways of speaking and of their practices. In this chapter, we have investigated several potential areas that have implications for intercultural communication in the workplace. We focused on interaction in the workplace in situations where activities are structured (meetings) and where the goal of talk is less task-oriented (small talk and humour). In doing so, we hope that we have demonstrated that interaction in the workplace is influenced by a variety of contextual factors such as power and social distance, genre of activity and goals of interaction, which intermix with cultural norms and expectations.

3 Business

With intensification of globalisation of the business world comes the need to appreciate the significance of languages and cultures in communication, a point well illustrated through the REFLECT project (reviewed in Bargiela-Chiappini et al., 2007) which carried out a survey of foreign language and cultural training needs in small to medium-sized businesses in the UK, Ireland, Poland and Portugal between 2000 and 2002. Their findings include the following:

a) Almost all the companies in the sample had experienced language and cultural barriers when they were working with companies from areas where languages other than their own languages were spoken.
b) About 30–40 per cent of the companies were expecting to explore new markets in the near future.
c) There were also discrepancies in the language and communication strategies across different countries, with England and Ireland showing less interest in establishing language strategies than their Polish or Portuguese counterparts.

In this chapter we are going to look at language and cultural issues in business communication. We will first look at two core business activities in which language serves as a major link and means, i.e. advertising and negotiation, before we review language and communication matters in other business contexts.

3.1 Advertising (Buy it, sell it, love it)

'Buy it, sell it, love it' is a commercial slogan for ebay, an on-line market place. Nowadays we are surrounded by advertisements which come our way through various media such as television, radio, print, internet, mobile phone and email, in various forms ranging from flyers to logos on T-shirts, and at various places such as airports, bus stops, supermarkets, etc. To serve their main purpose of influencing their audiences, advertisements have many features of their own. For example, they employ a range of attention-seeking and persuasive devices including the use of shocking or unusual images, manipulation of typographical or linguistic features, use of a combination of different means of communication such as music, pictures, paralanguage and discourse (more details on features of advertisements can be found in Goddard, 1998 and Cook, 2001). In this section, we are going to focus on advertising in a global context, in particular, cross-cultural differences in advertising in general, language matters, and the use of national images, cultural or linguistic stereotypes in advertising.

General attitudes towards publicity and advertising

Some recent studies compare cross-cultural perceptions of advertising through the internet or mobiles. Haghirian and Madlberger (2004) carried out a survey on the perception of mobile advertising among Austrian and Japanese students, and found that although mobile advertising allowed context-sensitive messages and a high level of customisation, both groups were sceptical towards mobile advertising. Despite shared concerns, the Japanese students perceived mobile advertising more positively than the Austrian students. The cross-cultural differences, according to the authors, could be due to the popularity of mobiles and the perception of mobile phones as a means of entertainment in Japan. In a separate study, Keshtgary and Khajehpour (2011) investigated factors affecting attitudes towards mobile advertising among Iranian users. They found that, similar to the Japanese students in Haghirian and Madlberger's study, Iranian users of mobiles also perceived mobile advertising, with the help of games, puzzles, jokes, songs, etc., to be entertaining. However, in contrast to the Japanese students, the Iranian users did not have negative attitudes towards mobile advertising but they preferred to be asked to consent to receiving advertisements. Incentives that offer free minutes on the phone also were found to have a more positive influence on the Iranian users' acceptance of mobile advertising.

Regulations and practices

Some countries have strict regulations on or even forbid advertising certain products such as pharmaceutical products or cigarettes. According to Usunier (2000), in Kuwait, advertisements for drugs are strictly controlled on the assumption that it is patients who ultimately bear the cost of advertising. Practices also differ on the use of foreign languages in advertisements. In France there is strict control over the use of language in advertising. The Toubon Law, which was adopted by the French Senate on 4 August 1994, requires the use of French in commercial advertisements, public announcements and product packaging along with other workplace-related activities. For advertisements originally designed in a foreign language, the minimal requirement is to add a footnote with everything translated into French. Legislation in various countries also differs concerning advertising to children and making claims that cannot be substantiated, among other things. In Canada rules have been laid out for advertisements directed at children. For example, advertisers must not use words such as 'new' or 'introducing' to describe a product for more than 1 year; advertisers may not promote craft and construction toys that the average child cannot put together; advertisers are not allowed to recommend that children buy or make parents buy their product. Schmidt et al. (1995) found that claims made by some Chinese commercials, such as promising that a particular medicine can cure a long list of diseases or health problems, would not have been allowed in the US. Usunier (2000) also pointed out the influence of religion and culture-specific practices on advertisements. For example, Quranic messages have special significance for the types of goods or products that can be promoted, when advertisements can be played (i.e. outside prayer time), what values advertisements should appeal to and how linguistic strategies may be used in advertisements (e.g. the use of Quranic phrases such as 'In the name of Allah', etc.).

Comparative advertising

Comparative advertising is the type of advertisement which explicitly or by implication identifies a competitor or goods or services offered by a competitor. It is an increasingly popular marketing strategy used by supermarkets, mobile phone, broadband and automobile companies, and banks. Comparative advertising is allowed in the United States. The rationale is that it provides information about available products and hence helps consumers to make well-informed choices. In Europe, mentioning a competitor's brand in an advertisement was illegal in many EU countries until new regulations came into force in 2000. Under the new regulations, comparative advertising is permitted if comparisons are made objectively without misleading consumers. However, objectivity is very often a matter of degree rather than being black-and-white. In a solicitor's e-bulletin, questions have been asked about whether the advertisement based on limited claims such as 'Out of 100 people we asked, 80 thought Jones's Baked Beans tasted nicest' should be considered 'objective' (Stan Turton Solicitors, 2012). In the same vein, concerns have been raised about the use of unspecified superiority claims such as 'Persil washes whiter'.

Advertising styles

Some cross-cultural differences are identified in advertising strategies and appeal. For example, according to the studies cited in de Mooij

(1998), a comparison between the UK and the United States shows that British commercials tend to contain more product information and focus on unique selling propositions, while American ones make more connection with lifestyle and use more personal testimonials. In general, British commercials adopt soft-sell strategies and make good use of humour. In contrast, American commercials tend to hard-sell, to focus on brand image and use emotive strategies. Comparison between the United States and East Asian countries confirms that countries such as Japan, China and Korea tend to use implicit or indirect appeal. Zandpour et al. (1992) summarised differences in advertising strategies between the United States, Taiwan and France in terms of different discourse styles: straight talk with dominant use of arguments in US commercials; story-telling with higher levels of information and obligation strategies in Taiwan; and symbolic association strategies in French commercials. Similarly, a study by Schmidt et al. (1995) also found that, when comparing prime-time television commercials in the US, Japan, Korea and China, American commercials use the speech act of suggestion to buy (e.g. 'Here, try this one') with the highest frequency, while Japanese commercials use the fewest number of speech acts of suggestion to buy. Korean and Chinese commercials fall in between these two styles. In contrast, other studies (e.g. Wu, 2008) reported the fusion of different styles in local advertising on the internet.

Advertising appeals and values

Since values influence one's evaluation and decision processes and play a critical role in assessing a product's attributes, advertisements often appeal to one's values in making a product particularly attractive or interesting to consumers. A number of studies have been dedicated to investigating how cultural values impact on the design and execution of advertisements. For example, Usunier (2000) reveals that although women are more likely to be shown in non-working roles than men in advertisements across cultures, differences exist in the type of gender roles to which advertisements appeal. In Swedish advertisements, women are rarely depicted in housework and childcare activities. In Malaysian television advertisements, targeted at a Muslim audience, women are typically presented as housewives whose main roles are looking after the house and children. On Singapore television, women are likely to appear in white-collar or clerical roles while men are shown in middle management roles. Family values and attitudes to the elderly are other potential areas of cross-cultural difference. In Japanese magazine advertisements, the elderly are shown more respect and given more prominent roles than their American counterparts (Javalgi et al., 1995; Mueller, 1987; both cited in Usunier, 2000,

p. 467). In anecdotal evidence cited by Goddard (1998), Volvo tried to market a car in the same way across Europe in 1990 but failed to attract much response from consumers. They then decided to use culturally specific approaches, which boosted the sale numbers significantly: promoting the car's safety to Swiss and UK audiences, its status to French audiences, its economy to Swedish audiences and its performance to German audiences. The following Task 3.1 gives an example of how advertisements for the same product can be manipulated to appeal to different values and thus reach different types of audience.

(TC)

Task 3.1 My Tempus does that

Read the following texts of two different versions of adverts (adapted from Hoeken et al., 2003, p. 205) for a watch, Tempus, which means 'time' in Latin. While the 'take home' message in both advertisements is that the watch is indispensible to a social evening or a date, two different scenarios for an evening out are presented. Which one appeals to security and which one promotes excitement? How do you know from the text? Which version is more appealing to you and why?

Table 3.1 My Tempus does that

Tonight?	Tonight?
First: dining out. In our favourite restaurant. We've gone there for years. It is a place we definitely like.	First: dining out in that new restaurant. Never been there before. Are not sure we will like it.
Then on to the theatre. A classical composition. It got rave reviews.	Then on to the theatre. An experimental composition. The reviews were mixed.
For us, an evening out is an evening in familiar surroundings – where we don't have to keep track of the time.	For us, an evening out is an evening full of new experiences – where we don't have to keep track of the time.
My Tempus does that.	My Tempus does that.

Language matters in advertising

> Language, be it through words or images, is the strongest link between advertisers and their potential audiences in marketing communications.
>
> (Usunier, 2000, p. 453)

Translating advertisements from one language to another is not a simple matter. To start with, there is a semantic issue when a brand name crosses borders. Intended connotations can be lost while unintended meanings can be brought in. Some hilarious examples can be found in Usunier (2000) and Goddard (1998). These include:

'Nova' as in the Vauxhall Nova car becomes 'won't go' (*no va*) when translated into Spanish; while Toyota's 'MR2' sounds very similar to *merde* (shit) in French.

Culturally specific symbolic meanings and connotations are also difficult to translate. The strapline for KitKat (a chocolate biscuit brand owned by Nestlé), 'Have a break, have a KitKat', is based on the tradition of eleven o'clock morning tea breaks in England dating back to before World War II when working people had their morning tea. According to de Mooij (1998, p. 61), the idea of a break is difficult to relate to other cultures where they do not have the same 'break memory' as the British. Interestingly, in 2004, the company decided to replace this strapline with 'Making the most of your break' to reflect change in society, i.e. people do not need to be reminded of the need to take a break from work for a snack. However, it reinstated the original strapline shortly afterwards.

Since most brands are originally conceived on a national level and in their source language, whether or not to keep the brand name in its original language is an important consideration in promoting a national brand name to an international audience. The following four cases show different approaches to brand management.

Case studies

Sony: rebranding to gain international recognition   Sony is often used as an example of rebranding success. Compared with its original name, Tokyo Trushin Kogyo (Tokyo Industrial Telecommunication Company), the name 'Sony' is easily memorable, recognisable internationally and plays a key role in making Sony a household name for electrical products. It is a combination of a Latin word, *sonus* meaning 'sound' or 'sonic' and an English slang word 'sonny' meaning 'little son' or 'young man'. The coined brand name 'Sony' is used to show that Sony is a 'very small group of young people who have the energy and passion towards unlimited creation' (Sony 2013, website).

Procter and Gamble: a twofold branding strategy to allow local adaptation   Procter and Gamble are the names of its founders. The company recognised that these names are difficult to pronounce in many languages and therefore simplified its name as 'P&G'. Many of its well-known products such as Pampers, Tide and Always are promoted almost independently of the company name.

Ma Griffe: preservation of the original brand name to reinforce its association with the country of origin   Keeping a brand name in its original form can invoke its association with the country of origin and bring in added value. Ma Griffe, a perfume produced by a French designer, literally means 'my designer label' or 'my claw mark'. It has several connotations such as good taste, wealth, passion and wildness. However, for English speakers who do not know the meaning of *griffe*, Ma Griffe may lose its connotations and become an index of Frenchness, thus invoking connotations of romance, sophistication, and so on (Cook, 2001).

Häagen-Dazs: deliberate use of 'foreign' brand name to manipulate perception and evaluation of product quality.   Leclerc et al. (1994, p. 263, cited in Usunier, 2000, p. 316) point out,

What do Klarbrunn waters, Giorgio di St Angelo design wear and Häagen-Dazs ice cream have in common? All three are successful brands, and all are not what they seem. Klarbrunn is not the clear mountain-spring mineral water from the German Alps that its brand name suggests; it is American water bottled in Wisconsin. Giorgio di St Angelo design wear is not the latest fashion from Milan but the product of U.S. designer Martin Price. And Häagen-Dazs is not Danish or Hungarian ice cream; It is American ice cream made by Pillsbury with headquarters in Minneapolis.

Foreign language or multilingualism found in headlines, subheads and straplines in advertising serves many purposes. Appearing in brand names or in texts alongside the source language, it indexes the cultural stereotypes, national images or language ideologies associated with the language(s) other than the source language. Under an intriguing chapter title, 'Intercultural communication for sale', Piller (2011, p. 99) states that ethno-cultural stereotypes drawn upon in advertisements are surprisingly similar across cultures:

French names have been found to carry connotations of high fashion, refined elegance, chic femininity and sophisticated cuisine in most advertising contexts outside the Francophone world. Outside the German-speaking countries, German is usually used to connote reliability, precision and superior technology. Italian is associated with good food and a positive attitude to life, and Spanish with freedom, adventure and masculinity.

There is a growing body of studies showing that other than invoking ethno-cultural or national images, English is frequently used as a marker of modernity, internationalisation and sophistication when it is used in advertisements outside English-speaking countries, for example in Brazil, China, Ecuador, France, Germany, Sweden and

Thailand. Examples of how English is used in German advertisements to create identities that are global, modern, sophisticated, fun-seeking, or attractive can be found in Piller (2001). English in advertising also acts as an agent of social change by introducing new concepts and lifestyles and appealing to its viewers with desirable identities.

There are also challenges with the use of foreign languages in advertising. In countries or regions where the national language is often seen as a symbol of unity and social cohesion, concerns have been raised about the increasing use or 'invasion' of English in advertising and media in general. The ethno-cultural or national images advertisements attempt to invoke with a foreign language can serve to 'reinforce national, linguistic, cultural and racial boundaries' (Piller, 2011, p. 100). The boundary between racism and jokes with good intentions can be very thin. 'Mock Spanish' is a case in point provided by Piller (2011). Mock Spanish phrases, such as *no problemo*, *el cheapo* or *muchos smoochos*, have become part of mainstream American discourse and their use indexes positive traits of being informal, easy-going and having a sense of fun. However, at the same time, it 'assigns Spanish and its speakers to a zone of foreignness and disorder, richly fleshed out with denigrating stereotypes' (Hill, 2008, p. 128f, cited in Piller, 2011, p. 100).

To conclude this section, cross-cultural differences exist in many aspects of advertising, as a number of empirical studies in the multidisciplinary fields of international marketing, business communication, intercultural communication and discourse-based studies discussed above have revealed. Language issues in advertising for an international market exist at different levels, ranging from brand names/straplines to a general policy of multilingualism in advertisements. These differences and matters bring challenges to international standardisation or local adaptation of advertisements.

3.2 International business negotiation (Why do they talk a lot about nothing really?)

International business negotiation, compared with other types of business discourse, is relatively well researched in some disciplines such as communication studies, management and marketing studies and social psychology, while gaining growing attention in discourse studies and business English lingua franca studies. The general consensus is that culture, among other factors, exerts influence on various aspects of negotiation, in particular, *how* to negotiate. A number of potential areas of cultural difference in how to negotiate have been identified in language-based studies as well as management, communication and anthropology studies. We are going to focus on cross-cultural differences in linguistic aspects of international business negotiation, i.e. point-making style and conversational styles, in this section first.

Point-making style, according to Garcez (1993), refers to the way that speakers make statements about their communicative intent, such as their wishes, demands, needs and so on, and provide supporting evidence. It is essentially a rhetorical style in which speakers make an argument for a case. When examining negotiation between an American importing company (Amage) and a Brazilian company (Courofatos), Garcez (1993) found that there were differences in point-making style between the two teams. In Example 3.1, Harry, the American, was arguing that if Courofatos placed an order directly with the Chinese company, the Chinese company would not be interested, since the quantity was not big enough. Garcez noted three things about the way Harry made the case in Lines 4–12. First, he used a straight line of development from the statement of communicative intent, the *point*, in Line 4, to the supporting evidence in the rest of the turn (Lines 5–12). Second, topic coherence was locally accomplished from start to finish, with each proposition being coherent with the next. Third, he also reiterated his point towards the end in Lines 11–12.

Example 3.1

H: Harry; R: Roberto

```
1    H:   I don't think you would be accomplishing anything. (2.8)
2    R:   Well, we wouldn't be talking about quantities (.) in this
3         case.
4    H:   if you can't buy quantities, they're not interested. (2.0)
5         the Chinese aren't interested. I mean if you're gonna
6         order three or four hundred pieces, ((or five hundred)) they're
7         not interested. (1.8) especially the factories we deal
8         with, which are the two biggest factories in China, (1.5)
9         they need quantities (.)? that's why we're important to them. (1.4)
10        y'know, we gave them almost two million dollars worth
11        of portfolio business? right on the spot. (1.8) that's
12        that's what they're interested in.
          [creaky voice]
13   R:   right.
```

(Garcez, 1993, p. 106, transcription altered slightly)

In contrast, in Example 3.2, Roberto, the representative from the Brazilian company, was trying to convince his American counterparts that his company could increase production. He followed a different point-making style. In Line 61, he declared his company's intention of increasing productivity. However, he did not provide any supporting evidence. His point is immediately challenged by Harry in Line 62. In his response, Roberto started with what they have done, the meetings and the trip to Argentina. His explicit statement of communicative intent only came at the end of a long turn in Line 69. Garcez argued that the Brazilian representative was using an indirect point-making style. The topical coherence was not locally accomplished, but managed upon completion of the statement of communicative intent. This kind of point-making style relies on the listener to work out the connection between the supporting evidence and the point.

Example 3.2

H: Harry; C: Charles; R: Roberto

```
55   H:   and we're gonna do more next year (1.5) and it's possible
56        we can double our volume [next year.
57   C:                            [oh, I think there's a
58        good possibility of that]
59   H:                            [the question is whether you
60        have the ability (1.8) to increase your production...
61   R:   we'd also like to do that to get there.
62   H:   well...I'm I'm not totally convinced (1.8)
63   R:   you know, as I told you, we...uh: (1.7) we had these uh
64        four meetings with uh two different engineers to talk
65        specifically about (1.5) productivity...I've been
66        down to Argentina about three or four times and because here
67        (()) our major problem is leather supply, especially leather supply,
68        you know once we have leather...here, to produce for you,
69        we are positive that we're gonna increase...uh. production. (1.3)
```
                        (Garcez, 1993, p. 107, transcription altered slightly)

In addition to differences in rhetoric styles, differences in the conversational style are reported in some studies. A study by Li et al. (2001), investigated conversational style in an international business negotiation conducted in English. Among the four people present at the negotiation, A was a native English speaker and from a large confectionery company based in the UK. He was trying to promote his company's products in the northern cities of mainland China. B was the senior manager of a supermarket and an executive member of a retailer's association in Beijing. C and D were from the marketing department of the association. When the participants were interviewed individually after the meeting, all of the Chinese participants said that the discussion went well. C and D in particular thought that their senior manager, B, was very keen on the project and were confident that a deal would be signed. However, A seemed to be less certain about the outcome and remarked upon the problems he had:

> Everything seems to take a long time. I'm used to that now, but I'm still having a little trouble with what we've agreed, or not agreed for that matter. They talk a lot, about nothing really. At the end of the day, I want to go home and tell my colleagues, yes we have a deal.

The impression of 'talking a lot about nothing really', according to the authors, partly results from a 'high involvement' conversational style adapted by the Chinese negotiators, in which a high degree of connectedness or solidarity among individuals in the conversation is shown through active participation. Among the three Chinese negotiators, B directed the conversation by using declaratives, offering opinions and drawing conclusions, almost all of which were supported and elaborated by C and D. There were many overlaps, repetitions and joint completions of utterances among the Chinese negotiators, as shown in the following Example 3.3.

Example 3.3

58	A:	Is that right?
59	B:	Because the smell. They [like the...
60	C:	[The flavour
61	D:	[Taste
62	B:	Flavour. It's very good flavour.
63	C:	很香哈]
		Hen xiang ha
		(Very aromatic)
64	B:	[对，他们就是喜欢
		Dui, tamen jiushi xihuan...
		(Correct, they truly like...)
65	D:	It's the taste.

(Li et al., 2001, p. 141)

So far we have argued that culture and language proficiency exert influence on the way negotiation is perceived and managed when the parties involved in the negotiation are from different cultural backgrounds or speak the common language used in the negotiation with different degrees of proficiency. Very often goals and purposes of business negotiations are perceived differently by different cultures. Some cultures are in favour of 'rational' behaviour in negotiating issues of conflict, and regard signing contracts and closing deals as the primary goal of negotiation. This kind of attitude towards negotiation is often referred to as 'game theory' which sees negotiation as a competition, a game in which one party wins and the other loses (for a review of the origin and development of game theory, see Leonard, 2010). Other cultures are likely to view negotiation as a process of social exchange by way of which a cooperative rather than competitive relationship needs to be established before deals can be made. It is important to understand that while business negotiation is inherently goal-oriented and the behaviour of participants reflects the nature of negotiation, it is also a balance between goal and relationship management. While we do not suppose that the Chinese would let the possibility of a good business deal slip by just for the sake of a harmonious feeling, understanding each other's ways of communication is crucial in business negotiation.

Task 3.2 Price or quantity first?

(TC)

Read the following extracts from Gimenez (2001, pp. 184–186). All the speakers are non-native speakers of English. The same seller discusses price with different buyers in each extract and there are some conflicts between him and the buyers regarding the price and quantity. How do you think the conflict is resolved in each extract? Why do you think there are differences in the way conflict is resolved? We deliberately withhold information on the cultural backgrounds of the seller and buyers. How much do you think the knowledge of seller's or buyer's cultural background would help you understand what happened in each extract? You can find out about the cultural background of the seller and buyers in the task commentaries.

Extract 1

S: How many do you want of the... [models]?
B: Well, give us your prices and we'll tell you.
S: Well, you see, the price is negotiable on the quantity.
B: Anyhow, give us your prices. If they are good, maybe we can add some more machines.
S: Well you see prices are all workable on quantities required.
B: ...[-quantity]. But it will depend on your price.
S: For that quantity I can make [-price-].

Extract 2

B: Let me tell you. There is a difference between you and your competitors.
S: Is it positive or negative?
B: Well, sometimes positive and sometimes not.
S: Let's concentrate on the positive differences and if you give me the quantities ...
B: No, I can't. I need to know the price to decide.
S: Well, prices, you see, are established on quantities, you know.
B: Well, in my case, quantities are established on prices, you know.

Extract 3

B: Are these prices CandF or Ex-works?
S: What do you think the Ex-works prices should be?
B: Well, I don't know. I can't say really. You tell me.
S: Well, these prices can be negotiable on the quantity you require.
B: I'm afraid...I'd need to know the real prices first.
S: But can't you give me an indication of the quantity you need?
B: To do that I'd need to know the real CandF and Ex-works prices.
(Gimenez, 2001, pp. 184–186, transcription altered; the name of the model, price and quantity are omitted in the first extract)

3.3 More language and communication matters (Dear Respected Mr Lin, How are you?)

Communication plays a key part in almost every aspect of a business. It is an essential means of relaying information and coordination within a business internally and of promoting a product or service externally. It also plays an indispensable role in establishing, maintaining and enhancing business relationships with a business's key stakeholders such as customers, manufacturers and collaborators. In the last two sections we have looked at two specific forms of business communication. One is advertising, an important tool of marketing communication, through which a company promotes its product, service or brand to the public. The other is negotiation, a business process which relies on interaction to establish common ground and to resolve conflict. In this section we will look at more language and communication matters in internal and external business communication.

Internal communication

For multinational corporations (abbreviated as MNCs), internal communication is often categorised into vertical and horizontal communication. The former refers to the information flow between head office and divisions/subsidiaries at different hierarchical levels, while the latter refers to the information flow between individuals at the same hierarchical level but in different units or subsidiaries. With their headquarters and subsidiaries based in different countries and the concomitant linguistic diversity among employees, MNCs need to make a decision on not only whether to adopt a common corporate language, and if so which language, but also on how to implement language policies in its management practices such as human resource management (HRM) and monitoring employee satisfaction.

It is widely accepted in the literature that the adoption of a common corporate language for internal communication has many advantages. It offsets the negative effects of language diversity, facilitates communication, coordination and central control, and creates and maintains a shared identity and vision. At a practical level, if managed well, it reduces the need for translation and incidence of miscommunication and speeds up decision-making and implementation processes. Three scenarios are identified regarding the choice of which language could be used as an official corporate language (Luo and Shenkar, 2006).

- The parent company's language: e.g. Japanese is used as the official language in the Japan-based Panasonic subsidiary in the United States.
- The local language: e.g. English serves as the official language in the Germany-based Siemens' subsidiary in the United States.
- A third language: e.g. English is used as the official language in a Mexican subsidiary of Airbus based in France.

While it is widely accepted that a common corporate language is useful for internal communication, its use and implementation often prove difficult and complex in practice. The question is which language should be used in internal communication: English or local language? If English, what English? (Louhiala-Salminen and Kankaanranta, 2012). Charles and Marschan-Piekkari (2002) investigated the use of English as the common corporate language in a Finland-based MNC, Kone Elevators. They found that although a common corporate language addressed the need to communicate to some extent, it did not solve all the problems. Some new issues emerged. These were (p. 19):

- the difficulty of finding a common language where none seemed to exist;
- comprehension problems due to insufficient translation of documentation into subsidiary languages;
- difficulty in understanding the various accents in which English was spoken internationally;

- centralisation of power into the hands of those who were able to obtain and disseminate information through knowing the official corporate language or the parent company language;
- feeling of isolation in those lacking or with inadequate skills in the corporate language.

Nickerson's study of the use of written English within British subsidiaries in the Netherlands (1998) further illustrates the problem that non-native speakers at the subsidiaries often find themselves in a situation where they have to make extra effort to accommodate the needs of their senior managers. Using data from 107 companies, she found that the majority of the subsidiaries regularly communicated with their head office in English in various forms of writing such as reports, minutes, letters and memos. What is interesting is that these reports were often written by Dutch employees and only in English (not in Dutch first and then summarised in English) despite the fact that the documents might be read by more non-native English users than native English speakers. The presence of senior English-speaking managers in subsidiaries required Dutch employees who usually did not have the benefit of additional language training to speak and write in English effectively. While communication in English was a necessity for keeping those in senior management roles informed, she noted that 'the needs (or requirements) of one powerful native speaker individual are likely to outweigh the interest of the non-native majority' (Nickerson, 1998, p. 291) and the onus was on Dutch employees.

Other context-specific factors challenging the applicability of a common corporate language across an MNC include practical and legal concerns. As reviewed in Fredriksson et al. (2006), one is employees' linguistic competence and this is particularly relevant in cases where the supposed common corporate language is a language other than English. For example, Japanese managers pay little attention to language competence when recruiting local employees because there is very often a mismatch between language skills and functional skills. Another is the local legislation. A US Fortune 10 MNC was given a substantial fine for issuing HR and benefits documents in English only to its subsidiaries in France. As a result, it is not surprising to see some hybrid language practices among MNCs, i.e. to standardise and localise simultaneously, out of recognition of the need for a common corporate language while appreciating the accompanying challenges.

A number of recommendations aimed at enhancing internal communication within MNCs have been made by Charles and Marschan-Piekkari (2002). These are:

- conducting a linguistic audit to find out potential problematic areas in communication and language use;
- making comprehension proficiency a priority as an interim measure;
- encouraging staff to understand and negotiate Global English, i.e. different varieties of English, and learn to use a variety of communicative strategies and meta-communicative expressions;
- including native English speakers in communication training as they also have and cause communication problems;
- making language and communication training a corporate-level function.

Communicating with the public and customers

In addition to internal communication, businesses also need to communicate externally with various stakeholder groups. Some issues which have implications for intercultural communication have been identified.

For example, a number of studies report language- and culture-specific features associated with the ways in which speech acts such as requests, compliments, disagreement and giving bad news are realised in business activities such as sales letters and emails (a review can be found in Yli-Jokipii, 2010). These studies generally support the argument that cross-cultural differences in concern for face, power, social distance, imposition and status often lead to different patterns in speech act realisations.

In addition to speech acts, cross-cultural differences also exist in rhetorical strategies used by businesses from different cultures in terms of organisation of arguments and orientations. The following two sales invitation letters (the first one by a New Zealand business and the second by a Chinese business) are from Zhu (2005). Both are invitation letters, but differ in the degree of formality and the way they get down to business (Table 3.2). The Chinese one uses a formal address term (e.g. 'Respected Mr Lin') and a personal greeting before introducing the background information about the exhibition. In contrast, the New Zealand one gets to the core business straightaway. It tries to impress the invitee with the scale and representativeness of the fair.

While business letters and emails are usually written with specific addressees and goals in mind, company websites are designed to provide general information about the company itself and its products or services, and to interact with customers. Some studies investigate how corporate organisations present themselves, in particular, their corporate credibility and ethos, on websites and in other business discourse such as brochures and advertisements. While HSBC's different points of view advertisement (which is available on the internet) is widely regarded as a successful example of promoting a

Table 3.2 Comparison of two business invitation letters

Dear Mr Jones,	Dear Respected Mr Lin,
Here's your personal invitation to join 6000 fellow retailers, and 280 leading industry suppliers enjoying the Christmas Stocking Fair experience.	How are you? 1998 arrived with hopes, opportunities and challenges. However, where are the opportunities and challenges? Please come and attend our 2000 Foreign Trade Expo. This event will be held December 1–3 in Beijing.
(from a company based in New Zealand)	(from a company based in China)

Source: Zhu, 2005, p. 1.

company's global standing, elsewhere less satisfactory communication has been reported. Fombrun and van Riel (2007, cited in Isaksson and Jørgensen, 2010) are critical of the communication of one US-based company which, in their view, is primarily about product and performance at the expense of communication that can showcase its leadership, citizenship, workplace, or organisation. In an attempt to unravel whether companies based in three different cultures converge or diverge from each other in their corporate self-presentation, Isaksson and Jørgensen (2010) examined discourse promoting corporate credibility on the corporate websites of sixty public relations agencies based in the UK, Denmark and Norway. They found that the PR agencies, irrespective of the countries they are based in, are more concerned with promoting their expertise than with attributes of trustworthiness and empathy. Empathy, which is defined as goodwill and caring, is paid the least attention on the websites of the PR companies based in these three countries. Some differences regarding the types of strategies used in evoking empathy are found among the companies based in the three countries. Although all the companies tend to employ the linguistic strategy of focusing on their own roles in contributing to the clients' success in business (me-attitude strategies in the authors' terms) rather than appealing to the client's role or benefit from associating with the company (you-attitude) and indicating a bond or partnership between the company and the clients (we-attitude), the British companies seem to use the 'we-attitude' type far less than their counterparts in Denmark and Norway. Some examples of linguistic strategies of invoking empathy are listed below in Table 3.3.

The discussion above reviews several key issues of internal and external communication facing business, particularly multinational corporations. For internal communication, the decisions on whether to adopt a common corporate language (and which language to

Table 3.3 Examples of linguistic strategies of invoking empathy
on company websites

Me-attitude	Our passion is for helping clients build their businesses
	We live for advertising and communication and would be delighted to help you.
You-attitude	Your advantages with POLARIS: You decide when, where and how often to train
	The team you hire will be the one that works on your account, round-the-clock
We-attitude	We set goals jointly with you…
	In close cooperation with you, we find solutions that best address your needs.

Source: Isaksson and Jørgensen, 2010, pp. 133–134.

choose) need to take into consideration the pros and cons of adopting a corporate language as well as practical and contextual constraints. For external communication, cross-cultural differences may exist in various aspects, including how a specific speech act or activity is realised, what rhetorical strategies are preferred, how information is conveyed on websites and how credibility of communication is managed.

3.4 Chapter summary

In this chapter, we have looked at two core business activities, i.e. advertising and negotiation, and reviewed language and communication matters in other business contexts. In a recent article by Neeley et al. (2012), the authors warn about the hidden turmoil of language-related 'inefficiencies' in international business, which largely remain unknown or overlooked as the use of a common language in global collaboration increases. 'English-only' policies or other similar language mandates, they argue, hurt and very often result in reduced or loss of information, apprehension, anxiety, disruption of the collaborative process, and productivity loss.

4 Family

This is a story about a mother, two daughters, and two dogs.
This was supposed to be a story of how Chinese parents are better at raising kids than Western ones.
But instead, it's about a bitter clash of cultures, a fleeting taste of glory and how I was humbled by a thirteen year old.
(From the blurb of *Battle Hymn of the Tiger Mother* by Amy Chua)

The family as a basic unit of society plays an important and indispensible role in not only fulfilling human beings' need to renew themselves as a biological species, but also in socialising the younger generation to become competent members of society. While family life is a universal human experience, cross-cultural differences have been observed, studied and reported over a range of aspects regarding family values, parenting and childrearing practices, socialisation practices and family interaction.

In her highly controversial book, *Battle Hymn of the Tiger Mother*, Amy Chua (2011), a Chinese American, described how she brought up her children in a traditional 'Chinese' way, a parenting style advocating strict discipline and obedience from children as well as sacrifice on the parents' part. Her book also gives a vivid account of how she, as a second generation Chinese immigrant and wife of a Jewish husband, navigates and lives with intercultural differences at home and in society at large. In this chapter, we shall focus on two cases where cross-cultural differences come into play perhaps at the most visible intensity, i.e. migrant families and intercultural couples who often find themselves at the crossroads of differing family values, language ideologies, norms of interaction and identities. It will be useful if you could read Amy Chua's book before reading the rest of the chapter (or the excerpts available on her website at http://amychua.com/) and preferably revisit her book after reading this chapter.

4.1 Migrant families (I'm British on paper, but am I English?)

To start with, we need to look at different types of migrants and associated terms used in the public domain and academia. The following terms and categories in Table 4.1 are synthesised on the basis of the categories presented in Castles (2000) and Knight (2002). These categories are not necessarily mutually exclusive.

In the context of this chapter, we use the term 'transnationals' to refer to those whose lives have been affected by global processes and who live outside their own countries. It includes those first- or second-generation immigrants who are sometimes described in the literature as 'transnationally affiliated individuals' (e.g. Hornberger, 2007), and those in intercultural relationships. Our main focus will be on those who have lived away from their home countries for a considerable period of time. We will leave the issue of study abroad to the next chapter.

Table 4.1 Types of migrants

Types of migrants	Examples
Educational migrants	International students, trainees and their dependents.
Highly skilled and business migrants	Professionals sent abroad by their companies (often referred to as *expatriates*, or *expats* for short) or those seeking employment outside their home countries.
Migrant workers	Seasonal, project-based or contract workers and their dependents.
Migrants for settlement	Anyone whose primary purpose in crossing geographical borders is to live in the host country for a variety of reasons: better climate or living conditions, family links, education, social mobility, etc.
Diaspora	Initially used to exclusively refer to Jews who were forced to leave their homeland, the term refers to any ethnic group or community that shares a common historical experience, a religious conviction, some tie to a specific geographic place or a strong desire to return home when the political, economic or social conditions are right (Knight, 2002, p. 15). Recently, the term has been used broadly to refer to any group that lives outside its ancestral homeland.
Irregular/illegal migrants	Those who enter a country through an illegal means and seek employment.
Refugees or asylum seekers	Those who live outside their own countries and are unable or unwilling to return either for fear of persecution or lack of basic economic and social infrastructure needed for survival following a natural disaster or war.
Return migrants or returnees	People who return to their countries of origin after staying away for a period of time.
Transnationals	People who have moved or are in the process of moving between national boundaries and have strong ties to more than one home country.

Reality link: migrants: facts and challenges

Number facts

The total number of migrants, worldwide, was estimated at 214 million in 2010, compared to 156 million in 1990. This data is supplied by the Population Division of the United Nations (website: www.un.org/esa/population/migration/index.html, accessed on 20 September 2011).

Three challenges

In his opening speech at the Third Global Forum on Migration and Development held in Athens, 4 November 2009, UN Secretary-General Ban Ki-Moon highlighted three challenges facing migrants (the speech can be accessed at www.un.org/esa/population/migration/index.html):

1 The vulnerability of migrants during the financial crisis: higher unemployment rates, concentrated in sectors hit hardest by the crisis such as construction, manufacturing and tourism, the lack of safety nets, taking blame for job losses or lower wages.
2 The impact of climate change on migration: the relocation of populations due to extreme weather conditions.
3 The 'abhorrent' practice in migrations: human trafficking.

Cultural acculturation

As transnationals leave their home countries and become residents in areas usually foreign and distant from their close relations, they often find that there are substantial differences in cultural traditions as well as social practices between what they are used to in their places of origin and those of the new local community. Some migrant communities, out of intention to preserve their cultural customs and identities, decide to adhere strictly to traditional cultural values and beliefs of their places of origin – sometimes deliberately shying away from the changes taking place in these settings as a result of globalisation and modernisation. Others, on the other hand, strive to develop new identities for themselves. Whatever the situation may be, new values and dynamics often emerge from the processes of migration and contacts with other groups. The 'cultural and psychological changes that result from the contact between cultural groups, including the attitudes and behaviours that are generated', is called cultural acculturation in the field of cross-cultural psychology (Berry et al., 2006, p. 1). In Berry's model of acculturation, he identifies four different levels of acculturation depending on two factors: degree to which native cultural identity is maintained and degree of contact with the host culture:

- Assimilation: the individual makes an effort to adopt the behaviours and practice of the host culture while discontinuing his or her native cultural identity.
- Integration: the individual desires a good level of contact with the host culture while maintaining his or her native cultural identity.
- Separation: the individual keeps a low level of interaction with the host culture while seeking a strong connection with his or her native culture.
- Marginalisation: the individual does not want to interact with the host culture nor his or her native culture.

Elsewhere, cultural assimilation has been used as a more general term to refer to the *process* by which members of an ethnic group adapt to the host culture, rather than an outcome. There have also been various models or theories of cultural diversity and assimilation. One is cultural pluralism, which advocates the co-existence of ethnic groups as separate entities. The other one is multiculturalism, which calls for interaction between different ethnic groups while maintaining and respecting each group's individual identity.

Cultural identity is an issue facing many transnationals, especially the second generation of migrant families. This second generation of migrant families, sometimes known as third culture kids (shortened as TCKs), have spent formative years in host countries (second culture) outside their parents' home countries (first culture). Being exposed to possibly conflicting sets of cultural values and practices, this generation faces unusually complex issues of developing their own socio-cultural identities and, at the same time, challenges in their transition to adulthood: e.g. being born in the host country but looking different; being seen as a member of the ethnic community by the larger society but rarely having lived in 'native' culture and not speaking the language; they may have access to their heritage culture and language to some extent, but maintaining the heritage culture and language requires tremendous effort and support from the host country. The complexity is well captured by Jerry, who was born in Jamaica and has lived in the UK since the age of 11 (Chamberlain, 2006, p. 100):

I see myself as a human being first, and as a black person of African-Caribbean descent. I've become a British person through rules and regulations, but I can never be English. Not even my sons, who were born here. They might be English on paper, but they will not... be regarded as such. They will always be Afro-Caribbean, or West Indian...And this is why I'm insistent about them learning about where their parents are from...I always thought that we've got this escape hatch in the back of our minds, those of us who are not born here, where we can always go back to. But those who are born here haven't got there, it is just stories to them, you know. But they're always being portrayed as being from somewhere else. Now, if you keep telling a young black kid that he's a West Indian, when he was born here, I mean, how does he feel?...To be apart from the society that he's grown up in?...The one thing they will feel, having gone back [to the Caribbean]...is that they realise, for the first time, that they are part of something...part of something else...[The Caribbean] will always be there for them as part of something that is their heritage.

Although having lived in the UK for most of his life, Jerry has a strong attachment to his African-Caribbean roots: he prefers his African-Caribbean identity over British identity and regards his home country as an 'escape hatch', a place where he can go back and seek protection. When it comes to his children, who were born and grew up in the UK, Jerry is aware that things are different. For them, the home country is just 'stories' that they have learned from their parents or grandparents, something unreal, abstract, constructed and lived in memory. However, being descendants of a black family, they will be attributed to and associated with that community by the larger society and therefore remain outsiders to the society where they have grown up. The answer to the problem of not being 'part of something' is, in Jerry's view, to go 'back' to visit their home country and reconnect with their heritage.

Language-related issues

Another challenge comes from language and its related issues. In recent years, a number of governments have adopted, or are proposing, a policy of making language tests mandatory for immigrants on the assumption that a certain level of proficiency in the official language is a prerequisite to integration into mainstream society. For example, in July 2010, the UK government proposed the introduction of English language tests, alongside the current citizenship test, for people applying to join spouses already living in the UK. However, for an immigrant, learning the language of the host country is not a simple task. It is a process of language socialisation, i.e. younger or newer members of communities are not only learning how to speak the language, but also socialised into the social-cultural values associated with the new ways of speaking. The analytical concept 'language socialisation' was originally developed to describe how child-directed speech helps children develop their language, communication and literacy skills in specific cultural contexts (Ochs and Schieffelin, 1995). In recent years, it has been extended beyond child development into the investigation of novices or newer members of communities or anyone who finds themself in a situation where there is an asymmetry in knowledge and power; for example, the elderly with deteriorating capacities.

Given the potential social and cultural differences, as well as differences in language ideologies (which are discussed next) and linguistic abilities between generations of speakers within diasporic families, how are members of the younger generation socialised into the social and cultural values of their parents? One of the angles to investigate the language socialisation taking place among transnational families is metalanguaging, i.e. 'talk about social, cultural and linguistic practices', or 'TSCLP' in short, between family members, initially proposed in my study of conflict talk between parent and children in Chinese transnationals' families in the UK (Zhu, 2008). It consists of comments made by participants, either explicitly or implicitly, about the degree of appropriateness of a social, cultural and linguistic behaviour in specific contexts. For example, in the following conversation, the son was asking for some money from the mother in Chinese and was immediately told off by his mother for using the informal second person pronoun.

Example 4.1

21   D: 你什么时候给我了？
         Ni shenme shihou gei wo le?
         (When did you give it to me?)
22   C: 不要老你你的。
         Buyao lao ni ni de.
         (Don't always say 'ni', 'ni' (informal form of you).)
23   D: 哎呀，您行了吧？
         Aiya, nin, xing le ba?
         (Interjection. 'Nin' (respectful form of you). Is that OK?)

                                                    (Zhu, 2008, pp. 1813–1814)

Examples such as the one above are abundant in interactions, not only at home, but also in schools. The comments may appear to be made casually or incidentally. They nevertheless reflect deep-rooted socio-cultural norms that are being passed down from generation to generation or are advocated by the host culture. In effect, they function as important means of socialising children or newer members into a specific community of practice. They provide an analytical focus and resource for researchers to understand the links between language practice and cultural values as well as language ideologies.

Language ideology is another potential area of tension between diasporic communities and the local communities as well as within the diasporic communities. Language ideology reflects speakers' views about the socio-cultural values of different languages. In transnational families, the socio-cultural values of different languages may well be different for speakers of different generations. For instance, many adult transnationals from East and South Asia in the UK regard English as the 'they-code' (Gumperz, 1982) and prefer to use their ethnic community language (e.g. Cantonese, Urdu, Punjabi) for family interaction, while their British-born children consider English as a 'we-code' and prefer it to their ethnic language. Language ideologies very often impact parents' language planning and practice with their children. In some cases, children speak their parents' native language at home and only begin to learn the mainstream language when they start school. For some families, children sometimes function as 'language brokers' to translate and interpret for their parents and communities. In other cases, however, parents may hold the belief that learning to speak the majority/ mainstream language will open a door in the job market. Out of their linguistic aspirations for their children, they might decide to bring the whole family into contact with new language varieties. For some parents, they might adjust their ways of speaking language(s) (e.g. the choice of language used with children) in order to promote desired linguistic competencies in their children either in the so-called 'heritage' language, 'mainstream' language, or 'desired' language which is different from either heritage or mainstream language. More and more successful stories of raising children speaking bilingually or multilingually have emerged in recent years. We will discuss the issue of language choice for the family and children in the next section on intercultural families.

It is important to note that some research evidence has emerged suggesting that children or younger members of communities play an active role in language socialisation such that the impact of language socialisation is bidirectional and not just on children alone. This influence of children on parents' language planning and practice is a good example of the indirect influence children can have on the language development process. We shall return to the process of language socialisation at large in Chapter 9, with a particular focus on the dialectic nature of parent–child or novice–mature member relationships.

Task 4.1 Language migrant

Anna Wierzbicka, a published author on cross-cultural pragmatics, has described her own experience as a Polish person living in Australia as a 'language migrant'. Read the excerpt below (1997a, p. 114). Relate your own experience in learning a language and adapting to new ways of speaking in a host country. Alternatively, you can interview someone who is adapting to a new culture or learning a new culture.

For example, when I was talking on the phone, from Australia, to my mother in Poland (15,000 km away), with my voice loud and excited, carrying much further than is customary in an Anglo conversation, my husband would signal to me: 'Don't shout!' For a long time, this perplexed and confused me: to me, this 'shouting' and this 'excitement' was an inherent part of my personality. Gradually, I came to realise that this very personality was in part culturally constituted.

I had to learn to 'calm down', to become less 'sharp' and less 'blunt', less 'excitable', less 'extreme' in my judgements, more 'tactful' in the expression. I had to learn the use of Anglo understatement (instead of more hyperbolic and more emphatic Polish ways of speaking). I had to avoid sounding 'dogmatic', 'argumentative', 'emotional'. Like the Polish-American writer Eva Hoffman (1989) I had to learn the use of English expressions such as 'on the one hand..., on the other hand', 'well yes', 'well no', or 'that's true, but on the other hand'.

4.2 Intercultural couples (Can love speak without words?)

Cross-linguistic and cross-cultural intimate relationships have been on the increase in recent decades. Unprecedented numbers of people cross national borders for a variety of reasons including work, study, holidays, etc. Some migrate to their chosen countries, some commute between home and the place where they work on a regular basis and some are only transient visitors. All these situations, together with growing diversity in the workforce, social networks or in local communities, mean that there are increasing chances of two persons from diverse linguistic and cultural backgrounds forming a close and intimate relationship. In a study carried out by Remennick (2009), one third of her participants met each other via work or studies, one third at the same military units and the rest met via mutual friends or internet dating sites.

Living with intercultural differences

For some time, intercultural differences have been the starting point of discussions on couples who are from different cultures. When people of difficult cultures marry, it is the meeting of two cultures, since an individual's value system reflects to some degree that of his or her culture of origin. In family studies and counselling research studies, a breakdown of the relationship between partners in an intercultural couple is often attributed to failure in the reconciliation of cultural differences between them. Instances of intercultural misunderstanding such as those below (Dodd and Baldwin, 2002) can be found frequently in the literature:

A husband from a Central Asian culture wants to send some money to his extended family back home while his wife from a Western culture sees the nuclear family as having sole ownership over time and financial resources.

The father from a Polynesian island culture prefers conformity from the children, while the mother from America prefers independent thoughts.

While seeing intercultural marriage as a meeting place of two cultures is intuitively appealing, recent years have seen a critical evaluation of the role of intercultural differences in the everyday lives of intercultural couples. Some studies have advocated that instead of seeing intercultural differences as an attributable variable, everyday practices of intercultural couples should be examined *progressively* over the time of the relationship (Piller, 2011) and through nuanced analysis of bilingual talk (for example, see Takigawa, 2010, for language expertise as a source of dispute in bilingual couple talk). Couples *do* intercultural differences through a variety of language and communication strategies.

In her publication in 2011, Piller argued,

Partners in an intimate relationship do not engage in intercultural communication by virtue of the fact that they come from different national and/or linguistic backgrounds, but by virtue of what they orient to. Intimate intercultural communication only takes place if partners orient to cultural difference, do culture and construct culture as a category.

(Piller, 2011, p. 114)

Her main supporting arguments for this *progressive* account are:

- Intercultural communication is not relevant all the time for intercultural couples, although it may be prominent in the early stages of a relationship.
- Intercultural couples tend to find themselves 'progressively less likely to frame their communication as intercultural as the relationship becomes more established'.
- Intercultural couples seek to construct similarities, deconstruct differences as well as to *accent* differences through their language and communication strategies.
- Some existing evidence suggests that for some couples, they tend to see themselves as individuals but their partners as representative of a different culture.

These arguments suggest that an alternative view of the role of intercultural differences in intercultural couples is in order. Its essence is to see intercultural differences as something to which people orient through interaction and practice, not as a precondition. We shall discuss this view further in Chapter 12.

Language choice

Language can make or break a relationship (Tannen, 1986). For intercultural couples from different linguistic backgrounds, the choice of which language to use as the language of communication between partners, with children, extended family, social network, local community, etc., is not a simple matter. One essential question is how intercultural couples decide which language to use and what factors contribute to their language choice.

For some years, it has been a common view that bilingual couples prefer the majority language, i.e. the dominant language where they live. For example, if a Russian woman marries a Turkish man and lives in Istanbul, the language of choice is likely to be Turkish. In fact, a preference towards the majority language among bilingual couples has been frequently cited as one of the driving forces behind language shift observed in many societies. However, some recent research, in particular Piller (2002, pp. 178–179) challenges this view on three grounds. One is that language choice, in real life, is not made across the board, but is sensitive to context and differs across various domains and genres of social interaction. The language choice may be different when couples are having a private conversation from the occasion when their children or members of their extended families are present. Likewise, couples may choose different languages when they have arguments compared to occasions when they celebrate their wedding anniversaries.

Second, the assumption that one language needs to be chosen over the other by a bilingual couple does not reflect the range of choices available or *made* available to them in reality. Apart from context-sensitive choices mentioned above, bilingual couples can choose not just between the two languages spoken by the partners, but between the two languages, a third shared language (if any) and mixed varieties, and between production, comprehension and a varied combination.

Third, although the place of living remains an important factor, other factors are equally and sometimes more important in language choice. A more nuanced and complex picture has emerged in the literature. For example, level of language proficiency may be significant. Good proficiency in the language of communication brings more choice and freedom in fulfilling one's communication needs, be it transactional or relational. In some cases, the language proficiency of partners decides which language can serve as the shared language. In Yamamoto's study of Japanese and American couples living in Japan (1995, cited in Piller, 2002), 65 per cent of her participants either exclusively or mainly use one language (i.e. Japanese or English), and among these 'monolingual households', two thirds use English rather than Japanese. The preference for English, an apparent minority language in the context of the study, can be attributed to the fact that Japanese-speaking partners appear more proficient and confident with their English than their English-speaking partners with Japanese.

Language proficiency aside, language choice is also about the power of the languages chosen, the dependency between partners, the language ideologies of the couples involved and the society in which they are living. The case is well exemplified in Walters's study (1996) of Anglophone wives in Tunisia, where varieties of Arabic and French are used. For these women, there are practical difficulties in learning Arabic: significant typological differences as a Semitic language; very limited teaching materials; busy schedules of the women as wives, mothers, and/or professionals. Despite these difficulties, all the women in her study learned some Tunisian Arabic. Some reported that they learned to speak Arabic so that they could communicate with their mother-in-law and other female relatives who not only had considerable influence on their husbands but also took the responsibility of socialising them into Tunisian society. There were also exceptions. One woman reported that she had made a 'strategic' decision not to spend a significant amount of time on learning Arabic so that she was not drawn into family conflicts and remained dependent on her husband, which she believed helped to balance power between herself and her husband. Some women also commented that their husbands were of two minds about their Arabic learning. While some husbands were keen to teach their wives Arabic, some husbands altogether discouraged their wives from learning Arabic for fear of losing the symbolic value these Anglophone women have as a 'trophy' wife in Tunisian society where a Tunisian man marrying a Western wife is highly valued.

In addition to these factors, Piller (2002) also mentioned that language choice could be just a shared habit, developed and subject to change over the duration of a relationship. The choice of the language of the partner who migrates to the place of the other partner can also be a means of compensation for the sacrifice he or she has made.

While there is an array of factors behind the language choice of partners when they interact with each other, there seems to be a clearer picture regarding the language choice for children of a bilingual marriage. Language choices of the children of bilingual parents are often influenced by the linguistic repertoire and language use of parents or the main carers of the children, the language(s) used by the school or nursery, and the sociolinguistic situation of the community at large and of the minority language community. As discussed earlier in this section, linguistic repertoires and language use are varied among bilingual couples: in some families, both partners are bilingual and they may decide to use one of the languages or both languages interchangeably as the primary language of family communication; in other families, one of the partners is bilingual and the other is monolingual and they may decide to use the monolingual one as the family language. The language of communication may also vary across different contexts. One couple may choose to use a different language to communicate, say, among the extended family, from the language they use when they are alone. The linguistic repertoire of a child's carer (who could be a grandparent, nanny or a nursery) also matters. Some research suggests that gender can make a difference to the language choice of their children: if the mother speaks a minority language, there is a higher success rate for children speaking the minority language. The language(s) used by the school or nursery also plays a key role in children's language choice. For example, a child of Mexican-American parentage learns Spanish at home, then goes to an English-speaking nursery or school and learns English as a second language. The sociolinguistic situation of the community at large and that of the minority language community also matter. Differences in the social status of the languages concerned, degree of closeness among members of the minority language community, the availability of institutional support and state language planning and policy all impact on the linguistic experience of children of bilingual couples.

Task 4.2 Language choices and practice in an intercultural and multilingual family (TC)

Read the following case. What do you think of their family language policy? Did the three languages – English, Spanish and Japanese – play an equal role in family interaction and why? What practical difficulties and challenges do you think the family might have in implementing the family language policy?

Fernando is an American computer scientist of Hispanic background. His wife Hiroko is of Japanese origin and her family migrated to America when she was 6. They live in Los Angeles, California. When their son Diego was born, they decided that they would each speak their 'heritage' language, Spanish for Fernando and Japanese for Hiroko, to Diego, while continuing to speak English to each other. Diego spends most of the day with Hiroko during the week and his evenings and weekends with Hiroko and Fernando. He watches English television programmes regularly.

Language mixing (i.e. alternating languages) caused a great deal of debate and disagreement between Fernando and Hiroko. Although they did it between themselves, they both felt that mixing languages with Diego would not be good for his linguistic and social development. However, Hiroko was stricter than Fernando in following their One Language at a Time policy. Fernando felt that Spanish was a lot more useful, especially in California, than Japanese and that it would not necessarily be a problem if Diego mixed some Spanish words with English. In any case, Fernando did not learn any Japanese, but Hiroko knew a reasonable amount of Spanish to be able to conduct simple conversations with Fernando's parents and other Spanish speaking neighbours. By the age of 3, Diego was able to speak Japanese and Spanish fluently. He understood English, but only spoke some English words occasionally.

4.3 Chapter summary

Two special cases of family situations, i.e. the migrant family and the intercultural family, offer us an opportunity to examine how a family, as a unit of social organisation, lives with differences with the outer society or differences between generations and couples, in particular, through language and interaction. It is essentially about how people involved negotiate, play down or accent differences. Amy Chua, author of *Battle Hymn of the Tiger Mother* cited at the beginning of the chapter, in the end, has to retreat partially from the strict Chinese parenting model and to give way to her daughters' individual choice. The book is in fact a poignant story of how people like us learn to adjust ourselves in the process of discovering and reconciling differences.

5 Study abroad and tourism

In this chapter, we are going to explore intercultural communication in the contexts of study abroad and tourism. In both contexts, people visit and stay in a place for a short period of time. We are interested in finding out what opportunities and problems these contexts bring for intercultural contact. Although we look at each context separately, the boundaries become blurred due to improved communication technology and cheap means of travel. Consider the following cases:

- Heather took a gap year and joined a study abroad programme in Spain. She stayed with a local family.
- Richard visited a town called Abadan in Nigeria on a regular basis, as part of the charity work with a local school there. He often took a few days off towards the end of his trip and toured around the area.
- Amy took her family on her visit to Wenzhou, South China, where her grandparents used to live before they migrated to Los Angeles in the 1930s.

The contexts presented in these cases are by no means mutually exclusive. Study abroad may entail living with 'locals'. Tourism takes all forms and shapes: while Richard is a regular visitor to Abadan, Amy is a diasporic tourist and visited her ancestral homeland for the first time.

5.1 Study abroad (Does 'real' experience help with my language and intercultural learning?)

Internationalisation has become a key aspect of the agenda for higher education in many parts of the world, and its main activities include the following (Jackson, 2010):

- international student recruitment: attracting international students for the purpose of revenue-generation, creating cultural diversity and promoting intercultural communication;

- 'internationalisation at home campus' through embedding international/intercultural perspectives into a local educational setting;
- 'internationalisation abroad' through offering educational programmes which are accessible to students who are not based in the same country as the institution;
- 'internationalisation of staff' through international collaboration, visits and exchange, and diversification of staff;
- 'programme mobility' through offshore programmes or branch campuses where students can take academic courses without leaving their countries; and
- 'student mobility' through a range of arrangements and formats available such as field trips, internships, volunteering, research collaboration and study abroad.

In the context of this chapter, we use the term 'study abroad' as an umbrella term to refer to educational activities in which students partake outside their home countries. According to UNESCO's estimation, there are 3.3 million students currently studying outside their own countries and by 2025, the number will rise to 8 million (Bhandari and Blumenthal, 2011). While each study abroad programme may have its own aims and objectives, two goals and outcomes are very often mentioned by programme providers. These are intercultural learning and language learning, both of which have a strong pedagogical preference for 'real' experience. For intercultural educators, experiential learning ('learning by doing', Kolb, 1984) is the key to intercultural learning; for language learning, immersion in a place where the target language is spoken brings unique opportunities for hearing how the language is used in real life, and most importantly for using the target language in real situations, such as finding one's way, service encounters, socialising with friends, etc.

To better differentiate what a period of study abroad can offer for student learning in terms of experience and educational goals, Engle and Engle (2003) identified the following seven 'defining elements' that can classify levels of study abroad programmes:

- duration of programme;
- entry target-language competence;
- language used in course work;
- academic work context, e.g. whether students are taught by home or destination institution staff, whether students study along with other study abroad students or destination home students;
- housing: home stay, staying with other study abroad students or destination home students;

- provision for cultural interaction, experiential learning, or integration activities; and
- guided reflection or mentoring on cultural experience.

The above defining elements have been put to the test in a number of empirical studies. In a large-scale longitudinal study, Vande Berg and his colleagues (Vande Berg, 2009; Vande Berg et al., 2009) tested oral proficiency and intercultural competence of the students enrolled in sixty-one study abroad programmes offered by the Georgetown Consortium Project. What they found was insightful. First of all, students enrolled in study abroad programmes improved their oral proficiency in the target language and developed their intercultural competence significantly more than the control group who did not take part in study abroad programmes. However, these overall positive findings are subject to a number of qualifications.

- Among those taking parting in study abroad, gender difference is evident: female students made significantly more progress on both oral proficiency and intercultural competence than their male counterparts.
- Being housed in a home-stay does not predict improved oral proficiency or intercultural competence. Students in home-stay made good progress only when they spent a large amount of time with their hosts.
- Similarly, studying alongside local students does not predict development. Those who studied in mixed classes with home, host or other international students made more progress than those with just host students.
- Programme duration is significantly associated with improved intercultural competence.
- Support from staff or cultural mentors makes a difference to students' intercultural learning. This applies to experiential activities as well.
- Study abroad students also benefit from second language classes during their period of stay.

Based on these findings, Vande Berg and his colleagues argue that while, traditionally, study abroad is founded on the thinking that immersion leads to success, merely exposing students to the target culture or language and leaving them to haphazard chance of discovery is problematic. For an optimal outcome, study abroad programmes need to get the balance right between challenge and support. The latter can take the form of interventions from 'cultural mentors', who can be members of staff from home or host institute, or of structured learning as part of students' experience in the host culture.

In some publications dedicated to investigating the benefits and challenges study abroad brings for language learning (e.g. Wilkinson, 2006; Vande Berg et al., 2012), a number of observations are made. First, in a study abroad context, 'need to know' (Dewey, 2006) and real communication and social needs rather than 'getting a good grade' become the driving force for learning. However, the study abroad context also poses new challenges for learners. For example, students may find fluency a pressing issue for keeping conversation partners' attention in real-life situations, compared with the simulated situations in language classrooms where accuracy weighs higher than fluency. Second, exposure alone is not adequate. Recursive exposure and a good awareness of linguistic differences and salient features are essential to effective language learning in a study context. Third, learning is a process and activity that takes place at an individual level. Each learner is unique and comes with their own learning style, life experiences, motives, attitudes and self-perceptions. Based on these observations, a range of classroom activity ideas which either simulate or facilitate study abroad experience in the language classroom were put forward. Examples include:

- interviews with native speakers
- observations
- portfolios
- research projects
- journal writing
- case studies
- role play with native speakers
- analysis of cultural documents
- classroom discussion.

In addition to intercultural awareness and language skills, other benefits of study abroad include opportunities to develop greater personal maturity, make friends and improve career prospects, etc. However, moving to and studying in a place away from one's own country is not problem-free and requires adjustment and adaptation. In the following section we are going to look at the process of adapting to change and settling in to a new environment.

Culture shock and cultural adaptation

Adaptation is fundamental to human existence. In the case of crossing borders, cultural adaptation – the process of adjusting to a new culture over a period of time – is a complex and dynamic process that brings challenges and opportunities to grow at the same time.

When moving to a new culture, one may experience anxiety, a phenomenon described as 'culture shock' by anthropologist Kalvero Oberg (1960) or alternatively as 'transition shock' (Bennett, 1977/1998). Loss of familiar signs, communication breakdown, and differences between cultural and social practices are very often mentioned as the cause of culture shock in the literature. The physical and psychological symptoms of culture shock are many, including tiredness, insomnia, loneliness, feeling lost, isolation and loss of control, lack of confidence, homesickness, irritability, resentment, developing obsessions about health and cleanliness, etc. The stress which occurs during culture shock very often results in 'cultural fatigue' (Taft, 1977). In essence, these terms reflect how people react when they find themselves relocated to a new culture and in a stage of transition – a process not unique to study abroad, but shared by many travellers and migrants.

There are several stages in culture shock. Two popular models describing culture shock and the process of cultural adaptation at large are the 'U-curve' and 'W-curve' hypotheses. These hypotheses exist in many variations and have been attributed to various authors. One of the earliest references to both models is in Brein and David (1971). According to these hypotheses, one's satisfaction is highest upon arrival. This stage is often referred to as the 'honeymoon' stage. The feeling of satisfaction soon changes to a feeling of anxiety and rejection when one faces the discomfort of adapting to a new culture. With time and appropriate strategies, satisfaction gradually returns and one recovers from culture shock and adjusts to the new culture. However, cultural adaptation is not just confined to moving to a new culture. After having stayed away and adjusted to the new culture, re-entry into one's own culture is also a process of adaptation, sharing a similar curve as that experienced when moving to a new culture: satisfaction is highest upon return and is then replaced with a feeling of disappointment and anxiety, since things may have changed during one's absence. Once one recovers, one's satisfaction level goes up again.

Feeling anxious when relocated to a new culture is not a surprise, and in many ways is to be expected. However, re-entry shock upon return home takes many people by surprise. Heather, whom we mentioned at the beginning of this chapter, is an American high school student, and has been on a study abroad programme in Spain for 9 months. This is what she said on her blog when she returned home:

I feel completely and utterly lost in my own home, in my own country. My first night in my house I actually was a bit scared. The house is so big and my bed room is like an elephant compared to my mouse sized room in Spain. Its [sic] as though I don't know the house or the neighbourhood, yet everything is so familiar. I went out to run errands for my mom the other day, after my family finally convinced me to get back behind the wheel again, and I felt like I was running errands on Mars...I've had times when I get frustrated that no one speaks Spanish. I can't express myself the same. I'm speaking in English but the words come out in the Spanish order. I'm a mess.

(Retrieved on 18 November 2011 from
http://hsa-spain.ciee.org/heather-kraft/)

In this narrative, Heather expressed her difficulties in adjusting to daily personal and work routines and socialising back in to her network. She also had linguistic problems. These three areas, i.e. cultural, social and linguistic, are very often at the top of the list of areas of adjustment for returnees. Other areas include political (a new political ideology may be required), educational (differences in educational systems and pedagogy), professional (resentment from and resistance to change by colleagues who stay behind) and financial (readjustment to different living costs and consumer habits).

Task 5.1 Curvy culture shock

Stages of culture shock have been described visually in terms of various curves to reflect changes in the level of satisfaction with time. Recall the experience you may have had in living in a new culture. In the following diagram, time spent in the new culture and returning home is divided into two parts with a vertical line in between. You can use the left side to describe how you feel in a new culture and the right side for your return to your own culture. Please pinpoint your level of satisfaction upon arrival and after you have stayed for a little while, and then link them up. While drawing the shape, ask the following questions:

- When is the level of satisfaction the highest and the lowest?
- How do these changes (if any) happen?
- Thinking back, what did you do that led to the changes, or is there anything you wish you could have done differently?

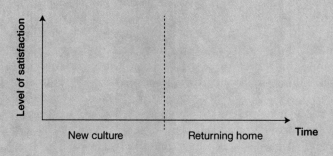

Figure 5.1 Curve of culture shock

U-curve and W-curve models are intuitively appealing and capture the emotional ups and downs visually. However, this strength also leads to (over)simplification (a critique can be found in Sobre-Denton and Hart, 2008). A model of culture shock needs to take into account individual variations in how one reacts in a new culture and for how long one stays satisfied or dissatisfied. Factors that impact on the nature and extent of culture shock include (e.g. Churchman and Mitrani, 1997; Lonner, 1986): how much control one has over relocation; intrapersonal factors such as age, previous travel, language skills, resourcefulness, independence, tolerance of ambiguity; physical or health condition; interpersonal factors such as support network and intercultural relationships; geopolitical factors such as international, national, regional or local tensions; cultural similarity between the new culture and one's native culture; quality of information about the new culture and the new system; host culture attitudes/politics towards newcomers.

There are things we can do to help us to adapt to a new culture. A number of strategies to manage culture shock are suggested in Neuliep (2006, pp. 434–435). For example,

- Study the host culture, including searching websites, and interviewing friends who have travelled or lived in the culture.
- Study the local environment and familiarise yourself with the new system.
- Learn basic verbal and non-verbal language skills.
- Develop intercultural friendships.
- Maintain your support network actively.
- Assume the principle of difference and be aware of your perceptual bias.
- Anticipate failure events and manage expectations.

In the conceptualisation of culture shock and its related models, transition from one culture to another is presented as a problem. There are several alternative models of cultural adaption that envisage anxiety, uncertainty and stress as necessary stimuli for development and transformation. One is the 'fight' or 'flight' transition model by Bennett (1977/1998) which focuses on the response and coping strategies one may have when facing a new cultural situation. Kim (2001, 2008) presents a transformative model which considers the dynamic and changing relationship between adaptation, stress and growth over time based on her review of the literature. The model builds on evolution theory and looks at the dialectic relationship between the need to adapt and 'natural' resistance to change. The paradox is that the very changes that lead to stress often motivate people to overcome difficulties and result in positive changes. In Kim's model, one responds to each stressful experience by reorganising oneself, which in turn leads to subtle positive changes. However, positive changes are not one-way in direction. They follow 'a pattern that juxtaposes novelty and confirmation, attachment and detachment, progression and regression, integration and disintegration, construction and destruction' (Kim, 2001, p. 57). With time, the fluctuations of stress and adaptation become diminished (see Figure 5.2). Kim also gives some empirical evidence from studies on international students and migrants. Those who (try to) integrate well into the host culture tend to have a higher level of stress or more intensive culture shock than those who integrate less well. Hence, Kim argues that stressful experiences may propel people to strive for survival and growth.

In this section, we have discussed the nature of learning and the process of cultural adaptation in the context of study abroad whereby students take part in educational activities outside their own cultures. Many issues discussed here are not confined to the context of study abroad. Professionals who work abroad for a period of time or those who move to a new culture with the intention of settling there share the same process of adaptation and change as those on study abroad programmes. What is unique about study abroad is that it has more specific learning aims and objectives, and the students are likely to have access to support and hence have greater chance of success in intercultural learning.

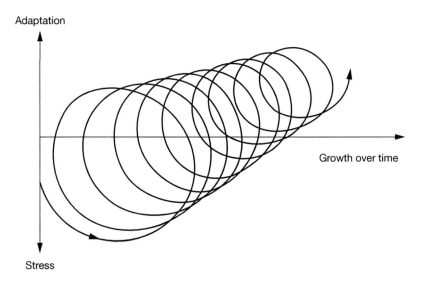

Figure 5.2 Diminishing stress–adaptation–growth fluctuation over time
Source: Kim, 2001, p. 59.

5.2 Tourism (Can I take a picture with you?)

Much of the thrill of travelling comes from steeping yourself in a foreign culture whose customs and traditions may be vastly different from the ones you're used to back home. But while confronting the unknown can be exciting, too much of it may be undesirable.

(Retrieved on 11 October 2011 from a website offering travel advice at www.traveletiquette.co.uk/)

The idea of travelling to a foreign country can be traced back to the grand tour, whereby in the seventeenth and eighteenth century young aristocrats embarked on a 2- or 3-year educational journey around Europe, accompanied by a 'tutor', from whose role the profession of the modern tour guide has developed. Nowadays, tourism is a common practice throughout much of the developed world. With a large number of people travelling for pleasure to a foreign country, tourism has become a promising site for cutting across religious, linguistic and cultural barriers, broadening people's knowledge of other cultures and creating opportunities for intercultural contact. The following facts are selected from the 2012 edition of *UNWTO Tourism Highlights*, a publication of the World Tourism Organization, a United Nations specialised agency.

Reality link: *Tourism Highlights*

- International tourist numbers grew by 4.6 per cent to 983 million worldwide in 2011, despite continuing economic uncertainty and uprisings in the Middle East. The number is expected to reach 1.8 billion by the year 2030.
- In 2011, travel for leisure accounted for just over half of all international travellers.
- The top ten world's tourism destinations are France, the United States, China, Spain, Italy, Turkey, the United Kingdom, Germany, Malaysia and Mexico.
- In terms of regions,
  - Europe hosts half a billion international tourists, making it the fastest-growing host region together with Asia and the Pacific;
  - In Asia and the Pacific, the growth is driven by Southeast Asian destinations such as Thailand, Burma, Cambodia and Vietnam.
  - South American countries such as Brazil, Uruguay, Paraguay, Peru and Chile continue to lead growth in the Americas.
  - Africa is a mixed picture, with the increase in tourists for Sub-Saharan destinations offset by losses in North Africa.
  - Tourism in the Middle East suffered a major setback as a result of the uprisings during 2011.

(UNWTO, 2012)

However, the reality is that tourism may take different forms and the intercultural contact involved differs in both nature and extent across different contexts. Tourists, who have been the main focus of most of the studies on tourism, are not the only group of people involved in the process. Hosts, tour guides and tour business establishments such as tour operators and companies also play an important part in intercultural learning. In what follows, we will look into the nature and extent of intercultural contact from the perspectives of tourists, tour guides and local people, as well as language matters.

Tourist roles and perspectives

Many labels have been used to describe different types of tourism. For example, in terms of aims and objectives, the term *cultural tourism* refers to a type of special interest tourism whereby visitors aim to learn about the past and present lifestyles of a destination from visiting historical or architectural landmarks, museums, galleries, scenic landscapes, heritage sites, artistic performances, festivals, and so on. Another well-known term, *mass tourism*, describes the phenomenon of travelling for pleasure in a foreign country by a large number of people.

For the purpose of understanding the nature of intercultural contact in tourism, it is useful to look at Cohen's classification, which is well cited in studies of tourism. As early as 1972, Cohen proposed a typology of four tourist roles according to tourists' travel arrangements, the extent to which they come into contact with the host country and the extent to which they seek 'familiarity' versus novelty. He also suggested the term 'environmental bubble' to describe vividly the way tourists seek to 'cushion' their level of contact with a new and different culture by retaining routines, habits or comfort of their home cultures.

1 'The organised mass tourist'. This is the type of tourist who signs up to a package tour and remains largely confined to their 'environmental bubble' throughout the trip. A typical scenario for this type of tourism is a guided tour in an air-conditioned bus in a group with stops fixed and planned in advance.
2 'The individual mass tourist'. Similar to the organised mass tourist, these tourists make travel arrangements through a travel agency and visit the selected tourist attractions. However, they have more control over their itineraries and do not stay in a group, and therefore have an opportunity to experience something unplanned.
3 'The explorer'. This type of tourist tends to arrange their own itinerary, often including places off the beaten track. They need an 'environmental bubble' much less than mass tourists and have more contact with local people. At the same time, they also retain some of the basic routines and comforts of their home cultures. Those

who travel on a low budget, stay in youth hostels and are known for carrying backpacks are a typical example.

4 'The drifter'. Compared with the explorer, this type of tourist has no fixed itinerary. They immerse themselves in the local culture to a greater extent through living with the locals. The boundaries between tourists and migrants become blurred.

Cohen (1972) further describes the first two types of tourist as 'institutionalised' in the sense that they are dealt with by the travel business in a routine way. Their experiences are often confined to tourist attractions and the 'novelty', if any, experienced by them is of a 'controlled' kind. The dilemma, as Cohen argued, is 'to enable the mass tourist to "take in" the novelty of the host country without experiencing any physical discomfort or, more accurately, to observe without actually experiencing' (p. 170). The problem is that, according to Cohen, it leads to loss of authenticity of tourist attractions, which very often undergo change and transformation in order to make them suitable for mass tourist consumption: 'They are supplied with facilities, reconstructed, landscaped, cleansed of unsuitable elements, staged, managed, and otherwise organised' (p. 170). At some popular tourist attractions, the tourist infrastructure has become separated or isolated from that of the local people. Some facilities such as nightclubs and shops serve tourists only and are out of bounds to the local population. The result is an 'ecological differentiation' of the tourist and the host, since

the mass tourist travels in a world of his own, surrounded by, but not integrated in, the host society. He meets the representatives of the tourist establishment – hotel managers, tourist agents, guides – but only seldom the natives. The natives, in turn, see the mass tourist as unreal. Neither has much of an opportunity to become an individual to the other.

(p. 175)

Cohen's doubts about the role of mass tourism in promoting intercultural communication are echoed by Hassan (1975). In his case study of fifteen Japanese tourists in Singapore, Hassan (1975) observed very little interaction between the tourists and the local Singaporeans. The tourists were met at the airport by a representative of the local tour agency and transported to a Hilton hotel in an air-conditioned coach. They were taken next day to visit the main attractions of Singapore including Mt Faber, Chinatown, a stop for picture taking at the Japanese embassy, the Singapore River, the City Centre, Johore Bahru (a Malaysian city), a Japanese cemetery and shopping with the tour guide. There was very little meaningful communication between the tourists and local people throughout: lunch was ordered by the guide for the group and the shop assistants in the shops where they were taken all spoke Japanese.

The intercultural contact in the type of tourism described by Cohen (1972) and Hassan (1975) is indeed very limited and leads many critics of tourism to conclude that what comes with tourism is only an opportunity to 'observe' foreignness of a place rather than 'experience' it. However, the situation has changed in a more positive way as Litvin (1999) discovered when he carried out a similar study on Japanese tourists in Singapore in order to revisit the issue raised by Hassan (1975), i.e. does tourism promote intercultural understanding and if so, to what extent? In his study, the Japanese tourists took part in a new tour product called the 'Heartlands of Singapore' tour, which is specially designed by the Singapore tourist industry to reflect the new image of 'being sophisticated and modern, and a blend of East and West' (Dhaliwal, 1997, cited in Litvin, 1999, p. 15). The tour started with Little India and Geylang Serai Market (a traditional Malay market), each of which is a 'living place' and still used by the local Indian and Malay communities respectively for their daily activities. As Litvin observed, the tourists seemed to enjoy the visits, though they had no interest in lingering. The tourists were then taken to a quiet neighbourhood park where some locals were strolling and fishing. This was followed by a silk warehouse not known among Singaporeans, but especially set up for Japanese tourists with prices all marked in yen and all the shop assistants speaking Japanese. Other places of interest the tourists visited include the National Museum, where they were handed a Japanese language headset, and then Raffles Hotel (a famous landmark) where the group ended up browsing a few famous-brand shops and taking pictures. The tour finished off with a visit to a duty-free shop at Millennium Walk where the primary customers were Japanese, Taiwanese and Korean. Compared with the group in Hassan's study (1975), the tourists in Litvin's study had more opportunities to observe differences and interact with the local people. However, although things are improving, intercultural contact is still more observational than interactive and intercultural learning is not in-depth.

Litvin also revealed that there seems to be a tourist mentality which is best summarised as 'been there, done it'. The tourists under his observation seemed pleased to experience authenticity offered by living places such as Little India and Malay wet market, but even more pleased when they took pictures of themselves, in front of, rather than inside, the market. While presence and observation seem to be priorities for many tourists, empirical studies on Japanese tourists' satisfaction with their experience suggest a different story. In Korzay and Alvarez's survey of 673 Japanese tourists to Turkey (2011), communication with the host Turkish people and the tourists' perception of friendliness and hospitality of the local people featured high on the list of things that lead to Japanese tourists' satisfaction. Other satisfactory factors included rich historical/natural heritage, appreciation of food, etc. What emerged from these empirical studies is that although some tourists may not actively look for intercultural interaction, their interaction with the hosts can enhance their experience to a significant extent.

Some scholars take a more positive position on the potential of tourism as transformative intercultural contact. Jack and Phipps (2005) in their book on tourism and intercultural exchange provided a nuanced analysis of intercultural learning opportunities embedded in travelling. They look at what tourists can do or learn to do to facilitate or hinder intercultural exchanges before, during and after tourism. In their view, packing, unpacking and repacking one's travel bags are learned practices and performances that reveal one's daily life, expectations, and readiness for intercultural exchanges. The 'baggage' which one takes with oneself on a visit can be metaphorically extended to describe any cultural, historical and perceptual bias that people may have. The potential of tourism, as they argue, lies in that it creates space and opportunities for a 'participatory set of interactions-in-the-world' (p. 6) and therefore, in their opinion, authenticity is not the priority.

Tour guides' roles and perspectives

As mentioned earlier, the role of tour guide is seen as having developed out of that of the grand tour tutor, who acted as a 'pathway finder' and 'mentor' to guide young aristocrats throughout their educational journey (Cohen, 1985, p. 9). Nowadays, tour guides are expected to perform a number of roles. A website offering career advice describes the job of a tour guide as follows:

> The job of a tour guide is dependent on an ability to interface with the public and provide accurate information concerning specialized interests. This position contains aspects of customer service, information dissemination, and continuing education in the venue or medium in which the tour guide is employed. Museums, theme parks and nature attractions are just a few of the venues that require a tour guide.
> (Retrieved on 10 November 2011 from www.ehow.co.uk/ about_6384288_tour-guide-job-description.html)

In this generic job description, tour guides have several roles. First, they act as 'interactive media'. Tour guides, similar to the 'tutor' in the grand tour, are a source of information. However, tour guides do not just relay factual information. Through selecting, filtering, foregrounding and endorsing information they pass on to tourists, they serve as 'interactive media' (a term used by Dioko et al., 2010) and

shape, confirm, correct or extend tourists' knowledge and understanding about the destination.

Second, they act as a mediator. Tour guides, working at the interface
with the public, serve as mediators between tourists and the hosts, and
between tourists and tourism operators. In many ways, as Scherle and
Nonnenmann (2008) argue, they are 'the most important link between
the tour operator, programme and customer satisfaction...It is they,
after all, who work directly with the customers, guiding and attending
to them, managing and organising, advising and innovating and last,
but not least, explaining and mediating' (Scherle and Nonnenmann,
2008, p. 123).

In international tourism where tourists travel to culturally and
linguistically different destinations, tour guides have additional roles.
The most important one is as intercultural mediator. In international
tourism, local tour guides are very often seen by tourists as
representatives of the local culture. Dioko et al. (2010, p. 3) describe
this as a process of 'personification of the destination brand itself, in
so far as they reflect or live in congruence with the ideals they are
presenting' (p. 3). The role of intercultural mediator is also reflected in
the way tour guides introduce tourists to cultural differences and
facilitate and guide them in their discovery and appreciation of
culturally specific customs and phenomena. To cite a quote from a
representative of a reputable German tour operator in Scherle and
Nonnenmann's interviews (2008, p. 129):

> We hear that from the customer feedback that they cannot get to
> know the country that the tour guide has shown them so intensively
> by themselves because there are various things where they simply
> do not find access to the countries. I see the study tour guide as an
> intercultural mediator and as a key, in other words, as a door
> opener in the key function of mediator.

Tour guides can create opportunities for intercultural contact and
stimulate meaningful exchanges between tourists and the local people.
They can make crucial differences when it comes to dispelling
stereotypes or misconceptions. Tourists come with expectations and
prior 'brand' knowledge of destinations. Tour guides have to work
very hard to disconfirm tourists' negative or out-of-date images or
stereotypes. A Chinese tour guide in Dioko et al.'s study gave insightful
comments on the problems caused by these misconceptions and the
struggle tour guides face.

> to be clear, even for Old China, they (tourists) don't have a
> comprehensive understanding. They always focus on its backward-
> ness, which is the answer they wanted to verify in Shanghai, in

China. Technically speaking, do they really know China? They possess a prejudiced impression towards old China, so it is even harder for them to know this Modern China. We ourselves don't know it well enough…What kind of country is China? Foreigners like to give definitions to things, so before coming to China, they put China in a certain frame, and they focus more on the results. But easterners, such as Chinese, pay more attention to the process instead of the results.

(Dioko et al., 2010, p. 6)

Task 5.2 Tourist websites and guidebooks: guidance or stereotypes?

Nowadays, tourists can get information about their destinations from tourist websites in addition to guidebooks. It is common for guidebooks and websites to offer some general advice on culturally specific etiquette, customs, practices and national character. Look through advice that you can find either from guidebooks or websites about your home country or a region you have been to before. In what ways do you think cultural information provided by these sources is useful? And in what ways do you think they perpetuate stereotypes?

The local and host roles and perspectives

By the local and the host, I am talking about several groups of people who fall under these umbrella terms. They include the local tourism business establishment, the local people who live near or use facilities offered in places of interest, and the local people who work for the tourist industry, including those who participate in cultural activities on site and hence constitute cultural artefacts themselves. They play different roles in intercultural contact in the context of tourism.

The role played by the tourism business establishment – the tour operators, agencies and various government tourism promotion and regulatory bodies – can be best described as 'mediator' or 'go-between', using Naidu's words (2011a). Similar to tour guides' role as mediators, they arrange, manage, filter and discipline as to what aspects of the culture should be packaged, displayed and consumed. The following 'brand promises' offered at the official websites of the respective countries are examples of subtle and indiscernible influence a tourist establishment may have in constructing, managing and manipulating regional identities.

- Egypt: 'Where it all begins'
- Austria: 'Arrive and revive'
- Thailand: 'Amazing Thailand always amazes you'
- Slovenia: 'I feel love'.

Tourist establishments also control and filter tourists' intercultural experiences on site. They arrange the sequence of events in encounters, with many tours finishing off at souvenir shops. They select which aspects of culture such as clothing, myths, dance, food, music-making, rituals, etc., are to be showcased. They also assess and decide how much 'environmental bubble' (a term used by Cohen, 1972) is needed to cushion the tourists' experience. As mentioned so often in tourism literature, tension exists between the desire to seek authenticity on the tourists' part and the reality that their experience is in fact staged and manufactured by tour operators.

There is also tension between the 'traditions' which tourists want to see and current practices among local people. The following case provides a nuanced account of a mismatch between the so-called 'cultural heritage' sought by tourists and the current cultural practices of a Zulu community.

Case study: 'Topless' Zulu dancers

Naidu (2011a, 2011b) investigates the 'topless' dance tradition of Zulu girls in a cultural village in KwaZula Natal, South Africa, and perceptions of indigenous cultural bodies in tourism. In the cultural village reported in Naidu's study, a small number of Zulu-speaking girls took part in a Zulu dance as 'ethnic' performers. As unmarried virgins, they wear no tops, only beaded skirts and some jewellery when dancing. However, although 'topless' has been a tradition for Zulu girls, things are very different now. As reported by two girls interviewed by Naidu (2011b), girls nowadays do not have to dance 'topless' to show that they are unmarried. Instead, they only do it at home and when there is a special celebration. Nevertheless, the girls feel that this is what tourists want to see and dancing 'topless' is a business exchange, despite the fact that they find it somewhat awkward when dancing in front of and posing along with tourists.

When asking the local Zulu-speaking people about their attitude to 'topless' dance practices, Naidu (2011a) found that while they felt very strongly that the dance indeed communicated the Zulu heritage for tourists, they also felt they were given little choice in what else to do and how to be showcased. The participants in Naidu's study commented: 'tourists see this and think this is who we are, always in skins and stuff'; 'they seem to enjoy seeing us Africans from Africa like this' (p. 33). They also raised the issue of tourists' stereotyped views of Zulu culture: 'The tourists come thinking they know what Zulus must look like'; 'they see all these postcards of African wearing bead' (p. 33).

Naidu's studies reiterated the question asked by many critics of cultural tourism, i.e. by showcasing what cultural heritage is, are we promoting cultural diversity or are we merely reducing culture to a 'commodity'?

To sum up this section, through an examination of the perspectives of tourists, tour guides and locals, we can see that the extent and nature of intercultural contact varies across different types of tourism. What is clear is that tourism has the potential to create opportunities for intercultural contact, but intercultural contact, as it is now, is managed and constructed by different stakeholders. There is a big gap between what tourism can offer within its current restraints and what is required in order for genuine intercultural interaction to take place.

Language matters

Language matters for tourism, a point made convincingly by Thurlow and Jaworski (2011) in their review of tourism discourse. To start with, local languages along with their traditional ways of communication often feature heavily in tourists' experience of authenticity. 'Along with material goods such as photographs and souvenirs, snippets of local languages are (re-) packaged and promoted as useful props (or trinkets) in the enactment of tourism's performances of exoticity' (p. 288). Take *hongi* as an example. As a traditional Maori greeting, it has been packaged as one of the key features of Maori heritage in New Zealand's tourist industry. It frequently appears on postcards, posters and tourism websites and is used as an activity or a 'game' in guided tours. However, in reality, as Thurlow and Jaworski point out, it is virtually impossible for a tourist to perform a *hongi* with a Maori person.

Related to their role as markers of authenticity and difference, local languages are frequently employed in travel shows as resources for relating 'foreignness' to audiences and sometimes as objects of play. In the following example provided by Thurlow and Jaworski (2011), the TV presenter John Savident was introducing the local greeting term, 'bula'. The staged nature of these types of televised programmes is given away by two details. One is the use of the presenter's name in the local's greeting. The other is the vendor's rendition of the English greeting phrase, 'how are you', immediately after the local greeting term. The transcript also shows that exchanges with local people can be very superficial.

Example 5.1

        (JS apparently wandering through a market place)

JS: Away from the hotel the town of Nandi [sic] is just ten minutes away. Fiji is such a friendly place and you're always greeted with a big smile (cut to a woman smiling) and a call of the local greeting (to a street vendor) bula

Vendor: bula bula John (JS continues walking past her stall, laughs to her) how are you bula bula la la la

                                      (Thurlow and Jaworski, 2011, p. 294)

Speaking the local language makes differences to tourists' experience. For without the language, sightseeing will become 'the world with the sound turned off' (Cronin, 2008, p. 82, cited in Thurlow and Jaworski, 2011, p. 288). However, the notion of language learning for tourism as constructed through guidebooks is problematic. For example, the 'glossaries' offered by many guidebooks, despite their intention of facilitating host–tourist communication, prepare very little for genuine interaction. Apart from some common phatic expressions such as hello, goodbye, thank you, etc., glossaries focus on the transactional demands of encounters, i.e. phrases one can use in cases of emergency, rather than interactional ones. Thurlow and Jaworski put together a short, hypothetical and hilarious conversational exchange using typical phrases found in glossaries. It reads like this:

Welcome! Hello Glad to meet you. **How are you?** Very well, thanks. **What's your name?** My name is...**Where are you from?** I'm from... I'm a tourist/student. I'm from Europe. **How old are you?** I'm 25. **Are you married?** How do you say...No (not so) Yes I want...No. I don't want it. **Do you like...?** I like it very much I don't like...May I? It doesn't matter. Can you please help me take a photo? Is it ok to take a photo? Goodbye.

                     (Thurlow and Jaworski, 2011, p. 299, emphases in original)

Thurlow and Jaworski argue that any conversation based on phrases in glossaries like the one above can only be described as a superficial, one-way exchange.

To sum up this section, language plays an important role in tourism. It can enhance tourists' experience of a different culture. However, its use and learning are not problem-free and require scrutiny if one aims for genuine intercultural experience in tourism.

5.3 Chapter summary

In this chapter we have looked at two potential sites of intercultural communication: study abroad and tourism. In both contexts, people come into contact with another culture in one way or the other. But unlike migrants and intercultural couples, whom we discussed in Chapter 4, intercultural contact in study abroad and tourism is time-bound and temporary, since people involved in these two contexts usually return to their home countries within a short period of time. There are differences between these two contexts: for tourism, intercultural contact is, at many levels, managed and constructed, while study abroad is about maximising intercultural learning through exposure to or immersion in the host culture. What has come through in this and previous chapters is the pervasiveness of intercultural communication in our life as well as its practical problems and challenges.

Part II

Developing intercultural communicative competence

How to communicate effectively and appropriately

As we have demonstrated in Part I of this book, intercultural issues permeate many aspects of modern life. While they bring challenges, they also create ample opportunities for intercultural learners to acquire knowledge about another culture and to apply and polish their intercultural communication skills. In this part, we are going to focus on the question 'how' by addressing factors and skills that lead to successful intercultural communication and interventions that facilitate the development of intercultural communicative competence. It starts with a cross-cultural comparative approach, exploring a number of culture-specific ways of communication (Chapter 6). It then examines conversational interactions among participants from different cultural backgrounds and/or with different levels of linguistic proficiency. In particular, it focuses on potential causes for misunderstanding and strategies of negotiating meaning in interactions (Chapter 7). Finally, it looks at the concept of intercultural communicative competence, which brings together various aspects of knowledge, cognitive factors and skills needed for successful intercultural communication (Chapter 8).

6 What are culture-specific ways of communication and why?

> When I first arrived in the UK I was very outgoing, I used to go up to total strangers in meetings and shake hands and say 'Hi, I'm John Deacon, I'm from the States, I just moved over here...' After a while, a colleague took me to one side and said, 'Look, John, people really do not need to know you that badly.'
>
> (Gidoomal et al., 2001, p. 170)

The incident above, experienced by John Deacon, an American businessman who was relocated to the UK by his employer, is just one of many examples of cross-cultural differences in communication. The seemingly trivial task of introducing oneself is in fact culturally bound. In her ethnographic study of the 'English', Fox (2004) observed that while an American tends to open conversation with an assertive self-introduction, the English follow a 'no-name' rule in social situations until a much greater degree of intimacy has been established. 'In fact, the only correct way to introduce yourself in such settings is not to introduce yourself at all, but find some other way of initiating a conversation – such as a remark about the weather' (Fox, 2004, p. 39).

In this chapter, we will look at several culture-specific ways of communication together with some empirical examples. The main questions we would like to address concern what culture-specific ways of communication are and why the ways of communication differ between cultures.

6.1 High versus low context: relationship and networks

In communication studies, anthropology and related fields, a number of dichotomies have been proposed to categorise cross-cultural differences in communication styles. One of the most widely cited terms is *high* vs. *low* context, suggested by Edward Hall (1976). As an anthropologist, Hall noticed that there were differences in the extent to which the meaning of a message primarily came from the context (the setting in which a message is conveyed) or the words themselves.

> A high context (HC) communication or message is one in which most of the information is already in the person, while very little is in the coded, explicit, transmitted part of the message. A low context (LC) communication is just the opposite; i.e., the mass of the information is vested in the explicit code.
>
> (Hall, 1976, p. 91)

Figure 6.1 gives some examples of cultures that prefer high versus low context communication.

According to Hall, the extent to which 'context' is relied upon to convey a message depends on the extent of the information networks to which people have access. In high context cultures, people usually maintain close relationships among family, friends, colleagues and clients and therefore, 'for most normal transactions in daily life they do not require, nor do they expect, much in-depth, background information' (Hall and Hall, 1990, p. 6). In contrast, in low context cultures, people 'compartmentalize their personal relationships, their work, and many aspects of day-to-day life' and one cannot assume that the other party in the conversation shares background information.

Some studies of intercultural communication have investigated the linguistic features of cultures which have a preference for high context style. Sachiko Ide's work on Japanese honorifics and *wakimae* (Ide, 1992, 2005) is such an example. Ide argued that in high context cultures such as the Japanese, there are three levels of communication. The first level is 'meta communication', which considers whether or not to say it, who is to speak, when and where to speak and how to take turns. The second level is 'meta-pragmatics', where the speaker needs to consider 'territory of information' (i.e. who, between the speaker and hearer, knows more about the information) and to acknowledge the distinction by means of modal expressions of evidentials (i.e. grammatical elements in a language which specify the

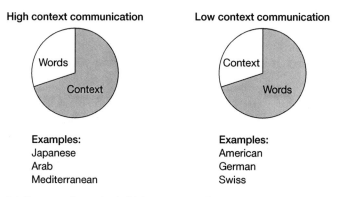

Figure 6.1 Sources of meaning in high context and low context communication styles

source of information, such as 'it is alleged'). The speaker also needs to consider situational factors such as the relationship between the speaker and the hearer and the formality of the situation. Appropriate use of expressions such as honorifics, person referent terms and sentence final particles is obligatory. On the listener's part, constant back-channelling or some other means of making the discourse pragmatically appropriate is expected. The third level is propositional communication, in which the speaker says the propositional content.

Ide argued that the obligatory nature of the full range of considerations in a high context culture is best described by a culture-specific term, *wakimae*. With 'discernment' as its near equivalent in English, *wakimae* means social norms which people are expected to observe in society. *Wakimae* is obligatory and essential to the Japanese culture. As Ide comments,

> speaking within the confines of *wakimae* is not an act of expressing the speaker's intention, but rather of complying with socially expected norms. The speaker's attention is paid not to what he or she intends to express, but rather to what is expected of him or her by social norms.
>
> (Ide, 1992, p. 299)

Ide (1992) gave the following example to show how *wakimae* is observed at different levels of communication. When a professor gives a seminar to graduate students in a Japanese university, this is what happens:

> Students keep listening to the professor speaking, sometimes nodding but not uttering any sound until the professor yields the floor to his/her students. Given the floor, the students speak, observing *wakimae* in regard to what to say and how to say it. They speak within the constraints of allowed topics. The greater the status difference, the greater the constraint on what is allowed to be said. There is less spontaneity allowed to students than to the professor. As to how to speak, it is an obligatory *wakimae* for a student to choose honorific forms in a seminar. His/her choice of honorifics indexes his/her sense of place in the situational context through expression of a formal attitude to the setting and a deferential attitude toward the professor, either as the addressee or as the bystander. The professor will speak with honorifics indexing his/her sense of place in the formal setting, the seminar. He/she may speak without honorifics outside of class, but the students will not reciprocate in non-honorific forms even in an informal setting.
>
> (p. 300)

The dichotomy of high vs. low context has often been applied as an explanation for patterns observed in cross-cultural management and marketing studies, and in discourse studies. Because high context communication tends to be more indirect and relies more on hearers' inferences, it poses challenges for internet communication, which is non-face-to-face and largely unilateral. Usunier and Roulin (2010) found that websites of companies based in low context communication countries differ from their counterparts which come from high context communication countries in the following aspects:

- information is more accessible;
- navigation interface is more attractive; greater and more effective use of colours and graphics;
- contain more corporate information and product information;
- more amenable to transactions; clear pricing information, stock availabilities and delivery updates;
- more interactive, with options of sending email messages or following up with phone calls; and
- more likely to have different language versions.

The authors argue that these differences could be explained by cultural orientation to high vs. low context communication, although there might be other interacting factors such as perceived purposes of websites, or accessibility of websites.

6.2 High involvement: solidarity and connectedness

Conversation involvement refers to the psychological solidarity and connectedness individuals show to each other through active participation in interaction. However, 'because of the paradoxical nature of closeness (and consequently of communication), speakers must constantly observe both the need for involvement and the need not to impose, or, expressed positively, for considerateness' (Tannen, 1984, p. 27). Based on her observations among residents of New York city, especially those of East European Jewish background, Tannen (1984) identified a range of linguistic features which she termed as 'high involvement style'. These features include (pp. 30–31):

- topics: prefer personal topics, shift topics abruptly, introduce topics without hesitance, persistence if a new topic is not immediately picked up;
- pacing: faster rate of speech, faster turn-taking, avoid interturn pauses, cooperative overlap, participatory listenership;
- expressive paralinguistics: expressive phonology, marked pitch and amplitude shifts, marked voice quality, strategic within-turn pauses.

The following excerpt selected from talk at a Thanksgiving dinner observed by Deborah Tannen shows how high involvement style operates. The conversation began when Steve concurred with Peter, who had commented previously that his son's teacher believed that television had limited children's fantasy lives. Deborah, the researcher herself, whose conversation style is typical of high involvement, then started asking questions like a 'machine-gun' over the next turn. Her questions not only changed the topic from an impersonal one to a personal one, but also either immediately latched onto or overlapped with other participants' turns. Her questions were fast and at times high-pitched.

Example 6.1

Steve:	I think it is basically done...damage to children.
	.... That was good it's done is .. outweighed by...
	The damage.]
Deborah:	[Did you two grow up with television?
Peter:	Very little. We had a TV [in the Quonset
Deborah:	[How old were you when your
	parents got it]
Steve:	[We had a TV but we didn't watch it all
	The time .... We were very young. I was four when my
	parents got a TV.]
Deborah:	[You were four?
Peter:	I even remember that ...... [I don't remember
Steve:	[I remember they got a TV

(Tannen, 1984, pp. 64–65, transcription slightly altered: the dots indicate length of pause).

Task 6.1 Performing 'high involvement'   (TC)

The following informal conversation took place between two female, middle-class friends (K and C) in English (recorded by Jennifer Coates, cited in Mercer, 2000, p. 31). K was worried that her neighbour might be able to see into her house, because she could see him in his living room. Please read it out with a partner, following 'high involvement' style. Discuss what you can do to make it into a conversation of high involvement style.

K:	and I thought my God
C:	yeh
K:	If I can see him
C:	he can see you
K:	and I don't always just get undressed in my living room
C:	(laugh)
K:	you know I mean Ok I'm sure he's not
C:	peeping

K:	peeping or anything
C:	but he
K:	but it just
C:	you accidentally saw him
K:	that's right
C:	oh I don't blame you I think it needs screening trees round it.

6.3 Directness or indirectness: face, politeness and rapport

Imagine the following case:

> A classmate of yours asked you whether you would like to go to a cinema with her and a couple of other classmates during the weekend. You do not particularly want to go, because you need time to prepare for an essay. How are you going to say 'no' to her? Which of the following reply sounds most like you?

A: Would you like to go together with me?

B1:   No, I can't. Thank you anyway.

B2:   I need to write an essay.

B3:   Let me have a think. I'm not sure that I'll be free though.

B4:   Thanks, but I can't. I have visitors at the weekend. I need to show them around.

The declinations by the second speaker vary in the degree of directness. While B1 is direct, B2, B3 and B4 are comparatively indirect. As early as 1975, John Searle found that speech acts (i.e. the actions that people perform through language, such as requests, apologies, invitations, refusals, and so on) can be roughly divided into either direct or indirect ones. In indirect speech acts, the speaker intends the other party to infer an additional meaning as well as the meaning conveyed by the words themselves. For example, 'can you tell the difference between a violin and a viola?' can be a direct speech act of question. In contrast, the utterance 'can you pass me the salt?' is an indirect speech act of request by enquiring the preparatory condition of the speaker. But why do conversational participants enact directness/indirectness?

To explain why people choose one particular linguistic form over another when they interact with each other, sometimes at the expense of clarity (in the case of B3 in the above example) or faithfulness (in the case of B4), Robin Lakoff (1973) proposed 'rules of politeness'. Rules of politeness consist of a set of three rules:

- Don't impose.
- Give options.
- Make addressee feel good – be friendly.

According to Lakoff, rules of politeness supersede 'rule of being clear' when there is a conflict between the two. So when the second speaker in the above example opts for an indirect refusal, she abides by the rules of politeness to make the first speaker feel good while, at the same time, breaking the rule of clarity.

Robin Lakoff's rules of politeness was the first attempt to explain language use in terms of linguistic politeness. A more elaborate model can be found in Brown and Levinson's politeness theory with the notion of face at its core (1978). In their framework, every 'model person' is assumed to possess a self-image, i.e. face. Face is a socio-psychological construct consisting of two dimensions: the desire to be approved of by others (positive face) and the desire to be unimpeded in one's actions (negative face). Any rational face-bearing model person will employ a number of ranked strategies when he performs acts potentially threatening the other party's face (see Table 6.1).

Table 6.1 Politeness strategies

Strategies in B&L's framework	What they mean	Examples
'Without redressive action, baldly'	The most direct, unambiguous and concise way of putting one's intention across. It usually occurs in cases of urgency or when the degree of face-threatening is minimally small.	Close the door.
Positive politeness	A set of strategies aimed to reduce the threat to positive face of the hearer. These include claiming common ground, conveying that speakers and hearers are cooperators and fulfilling hearers' wants.	I like your jacket.
Negative politeness	A set of strategies aimed at reducing the threat to negative face of the hearer. These include being direct; do not presume/assume; do not coerce; communicate speakers' wish to not impinge on hearers; and redress hearers' other wants.	I know it will be late, but do you have time to meet after class for a few minutes?
'Off record'	Using hints to deliberately make her intention ambiguous.	Is anyone cold here?
Don't do the FTA (face-threatening act)	The speaker gives up her communicative intention when the face threat is too great.	

Brown and Levinson argued that a speaker usually bases his/her selection of a specific strategy in a certain situation on the payoffs that come with the strategy and the *weightiness* of an FTA (face threatening act). The weightiness of an FTA is decided by the distance between S (speaker) and H (hearer), H's power over S and the degree of imposition, as the following formula shows.

$$W_x = D\ (S,\ H) + P\ (H,\ S) + R_x$$

W: weightiness;
D: social distance (e.g. strangers or intimates);
P: power difference (e.g. speakers' relative positions in social hierarchies as the result of role, age, gender and so on);
R: Rank of imposition degree; the degree of S's imposition on H's negative or positive face (e.g. asking H to pass the salt vs. asking H to move a piano).

The variables such as D, P and R are culture- and context-dependent. Social distance can become narrower when, for example, two people from Brisbane meet in London. In some communities, the concept of family extends beyond close family members to distant relatives. In some cultures, power comes with age, masculinity, wealth or certain jobs.

The politeness theory has inspired numerous studies that have either tried to apply it to various cultures and languages or to refine, expand or challenge it. Scollon and Scollon (2001) revisited the influential factors in politeness/face systems from the perspective of interpersonal communication. They chose to classify 'face' as involvement vs. independence, rather than positive vs. negative. They also proposed three politeness systems based primarily on whether there is power difference and/or distance between S and H (see Table 6.2).

Table 6.2 Scollon and Scollon's politeness and face systems

Politeness systems	Power and/or distance	Examples
Deference politeness system	Symmetrical power (−P) Distant (+D)	Two travellers talk to each other while waiting at the train station.
Solidarity politeness system	Symmetrical power (−P) Close (−D)	Two close friends have a chat.
Hierarchical politeness system	Asymmetrical power (+P) Close or Distant (±D)	A senior manager talks to his PA in the office.

Spencer-Oatey (2002) further extended the debate on the effectiveness of the politeness theory by proposing a 'rapport management' framework. She argued that it is important to consider the motivational concerns in interactions to take account of the situated social psychological context in which interactions occur. In her framework, face has two interrelated aspects: quality face (the desire to be evaluated positively) and social identity face (the desire for others to acknowledge and uphold their social identities or roles). The crucial difference between Spencer-Oatey's model and that of Brown and Levinson is that the former brings motivational concerns into focus.

The concept of face is also central to Ting-Toomey's conflict face-negotiation theory, which seeks to interpret verbal and non-verbal behaviours in perceived and actual conflict in terms of facework (Ting-Toomey, 2005). Differentiating the cause of conflicts to differences in content, relational or identity-based goals, Ting-Toomey argued that face-saving and face-honouring issues are most relevant and problematic when the situated identities of the participants are called into question. The facework interaction strategies, i.e. strategies participants use to prevent or restore face loss and to uphold and honour face gain, are subject to cultural variations and individual, relational and situational factors.

While the notions of politeness and face have inspired numerous subsequent studies on various languages to account for observed intercultural differences, their very universal appeal is under constant challenge. A number of studies, for example, Yoshiko Matsumoto (1988, 1989), Ide (1989), Mao (1994), de Kadt (1998) and Gu (1990), have challenged the universality of these notions and argued for culture- and language-specific renditions of such key notions. Some studies have also made an attempt to differentiate 'common sense politeness', whereby politeness is associated with courtesy and good manners, from 'linguistic politeness', a technical term to describe whether and how speakers address the face-want in interactions (Ehlich, 1992). Watts (2003) further proposed the term 'politic behaviour' to describe both linguistic and non-linguistic behaviours which the participants construct as being appropriate to the ongoing social interaction. Below we will look at three cases of the application of politeness and face in culture-specific contexts, in particular, with regard to the degree of directness with which a speech act is performed.

The *dugri* talk

The *dugri* talk is an example of a speech activity in which face work is temporarily suspended in order to allow the speaker to be direct in his way of speaking. Tamar Katriel (1986) observed that in the discourse of native-born Israelis of Jewish heritage, there is an Israeli style of directness, the *dugri* talk. Translated as straight or direct talk, the *dugri* talk gives the speaker an opportunity to confront the hearer explicitly and directly. For example, an employee can start the *dugri* talk with his boss by stating 'I want to speak to you *dugri*. I don't like the way this department is being run.' The boss is expected to accept the *dugri* approach in good spirit and to refrain from interpreting it as a personal affront. The *dugri* talk can be emotionally intense with the initiator sounding resolute, sincere and defiant while the respondent may be open and prepared to listen. In essence, the *dugri* talk serves to counteract what is 'considered the tendency to gloss over interpersonal relations in the service of a false, superficial consensus, a concern with harmony in interpersonal relations at the expense of dealing with basic issues and matters of principle' (p. 59). It works on a seemingly paradoxical understanding between the initiator and respondent that 'face' is maximally challenged to the extent that 'facework' has to be suspended.

Gift offering and accepting

Zhu et al. (2000) investigated the sequential organisation of gift offering and acceptance in close, friendly relationships in the Chinese context. They found that there is a schematised cycle of gift offer and acceptance, as shown in Figure 6.2.

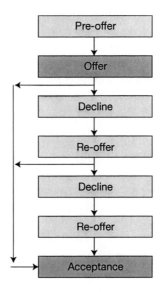

Figure 6.2 Sequential organisation of gift offering and accepting in the Chinese context

This analysis by Zhu et al. shows that the boundary between direct or indirect speech acts becomes blurry when the speaker's intentions in uttering these speech acts are viewed in the overall sequential organisation of gift offering and accepting. On one hand, gift offers in the Chinese cultural context are almost always structurally marked, with either pre-sequences or additional elaboration of various kinds. The giver behaves as if their act of offering was unacceptable and inappropriate to the recipient, and had to be hidden, heavily masked, or downplayed. On the other hand, the recipient needs to balance between showing their gratitude for the cost and effort incurred by the person making the offer and showing their modesty and lack of greediness. As the result, they need to enact a speech act of declination through one of the following strategies: complaining about the gift being too much or too expensive, questioning the reason for the offer, highlighting the already existing close relationship, or insisting that they do not need the gift. The data show that whether a speech act is direct or indirect cannot be viewed in isolation. Considerations need to be made to take account of the sequential organisation of the event in which a speech act occurs, the context where the speech event takes place, and also participants' knowledge of and expectation towards the local organisation of the interaction.

Quranic verses

Nazzal (2005) investigates the recitation of Quranic verses as a communicative resource among Muslims and the interplay between religious, linguistic and cultural identities. *Insha' Allah*, translated as 'God willing', implies that instead of being in control of the outcome, one is at the mercy of God – an Islamic belief. The author argues that the phrase, used in daily conversation, serves to mitigate one's commitment, to indirectly refuse or reject a request or invitation, to avoid undesirable consequences and to protect one's self-image. The phrase can also be used as a rhetorical strategy of indirect persuasion to lend credibility to the speaker's claim. In the following excerpt, an Egyptian couple living in Albany County in New York State are discussing whether to settle in the US or to go back to Egypt.

Example 6.2

1 H: But people are sick because of the pollution
2 W: My daughter wants to go back to Egypt because of the cold weather/climate here.
3 H: No your daughter is not going back to Egypt because the weather there is polluted.
4   And she got sick because of that and she does not like it either.
5   So how do you say that your daughter wants to go back to Egypt?

6   W: No, she does not want to settle here in the US.

7   H: That is up to her.

8   W: It is very clear that she does not want live here in America

9   H: That is up to her really.

10 W: It is better for her there.

11 H: Do you want to go back to Egypt too.

12 W: *Insha' allah and with his permission insha' allah*

13 H: *Insha' allah.*

(Nazzal, 2005, p. 267)

The author argues that the wife's enactment of *Insha' Allah* has several payoffs. With this recitation, the wife avoided making a direct, explicit statement which she knew was not what her husband wanted to hear. She also managed to deflect her responsibility and to mitigate a future commitment in order to save herself from any embarrassment if things go wrong.

6.4 Turn-taking: Universals vs. cultural variations

In an article with the title of 'A simplest systematics for the organization of turn taking in conversations', Sacks et al. (1974) identified a number of key features of how turns are allocated and transit from one speaker to another in conversation. These are:

- One party talks at a time.
- Overlaps occur, but are usually very brief.
- Turn order and size are not fixed, but vary.
- Turn allocation techniques are used either for self-selection or for the current speaker to select next.

Cross-cultural differences in the length of pause or gap between turns are reported in the literature. Jefferson (1989) found that in normal American English and Dutch conversations, a 1-second interval (in a range of 0.9–1.2 second) was the standard maximum gap between turns. Any pause longer than that would either be treated as 'problematic' by participants and require 'repair' such as topic shift, or be understood as a strategy to hedge a dispreferred response. In contrast, as mentioned in Chapter 2, studies on Athabaskan (Scollon and Scollon, 1981), Apache (Basso, 1990) and Australian Aboriginal cultures (Eades, 2000; Mushin and Gardner, 2009) suggest that these cultures allow a longer silence than the 1-second norm between turns noted by Jefferson.

In a ground-breaking study by Stivers and her colleagues (2009), a systematic comparison was made of the length of time speakers from ten languages (including Danish, Italian, Dutch, Tzeltal, Akhoe

Haillom – a language spoken in northern Namibia – English, Yélî-Dnye, Japanese, Lao and Korean) take to respond to polar questions (i.e. questions that expect a yes or no answer) in informal natural conversation. The study found there are some cross-linguistic differences in the average gap between turns. Danish has the slowest response time on average (469 ms), followed by Akhoe Haillom, Lao and Italian. English (236 ms) is slightly above the cross-linguistic mean. Japanese has the fastest response time (7 ms), contradicting anecdotal observations which suggest that Japanese tend to leave substantial gaps between turns. However, the authors stress that these cross-linguistic differences are in fact minimal. The cross-linguistic average for response time is 208 ms with the language-specific means falling within 250 ms on either side of this, which is equivalent to the length of time to produce a single English syllable. There is a general tendency to avoid overlapping talk and to minimise silence between conversational turns in all the languages tested. The discrepancies between their findings and ethnographic observations reported elsewhere, according to Stivers et al., may be due to a natural sensitivity to gaps in turns that are measured in milliseconds which result in 'subjective perception of dramatic or even fundamental differences' (p. 10587).

6.5 Space: The silent language

In his book *The Silent Language*, Hall (1959/1973) argues that 'space speaks' and 'time talks' and both space and time communicate as powerfully as language. His work has highlighted the relevance of non-verbal communication to interaction and brought well-deserved attention to non-verbal stimuli such as space, time, touch, gesture, facial expressions, paralanguages and so on. It has now been widely accepted that non-verbal communication plays an indispensible role in communication. It can be used to support speech by replacing the spoken message when words cannot be used, sending uncomfortable messages, regulating and managing communication and reinforcing and modifying verbal messages. It can also be used to convey emotions.

In this section, we will examine how meaning is conveyed through space (i.e. the study of proxemics) as an example of non-verbal communication. Klopf (1998) suggested that space reflects the personal relationship between the speaker and other people in the following way:

> Each of us carries around with us a personal space, a movable, portable space like an invisible bubble. It becomes larger or smaller depending upon whom we are speaking to. We take our friends and

people we like into our bubble. With those we do not like, our bubble contracts, shutting them out.

(p. 232)

Indeed, Hall suggests (1966) that, generally speaking, there are four levels of personal space among middle-class Americans, as depicted in Figure 6.3.

- *Intimate* distance: the distance for close or maximum contact among close family members or in intimate relationships such as parents and children or lovers. This is the distance where vocalisations are delivered in a soft voice or whisper.
- *Personal* distance: the distance for informal conversation between family members or relatives, friends or colleagues. Compared with intimate distance, the speakers are further apart and body touch is limited. Speech is louder, but remains casual.
- *Social* distance: the distance for more formal conversation, either for exchange of information or about non-personal matters. Speech is louder than that in intimate and personal distances and can be heard easily.
- *Public* distance: the distance for the most formal occasions such as giving a speech to a group. Speech is loud in order to get attention and to be heard. The conversation style is formal with a careful choice of words and phrasing of sentences.

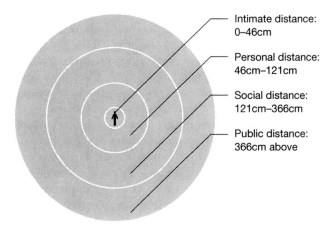

Figure 6.3 Four levels of personal space among middle-class Americans: an example of 'space speaks'

The following Task 6.2 is designed to discover your (unconscious) preference on how space is managed in daily life.

Task 6.2 Where would you stand/sit? (TC)

Elevator behaviour

When you get into an elevator, where do you usually stand and look in the following situations: (a) there is no one in the lift, (b) there is one person in the lift already, and (c) it is crowded?

Seating in a train

When you get into an underground train and find there are some empty seats as the picture below shows, where you would sit?

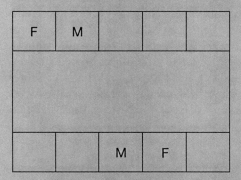

Figure 6.4 Seating in a train
Note: F: female; M: male

Axtell (1991) observes that there is a silent set of rules for elevator behaviour in America: when one or two enter an elevator, each of them would lean against the walls of the elevator; if it is four people, each would occupy a corner; in the case of five people or more, all turn to face the door and they seem to get 'taller and thinner' with their hands, handbags or briefcases hanging down in front of the body in a 'fig leaf position'. They are also likely to stare at the illuminated floor indicator. Members of other cultures may differ in their use and interpretation of space in general and in how comfortable they feel when they sit/stand close to each other. Cultural orientations to space can have ubiquitous influence on the way we do things, such as furniture arrangements, office arrangements, sleeping arrangements and architecture (Hall, 1959/1973). For example, how seating is arranged in a living room, how desks are arranged in an open-plan office and how buildings are designed very often reflect cultural orientations to space.

Apart from turn-taking and space, there are a number of aspects of non-verbal communication (NVC) which may have potential cross-cultural variations. One is emotion recognition. Although facial expressions such as happiness, surprise, fear, sadness, contempt, disgust and anger are generally believed to communicate the same feelings across cultures (Elfenbein et al., 2002), each culture may have different expectations of when, how, where and to whom facial expressions are displayed. The very social nature of emotional expressions such as fear is demonstrated in Ekman and Friesen's well-cited early study (1975). In their study, Japanese and American subjects revealed the same facial expression when shown a horror film alone. However, when viewing the film in the presence of others, Japanese participants manifested only neutral expressions. Since then, other empirical evidence supporting cross-cultural differences have been reported. For example, Markus and Kitayama (1994) argued that in Asian contexts emotions might reflect the feelings and responses of the larger group rather than those of the idiosyncratic self. David Matsumoto (1989, 1992) reported that some cultural groups tend to avoid recognising negative emotion in order to preserve social order. Recently, Masuda et al. (2008) found that when inferring individual emotions, Japanese will display greater sensitivity to social context than Westerners. A review can be found in Matsumoto and Hwang (2012).

6.6 Chapter summary

We have described some culture-specific ways of communication in this chapter. These are:

- the degree of directness in conveying intentions;
- the amount of information embedded in the context;
- the degree of involvement in conversation;
- the amount of gap between turns; and
- the distance and space between people.

We have also looked into some notions and models behind these culture-specific ways of communication. These include:

- face and politeness
- rapport
- *wakimae*: a key Japanese cultural term
- connectedness and solidarity.

In addition, we have compared how the notions of directness and indirectness are accomplished and negotiated in conversation in different cultures. Critiques of the approaches adopted in the studies discussed, particularly with regard to the use of local cultural terms vs. culturally general constructs, can be found in Section 11.6.

7 What are the key factors that may cause misunderstanding in intercultural communication?

During Hillary Clinton's trip to Africa in August, 2009, a Congolese university student asked her what her husband, Bill Clinton, thought about the involvement of China and the World Bank in the Democratic Republic of Congo.

'What does Mr Clinton think about it?' he asked through an interpreter.

'You want me to tell you what my husband thinks? My husband is not the secretary of state, I am,' Clinton retorted. 'You ask my opinion; I will tell you my opinion. I'm not going to be channelling my husband.'

Something clearly went wrong in this exchange. The US State Department official later claimed that the student told Hillary Clinton afterwards that he meant President Barack Obama, not Bill Clinton. If this were indeed the case, Hillary Clinton may have 'overreacted'. For her, however, the timing of the question could not have been worse. Her trip took place just one week after her husband had succeeded in a high-profile mission to free two American journalists from North Korea. The student's question could be easily interpreted as an attempt to marginalise her as a female politician in her own right and to trivialise her political agenda for this trip. The incident shows that misunderstandings can occur, more easily than we might expect, in conversations when different people bring in different contextual information to interactions. It also shows the cost of misunderstanding: in this case, Hillary Clinton displayed her upset and frustration. In some other cases, misunderstanding can lead to financial loss among business partners, distrust between friends or family dispute.

In this chapter, we are going to explore some main sources of misunderstanding in intercultural communication. We will first define what counts as misunderstanding and then look at several sources of misunderstanding. We will also explore the process of meaning-making in conversation, in particular, how speakers use information made available through conversation and relate it to their knowledge about the context in conversation.

7.1 Defining misunderstanding

Although the term 'misunderstanding' is often talked about, it is frequently used either intuitively or put down as a convenient diagnostic label for what goes wrong in a conversation, especially when the conversation concerned involves people from different cultural and ethnic backgrounds or there are discrepancies in linguistic proficiencies (e.g. the often used dichotomy of native vs. non-native speakers). In the context of the current chapter, it is useful to first have a close examination of some available definitions of misunderstanding, before we look into some sources of misunderstandings.

Mauranen (2006) defines a misunderstanding as a 'potential breakdown point in conversation, or at least a kind of communicative turbulence' (Mauranen, 2006, p. 128). It happens when a listener fails to make sense of what is going on. The question is: is the listener concerned aware of the problem? To reflect that the participants may have different awareness of the problem, Bremer (1996, p. 40) uses the term 'misunderstanding' to refer to the occasions on which 'the listener achieves an interpretation, which makes sense to her or him – but it wasn't the one the speaker meant' and the term 'non-understanding' to describe those occasions when the listener fails to make sense of what has been said by the speaker. Differentiating the two types of problem, according to Bremer, helps us to see the 'traces' the participants leave in the actual interaction and to identify what misunderstandings are, how and when they happen, and why. In cases of non-understanding, the person involved usually indicates that there is a problem with her understanding. In Example 7.1, the listener signalled her non-understanding by asking a 'who' question. In contrast, when misunderstandings happen, the problem is only revealed later in the course of conversation, e.g. through an 'incoherent' answer to the misunderstood question, or emerge later in the analysis or upon reflection. In Example 7.2, the Dutch housing officer was trying to find out whether the Turkish worker and his family had any circumstance that he needed to consider in housing, e.g. having a baby. He tried to reformulate his question about the baby several times, in Lines 2, 6 and 10. The Turkish worker went along with the housing officer's questions, not aware that he did not understand the question correctly until Line 15 when the Dutch housing officer heard an 'unlikely' answer.

Both Bremer (1996) and Roberts (1996) warn against any attempt to use misunderstanding or non-understanding as an absolute dichotomy. Rather, they see these two terms as poles of a continuum with partial lack of understanding in between, due to the largely 'invisible' nature of misunderstanding. In real-life communication, especially among participants with limited command of the language in which the conversation takes place, participants often make do with whatever information they can process to keep conversation going rather than signal the 'problem', just as the Turkish worker did in Example 7.2. This means that the extent of understanding is by no means evident from the conversation.

Example 7.1

A: well who'r you workin for.

B: 'hhh Well I'm working through the Amfat Corporation.

A: The who?

B: Amfah Corporation. T's a holding company.

A: Oh

A: Yeah

(Schegloff et al., 1977, p. 368; transcription slightly altered)

Example 7.2

An interview between a Dutch housing officer (N) and Ergün, a Turkish worker (E)

1	E:	ja
		yes
2	N:	vrouw wel in verwachting?
		wife is expecting?
3	E:	jawel
		Yes
4	N:	wel in verwachting?
		is expecting?
5	E:	ja wacht
		yes wait
6	N:	wanneer komt de baby?
		When will the baby come?
7	E:	weet ik niet
		I do not know
8	N:	niet?
		not
9	E:	Nee
		no
10	N:	hoe lang is ze in verwachting dan?
		how long has she been expecting then?
11	E:	oo misschien een jaar twee jaar [ik
		oh maybe one year two year I
12	N:	oh
		oh
13	E:	weet ik ook niet [laughs]
		I don't know – me either

14   N: dat lijkt me wat onwaarschijnlijk (.) nee kijk
             that seems unlikely to me + no look
15   ik denk dat je me verkeerd begrijpt
             I don't think you understand me correctly

(Roberts, 1996, pp. 17–18; transcription slightly altered)

In the next few sections, we are going to look at sources of misunderstanding in intercultural communication. Although these sources are presented separately under different headings, in reality they may interact with each other and it is likely that a misunderstanding can be attributed to several sources.

7.2 Inadequate linguistic proficiency

In intercultural communication participants more often than not speak the shared language with different degrees of proficiency. Bremer (1996) identified several problems of understanding that are located at the linguistic level and can be attributed to inadequate linguistic proficiency. These are described below.

Lexical comprehension problem. Participants may have difficulties in understanding lexical items that have relatively low frequency or are highly specialised. This type of problem is usually indicated more frequently, explicitly and willingly by the participant. In Example 7.3, Mahmut repeated the word *gekeurd* in rising tone in Line 2 to indicate that he did not understand the word and asked explicitly what the word means in Line 4.

'Mishearing' a lexical element. This type of misunderstanding happens when the participant perceives one or more phonetic/phonemic features differently. Similar to the previous lexical comprehension problem, it frequently happens when the lexical items are less familiar. In many ways, a mishearing, signalled and negotiated in the interaction, displays the interpretative process of the participant. In Example 7.2 cited above, it is possible that Ergün, the Turkish worker, misheard *verwacht* (expecting) as *wacht* (waiting).

Syntactic complexity. Complex utterances, elliptical utterances, contracted utterances, pronominal forms, hypothetical questions, etc., are often difficult to understand. In Example 7.4, Abdelmalek did not understand that *où* (where), a location pro-form, can be used to describe the temporal development of the situation.

Example 7.3

Context: Mahmut (M), a Turkish speaker, went for an interview in a bakery. The interview was conducted in Dutch. N: interviewer.

1	N:	uh nou u moet nog gekeurd worden
		ur well you have to have examined
2	M:	gekeurd?
		Examined?
3	N:	ja
		yes
4	M:	wat is dat die?
		what is that?
5	N:	gekeurd u moet naar arts naar dokter
		examined you have to go to a doctor to a physician
6	M:	keuring
		yes examination

(Bremer, 1996, p. 43; transcription slightly altered)

Example 7.4

Context: Abdelmalek (A), originally from Morocco, was seeking some advice from a lawyer (N). He has just explained that after a serious accident at work he has been unable to pay his rent and that the landlord has already locked up his room once.

1	N:	oui et alors ça en est où pour l'instant ?
		yes and so that's where at the moment?
2	A:	euh ici à la premiere arrondissement
		here in the first district
3	N:	non mais la situation elle en est à quel point
		no but the situation its got to what point
4		Je veux dire vis-à-vis de (.) du responsable du + de l'endroit ou vous habitez?
		I mean as far as the the person responsible for the place where you live?

(Bremer, 1996, p. 55; transcription slightly altered)

7.3 Pragmatic mismatch

When someone says 'the window is still open', she is performing a speech act at three levels: a locutionary act (said the meaning of the words), an illocutionary act (what is intended by the speaker, e.g. she may be suggesting shutting the window) and a perlocutionary act (the consequence of what has been said, e.g. the hearer went and shut the window). Misunderstanding can occur when the hearer has difficulty in understanding a locutionary act or illocutionary act. In the previous section, we have discussed several possible causes of misunderstanding at locutionary level. In this section, we are going to look at misunderstandings at illocutionary level, which can be broadly termed as pragmatic mismatch.

The first type of pragmatic mismatch is lack of understanding of the illocutionary force of a speech act. Some speech acts such as greetings and goodbye are more formulaic and more easily recognised than other speech acts, the intentions of which are either ambiguous or very much context-dependent. In Example 7.5, the receptionist at a dentist in a town called Walsall was asking the patient where he lived. Although her question could be interpreted as a more general one elsewhere, the context of the conversation requires the patient to give a specific answer rather than a general one.

Example 7.5

T: fine and erm where do you live?
R: (.)Walsall
T: what's the address sorry

(Bremer, 1996, p. 62; transcription slightly altered)

So far, we have looked at situations in which participants fail to *interpret* what is actually said or implied in utterances. There are times when participants as second language users fail to *convey* what they intend to say and hence cause misunderstanding. This phenomenon has been referred to as 'pragmatic failure'. According to Thomas (1983), there are two types of failure: pragmalinguistic failure and sociopragmatic failure. The former occurs when the pragmatic force in an utterance by a second language user does not match the force most frequently assigned to it by native speakers of the target language. As an example of pragmalinguistic failure caused by inappropriate pragmatic transfer, Thomas compared the way the phrase 'of course' is used in Russian and English. In Russian, *konesno* is often used in cases of enthusiastic agreement similarly to 'of course' in English. However, 'of course' in English can also be used in cases when something is obvious and cannot be argued. When directly transferring their use of *konesno* into English, Russian speakers may sound 'at best peremptory and at worst insulting' as shown in Example 7.6.

Example 7.6

A: Is it a good restaurant?
B: Of course
[Gloss (for Russian speaker): Yes, (indeed) it is. For English listener: what a stupid question!]

(Thomas, 1983, p. 102)

Sociopragmatic failure, in contrast, is more concerned with those hidden rules governing the applicability of pragmatic concepts such as politeness, face, directness, sincerity, etc., and is caused by inappropriate assessment of the degree of imposition, cost/benefit, social distance and relative rights and obligations, etc. In Chapter 1, we have observed that emails have become the most frequent means of communication between students and teachers in many parts of the world. But when you as a student draft an email request to your lecturer, how do you phrase your request? What are the challenges for second language users of English? These are the questions addressed in Task 7.1.

Ⓣ©

Task 7.1 Please answer me as soon as possible

As discussed earlier in Chapter 1, nowadays email has become an important means of communication between students and staff. It can be used to maintain relations, to engage in activities outside the classroom and/or to perform functions such as making requests, relaying information, etc. Read the following example, written by a Greek Cypriot university student who was seeking some guidance, and answer the following questions:

- If you were the recipient of the sample email, what would you think of its appropriateness?
- Can you find any features in the sample email that suggest that it is written by a non-native speaker? Does the fact that the email is written by a non-native speaker change your view of its appropriateness?

The sample email (adapted from Econonmidou-Kogetsidis, 2011, p. 3212):

Mary

I collected some 'chunks' about professional identity from the chapters that I read. I'm going to use them in my literature review that I will write tomorrow. Please take a look and see whether what I collected are necessary and important but also whether my references are ok.

Shall I include a quotation as it is…or shall I paraphrase?

Please answer me as soon as possible.

Thanx

C [student's name]

Pragmatic failure is essentially about the impact of one's first language on the use of a second language. A number of fields and disciplines provide particular insight in understanding the relationship between first and second languages. One is cross-cultural pragmatics. This is the study of speech acts by language users from different linguistic and cultural backgrounds. It mainly investigates how speech acts or events, such as requests, apologies, greetings, refusals, persuasions, invitations, gift offering and acceptance, etc., are realised in different languages and to what extent a speaker's choice of linguistic politeness strategy is influenced by factors such as relative power, social distance, and degree of imposition in a given culture. The first systematic study in this line of enquiry was the CCSARP (a cross-cultural study of speech act realisation patterns) project reported in Blum-Kulka and Olshtain (1984). Since then, a growing body of comparative studies of speech acts in different languages has emerged. These studies provide a wealth of information on cross-linguistic differences and similarities in speech acts, which could be used to explain what has gone wrong in intercultural (mis)communication.

Recent research on emotion and multilingualism represented by the work of Pavlenko (2005b) and Dewaele (2010) brings a multilingual perspective to the relationship between first and second languages. These authors take the view that multilingual speakers perceive the emotional force of the same emotion words – such as swear words, taboo words, and words expressing love or anger – differently in the different languages at their disposal, and therefore often resort to different languages to express these emotions. This argument is well illustrated in a quote from an interview with a multilingual speaker in Example 7.7.

Example 7.7

A participant who speaks Finnish as L1, English as L2, Swedish as L3 and German as L4 commented:

> I very rarely swear in Finnish but 'oh shit' or 'fuck' can easily escape my mouth even in quite trivial occasions – they just do not feel that serious to my (or my hearers') ears, even though I know they would sound quite horrible to a native speaker (milder English swear words like 'damn' for example do not even sound like swear words to me). If I would happen to hit myself with a hammer the words coming out of my mouth would definitely be in Finnish.
>
> (Dewaele, 2004, p. 213)

Among some of the main findings in this area are:

- Perceived emotional force of swear words and taboo words is in general correlated with the order in which languages are learned by the same speaker: highest in L1 and gradually lower in languages learned subsequently.
- Participants who learned their languages in a naturalistic – or partly naturalistic – context gave higher ratings to the emotional force of swear words and taboo words in that language than instructed language learners.
- Self-rated proficiency in a language and frequency of use of language significantly predicted perception of the emotional force of swear and taboo words.

Instead of attributing unique features associated with second language users to 'transfer' from L1 to L2 or 'failure', the work on emotion and multilingualism foregrounds emotion as the driving force for language choice, learning and use in multilingual contexts, and legitimises affective use of language by second language speakers.

7.4 Clash of styles

Misunderstandings can be caused by clashes of different styles of communication. In Chapter 6, we elaborated on some communicative styles and aspects of communication that are likely to have culture-specific variations. We have also discussed some examples where speakers apply different styles of conversation, for example, small talk in Section 2.3 and point-making styles in Section 3.2. Unlike misunderstandings caused by inadequate linguistic proficiency and pragmatic mismatch, clashes of style often leave very little trace in interactions in the sense that no conversational trouble or 'breakdown' is usually visible in interaction. The clash often runs across a longer stretch of conversation. Below we are going to look at an example from a study by Bailey (1997). The conversation took place between an immigrant Korean shopkeeper/cashier and African-American customer in Los Angeles. It begins with the customer speaking to his nephew while walking into the shop.

In the extract, the cashier's response to the customer's requests was minimal in the first half of the extract ('nods' in Line 4; 'eh' in Line 6). He only began to show some interest in sustaining the conversation when the customer asked him a specific question ('you remember me', in Line 13). But his contributions in the second half of the extract were mainly a mixture of clarification ('Oh yesterday, last night' in Line 14) and confirmation ('I know you' in Line 20) and business transaction ('there you go' in Line 24).

In contrast, the customer engaged in a different conversational style which resembles the 'high involvement style' we discussed in Chapter 6.

He was informal and intimate ('how's it going partner' in Line 4) and direct ('you got them little bottles', in Line 5). He spoke in high volume and used a swear word in Lines 2 and 17. He volunteered personal topics in Line 13 and explicitly asked the cashier to 'know' him.

Bailey argues that the contrast in conversational style between the shopkeeper and the customer suggests that each side has different ideas about the relationship between customers and shopkeepers and about the corresponding service encounter style. While the customer's interactional style is 'emotionally intense, dynamic and demonstrative', the shopkeeper remains detached and impersonal. When the customer revisited the topic of getting to know each other in Line 21, the shopkeeper reframed the conversation as a business transaction by saying 'there you go' in Line 24 and signalled the end of the interaction by physically removing himself from the counter. According to Bailey (1997), the clash in conversation styles between members of two different ethnic groups, as evident in this extract, often leads to tension in interethnic relationships between two groups. In this case,

> the seeming avoidance of involvement on the part of immigrant Koreans is frequently seen by African Americans as the disdain and arrogance of racism. The relative stress on interpersonal involvement among African Americans in service encounters is typically perceived by immigrant Korean retailers as a sign of selfishness, interpersonal imposition, or poor breeding.
>
> (Bailey, 1997, p. 353)

Example 7.8

Context: customer arrives talking to his companion, who is later identified as his nephew.

1	Cust:	(()) thirty-seven years old ((in this)) ass
2	Cust:	Motherfucker
3	Cash:	Hi [Customer approaches counter]
4	Cust:	How's it going partner? euh [Cashier nods]
5	Cust:	You got them little bottles?
6	Cash:	(eh) [Customer's gaze falls on the little bottles]
7	Cust:	One seventy-fi:ve! [Customer gazes at display of bottles]
8	Cust:	You ain't got no bourbon?
9	Cash:	No: we don't have bourbon
10	Cust:	I'll get a beer then.
11	Cust:	((turns to nephew)) What would you like to drink? what do you want? [Customer selects beverages and brings them to the cash register.]
12	Cash:	Two fifty [Cashier rings up purchase and bags beer.]
13	Cust:	I just moved in the area. I talked to you the other day. You [remember me]?

14 Cash: [Oh yesterday] last night
15 Cust: Yeah
16 Cash: [(O:h yeah)] [Cashier smiles and nods]
17 Cust: [Goddamn, shit] [then you don't –]
18 Cash: [new neighbor, huh?] [Customer turns halfway to the side toward the owner]
19 Cust: Then you don't know me
20 Cash: [(I know you)] [Cashier gets change at register]
21 Cust: [I want you to know] me so when I walk in here you'll know me I smoke Winstons. Your son knows me
22 Cash: [Ye::ah]
23 Cust: [The yo]ung guy
24 Cash: There you go [Cashier proffers change]
25 Cust: [Okay then]
26 Cash: [Three four] five ten [Cashier steps back from counter]

(Bailey, 1997, pp. 345–346; transcription slightly altered)

7.5 Mismatch in schemas and cultural stereotypes

During my first trip to the UK a few years ago, I went to a supermarket to buy some groceries. When I was checking out, the cashier asked me 'Any cash back?' Although I heard every syllable of the question, I was bewildered: why was she offering me money? New to the system, I did not know at that time that many supermarkets offer their customers the option of withdrawing cash if they pay with a debit card.

This kind of mis- or non-understanding triggered by lack of knowledge about the system and procedures can be referred to as a mismatch in schemas, a term having its root in psychology and cognitive science. Schemas are 'generalized collections of knowledge of past experiences that are organised into related knowledge groups and are used to guide our behaviours in familiar situations' (Nishida, 2005, p. 402). They are the knowledge we have learned, accumulated and stored in our memory since the moment we were born. They are important because we rely on them to make sense of an interaction, a person, an event, or a place on the basis of whatever information is available to use. They also guide our attention to certain things and ultimately influence the way we understand our world.

According to Nishida (2005, pp. 405–407), there are different types of schemas.

- Fact-and-concept schemas: general information about facts, e.g. 'London is the capital of the United Kingdom.'
- Person schemas: knowledge about different types of people, including personality traits, e.g. Mary is easy-going.
- Self schemas: knowledge about ourselves (i.e. how we see ourselves, and how others see us).
- Role schemas: knowledge about social roles and behaviours that are expected of people in particular social positions.
- Context schemas: information about the situation and appropriate settings of behavioural parameters.
- Procedure schemas: knowledge about the appropriate sequence of events in common situations.
- Strategy schemas: knowledge about problem-solving strategies.
- Emotion schemas: information about emotional states and affect association with events, activities or states.

Some of the examples previously given in pragmatic failures and clash of styles can be alternatively interpreted as mismatch in schemas. In Example 7.5, the patient failed to draw from the context schema of 'going to a local dentist', i.e. at the dentist, checking a patient's address is part of the identification process. In Example 7.8, the shopkeeper and the customer clearly have different expectations, i.e. person and role schemas, about the degree of solidarity in service encounters.

Task 7.2 What brings you here?   (TC)

Read the following conversation recalled by Donal Carbaugh, author of *Cultures in Conversation* (Carbaugh, 2005, p. 15). He was talking with a gentleman in a pub during his residence at the University of Oxford's Linacre College as a visiting senior member. Discuss why the conversation did not seem to go anywhere. What does the conversation tell us about the role of schemas in conversations?

1	He said:	Hello.
2	I replied:	Hello.
3	He said:	What brings you here?
4	I:	I'm visiting Linacre College.
5	He said:	Oh, yes, are you a student?
6	I:	in a broad sense, yes (laughing) but I've come to join two research teams.
7	He:	Oh. What are you studying?
8	I:	One group is studying communication and identity. The other is studying environmental discourses.
9	He:	Oh, yes, mighty interesting. Are you a member of the college?
10	I:	(pause) I'm here at the invitation of Professor Harré.
11		(pause)

12 He:	What is it that you study?
13 I:	Cultural patterns of communication and intercultural encounters.
14 He:	Oh, you're an anthropologist?
15 I:	No, not really, although my undergraduate degrees were in anthropology and communication, but what I study mostly are communication processes. In the United States we have academic departments whose primary purpose is to study communication.
16 He:	(surprised) Oh, yes, uh-huh.

Schemas can operate at different levels. Those that emerge from a cultural group's collective knowledge and are shared by the members of a cultural group are described as 'cultural schemas' by Sharifian (2005) or 'cultural models' by Quinn and Holland (1987, p. 4). Example 7.9 is a conversation between an Iranian student and an Australian lecturer. The lecturer found the student's reply to his congratulations uncomfortable and lacking in sincerity to say the least, while the student on the other hand could not think of anything wrong with her reply. Sharifian explained that the misunderstanding was a result of discrepancy in cultural schemas. While the Australian lecturer used his Australian schema of 'individual merit', the Iranian student drew upon her Persian cultural schema of *shekasteh-nafsi*, which 'motivates the speakers to downplay their talents, skills, achievements, etc.... and also encourages the speakers to reassign the compliment to the giver of the compliment, a family member, a friend, or another associate' (Sharifian, 2005, p. 337). In this way, cultural schemas provide an alternative interpretation of cross-cultural differences in norms and patterns of interactions.

Example 7.9

Lecturer: I heard you've won a prestigious award. Congratulations! This is fantastic.
Student: Thanks so much. I haven't done anything. It is the result of your effort and your knowledge. I owe it all to you.
Lecturer: Oh, No!!! Don't be ridiculous. It's all your work.

(Sharifian, 2005, pp. 337–338)

In the list of different types of schemas provided by Nishida (2005), person schemas are about knowledge about other individuals or groups of people including their traits, roles and behaviours. Within this type of schema, knowledge about other cultural or ethnic groups (e.g. Italians, Latin Americans, etc.) is also called 'cultural stereotypes'. It is difficult to miss the presence of cultural stereotypes in everyday life. Many of the examples in the previous chapters either explicitly build on or insinuate the idea of cultural stereotypes: the 'suitcase' of cultural stereotypes in Section 1.1 shows how cultural stereotypes might be used to facilitate language learning; the case of Volvo in diversifying their marketing strategies using culture-specific approaches (promoting the car's safety to Swiss and UK audiences, its status to French audiences, its economy to Swedish audiences and its performance to German audiences) in Section 3.1 shows how cultural stereotypes can be turned into advertising appeals.

Cultural stereotypes, similar to other types of schema, filter our attention. If we have negative stereotypes, we tend to look for evidence to confirm them, ignoring the fact that these cultural stereotypes can be wrong and they are no more than 'best guesses'. An example of how cultural stereotypes affect our perceptions is provided by Correll and his colleagues (2002). Using a videogame with images of African- or White Americans holding guns or other non-threatening objects, their study examined the effect of ethnicity of the target on shoot/don't shoot decisions both among university students and a community sample. They found that participants, including both Whites and African-Americans, showed a bias to shoot African-American targets more rapidly and/or more frequently than White targets, primarily because of the cultural schema associated with African-Americans, namely 'violent' or 'dangerous'.

Some examples are available in the literature showing how cultural stereotypes can lead to misunderstandings in interactions. Example 7.10 took place during a genetic counselling session in a university clinic in southern Germany. A Turkish couple (referred to as PtM and PtF) were referred to the clinic by their doctor after the doctor discovered that the cause of their child's mental retardedness was a faulty gene carried by the mother. The geneticist conducting the session (DocM) was German. A Turkish trainee doctor (IntM) acted as interpreter. The following simplified transcript in English has been adapted from the original transcript.

Example 7.10

DocM: German male medical doctor, specialist in human genetics
PtM: Turkish male patient
PtF: Turkish female patient
IntM: Turkish male doctor-in-training.

1 IntM: [to the patients] *if too much goes across, the child will be sick,* (1s) *if the normal one goes across the child will be normal. That's what we'll show you now. That is, we know it comes from there.*
2 PtF: *That is, too much from me went across.*
3 IntM: hmhm
4 DocM: (3s) hmhm

5 PtM: [speaking to his wife] [breathes in deeply] *Wife, ought I to marry again? What ought I do?* [laughs]
6 PtF: [laughs]
7 IntM: [to the doctor] whether he should marry again/once more or what he ought to do. Mr. Güneş, he asks himself or he asks Mrs. Güneş.
8 DocM: (1s) I don't think you have to consider these thoughts.
9 PtM: [in German] I making joke, yes! I love my wife.
10 DocM: Yes! [Slightly laughing] (1s) I'd like to explain to you simply what can happen and uhm what the heredity looks like.

(Hartog, 2006, pp. 178–180; transcription altered. Sentences produced in Turkish originally are in italics to differentiate from those in German)

The misunderstanding in the conversation was triggered by the male patient's rhetorical question to his wife in Line 5. From the way he said it and the wife's response, it was clear that he meant it as a joke. However, when the interpreter attempted to translate the conversation between the patients from Turkish to German, he did not foreground it as a joke, perhaps because he thought that it was obvious. Without knowing that it was meant to be a joke, the doctor drew upon his cultural stereotype, i.e. the Turkish man was going to repudiate his wife, and began to make his position clear in Line 8. The male patient quickly realised that he had been misunderstood and spoke out in German for the first time in the transcript in Line 9 to the effect of 'de-stereotyping' (the term used by Hartog to describe the process of 'undoing a stereotype').

7.6 Mismatch in contextualisation and framing

In the previous sections, we have discussed various cases of misunderstanding as the result of inadequate linguistic proficiency, pragmatic mismatch, clash of styles and mismatch in schemas. To understand each other, conversation participants not only need to make sense of what is accessible and available to them in the immediate context but also to draw upon relevant schemas. Such a process is called 'contextualisation' by Gumperz (1982, 1992). As an analytical tool, contextualisation describes the process whereby

speakers' and listeners' use of verbal and nonverbal signs to relate what is said at any one time and in any one place to knowledge acquired through past experience, in order to retrieve the presuppositions they must rely on to maintain conversation involvement and assess what is intended.

(Gumperz, 1992, p. 230)

The verbal and non-verbal signs are 'contextualisation cues' and they operate at the following several levels (Gumperz, 1992).

- prosody: intonation, stress, accenting, pitch, register shifts, etc.;
- paralinguistic signs: tempo, pausing, hesitation, tone of voice, turn-taking, etc.;
- code choice: code switching (alternating languages), style switching, or selection among phonetic, phonological or morphosyntactic options;
- choice of lexical forms or formulaic expressions: similar to code choice, the choice of lexical forms or formulaic expressions such as opening or closing routines or metaphoric expressions is meaningful.

The breakdown of contextualisation cues given above helps to identify aspects of conversations, particularly prosody, paralinguistic signs and code switching, which have received little attention in the field but are important for interpretive processes. Gumperz's well-cited study on 'gravy' is an excellent example of how prosody is not only relevant but also significant to intercultural relationship (1992).

Research summary: 'gravy!' versus 'gravy?'

Gumperz's study (1992) started with a puzzling problem: newly hired Indian and Pakistani assistants in a staff cafeteria at Heathrow airport were often perceived as rude or uncooperative by their supervisors and the airport staff, while the Indian and Pakistani women complained of discrimination. The analysis of tape-recorded conversations revealed that differences in prosodies were the primary cause. When the staff ordered meat, the cafeteria assistant was supposed to ask them whether they would like to have some gravy. Instead of saying 'gravy?' with a rising intonation, the Asian assistants would say 'gravy' with a falling intonation, which is their normal way of asking a question. However, this may appear rude to native speakers of English: 'gravy' with falling intonation came across as a statement, suggesting 'This is gravy. Take it or leave it.'

For contextualisation cues to enter into the inferential process, Gumperz (1992) argues that conversation participants need to first of all receive and categorise communicative signals; second, to make inference on 'communicative intent'; and third, to frame and signal what is expected in the interaction at any one stage. The third level, 'frames', are interactional devices used by conversation participants to define the boundary of an event and foreground the contextual information in interactions. They are, as Roberts (1996) points out, 'a particularly important notion in intercultural communication because shared frames are central to creating the conditions for shared interpretations' (p. 24). In Example 7.11, there are several occasions in the conversation when new frames are introduced. In Line 1, the interviewer/counsellor began to probe A's qualifications with a direct request ('Well tell me what you have been studying'). The second frame was introduced when B commented 'Oh, so you have *done* some teaching' in Line 9. This comment was in fact an invitation for A to tell her about his teaching experience. However, A missed the frame and merely rephrased his words. The third frame was introduced by A himself when he realised that B seemed to have attributed his difficulty in finding a job to his uncompleted probation. In Lines 23 and 25, he rejected B's assumption explicitly and made it clear that his account was not complete yet. By doing so, he signalled his forthcoming recounting of what happened to him.

Example 7.11

A: Indian male speaker
B: British female speaker.

The conversation took place at an interview-counselling session in London.

1	B:	well tell me what you have been studying
2	A:	um
3	B:	Up till now
4	A:	um, I have done my MSc from N. University
5	B:	huh
6	A:	I have done my graduate certificate in Education from L. Uni-
7		versity. I had been teaching after getting that teachers' training in
8		H., in H.
9	B:	oh, so you have <u>done</u> some teaching
10	A:	Some [I have done I have done some [teaching
11	B:	[in H. [I see
12	A:	Um ... I completed two terms ... uh, unfortunately I had to
13		Leave from that place [uh I was appointed only
14	B:	[oh
15	A:	for two terms
16	B:	Oh so you didn't get to finish your probation, I suppose
17	A:	(sighs) so that is uh [my start was alright but later
18	B:	[oh
19	A:	on what happened it is a mi – a great chaos, I don't know
20		Where I stand or what I can do, um, [after

21   B: [and now you find
22   You can't get a job
23   A: no this is not actually the situation, [I have not
24   B: [oh
25   A: completely explained [my position
26   B: [yes yes
          (Gumperz, 1982, reprinted in 2005, pp. 41–42 in 2005; transcription slightly
                                                                          altered)

The example shows how frames which are initiated by one party can
be either taken up or missed by the other party in the conversation and
how they can be used as interactional devices to signal and negotiate
what is to be expected at a point in a conversation.

7.7 Chapter summary

In this chapter we have looked at a variety of sources of misunderstanding in intercultural communication. These include:

- inadequate linguistic proficiency;
- pragmatic mismatch;
- clash of styles;
- mismatch in schemas and cultural stereotypes;
- mismatch in contextualisation cues and framing.

We also discussed:

- understanding vs. non-understanding in a process of negotiation
  among participants;
- a misunderstanding may have several sources.

The question is: are all the misunderstandings we have discussed so far
intercultural? While misunderstandings caused by cultural stereotypes
are clearly intercultural in nature, not all misunderstandings are caused
by the fact that the participants are from different cultural backgrounds.
Some sources, such as misinterpretation of the propositional meaning
of certain words or mishearing of what is said, are generic. They can
happen to anyone in any context and are not limited to communication
between people from different cultural backgrounds. Some sources
such as pragmatic mismatch and inadequate linguistic proficiency are
likely to occur in intercultural communication, not because of the
nature of intercultural communication *per se*, but because the
participants in intercultural communication are very often second
language speakers or lingua franca users of the language of communication. However, the challenge for intercultural communication

is that when things go wrong in communicating with people from different cultural and ethnic groups, it is minority groups or non-native speakers who tend to get the blame even if misunderstandings are not always intercultural.

8 What contributes to successful communication?

As discussed in Chapter 7, misunderstanding in intercultural communication can arise for a variety of reasons. In this chapter, we are going to look at what we can do to facilitate successful communication in intercultural encounters. We will first discuss Communication Accommodation Theory (CAT), which aims to understand what people do *naturally* when there are communicative and linguistic differences between conversation participants. We will then discuss strategies of collaboratively negotiating meaning and achieving understanding, followed by a section on interpreter-mediated interactions. In the last section, we will explore how knowledge of professional and institutional discourse can contribute to successful communication.

8. 1 Accommodating towards your audience

Why did Joey Barton put on a French accent?

This is the headline which appeared in a November 2012 issue of the *BBC News Magazine*. English footballer Joey Barton appeared at a press conference in Marseilles, France, and spoke to reporters in a 'French' accent reminiscent of the BBC sitcom *'Allo 'Allo!*, in which British actors playing French characters mimicked the 'French' accent to humorous effect.

Barton, defending his action, tweeted about the difficulty of speaking in Scouse (an English dialect spoken in Liverpool) to a room full of French journalists, and claimed that the only way he could be understood was to adopt the accent of an *'Allo 'Allo!* character.

While Barton's idea of making himself understood is debatable, what he expressed was a desire to accommodate the needs of his audience. The psychological model for speakers to adjust and shift their speech styles either consciously or unconsciously according to the context is Communication Accommodation Theory (CAT). It originates from Howard Giles's work in the field of social psychology of language. The model was initially named 'Speech Accommodation

Theory' (Giles, 1973; Street and Giles, 1982) and later renamed 'Communication Accommodation Theory' when Giles and his colleagues realised that adjustments took place not only to accents, but also at non-verbal and discursive levels such as speech rate, patterns of pausing, utterance length, gesture, posture, smiling, gaze and so on (Giles et al., 1991). Reviews of the main arguments on CAT can be found in Ylänne-McEwen and Coupland (2000) and Gallois et al. (2005).

Broadly speaking, there are three types of adjustment:

- Convergence: a speaker converges towards her conversation partner working on the principle of 'similarity attraction' (a hypothesis proposed by Byrne, 1971).
- Divergence: a speaker seeks to accentuate communicative differences between her conversation partner and herself.
- Maintenance: a speaker chooses not to modify her way of speaking relative to her conversation partner.

Communication accommodative behaviours are believed to be motivated by three goals: seeking approval, maintaining group identity and attaining communicative efficiency. The first two motivations are relational in nature: a speaker who wants to cooperate and seeks her addressee's approval is likely to show convergence behaviour, and a speaker who wants to dissociate herself from her addressee is likely to diverge from her addressee. The third goal of communication accommodative behaviour, attaining communicative efficiency, is functional in nature and particularly relevant to the theme of this chapter. It describes what a speaker does to improve her chances of being understood. For example, when we speak to a 2-year-old child, we are likely to speak slowly and clearly and to choose our words carefully. This is known as baby talk. Accommodative behaviours are also reported in the way we talk to the elderly (Coupland et al., 1988; de Bot and Lintsen, 1989). In order for accommodation to be successful, speakers need to modify their way of speaking on the basis of their assessment of addressees' linguistic ability. Coupland et al. (1988) argued that 'accommodative talk is not necessarily talk wherein participants share any obvious speech characteristic...Rather, it is talk wherein actors achieve a high degree of fit between their typically different, but potentially attunable, behaviours' (p. 28). They differentiated the following four types of communicative accommodation behaviours which have a clear focus on addressees.

- Approximation strategies: converging towards the addressee's productive performance such as accent, speech rate, etc.

- Interpretability strategies: modification of the complexity of communication and improvement of clarity through attending to the addressee's receptive competence.
- Discourse management strategies: being facilitative in turn-taking and topic-selection and attentive to the addressee's face wants and conversational needs.
- Interpersonal control strategies: allowing the addressee's discretion in the communicative roles to be adopted in face-to-face interaction.

These four types of discursive strategies highlight areas where adjustments can be made beyond speech styles between conversation participants. In the process of accommodating, a speaker needs to take into account not only the conversation partner's productive performance, but also the latter's receptive competence and interpersonal needs. The addressee's role in influencing a speaker's way of speaking is well illustrated in the idea of 'audience design', which proposes that whether the audience is known, ratified and directly spoken to by the speaker influences the speaker's way of speaking. Bell (1984, 2001) categorised four types of audience: addressee (listeners who are known, ratified and addressed), auditor (listeners not directly addressed, but are known and ratified), overhearer (non-ratified listeners of whom the speaker is aware), and eavesdropper (non-ratified listeners of whom the speaker is not aware). For example, in a news interview on a radio station, the interviewee may be 'known' to the interviewer while a listener is acknowledged by the interviewer, but not known to the interviewer and not directly addressed by the interviewer. However, the knowledge of the presence of the listener can influence the interviewer's way of speaking. In Bell's study (1984), four news broadcasters working for two New Zealand radio stations were found to systematically adjust their speech according to the perceived backgrounds of the listeners of each station: they tended to use more standard pronunciations on one station whose listeners were thought to be of higher socio-economic status, and less standard pronunciations for the other station whose listeners were believed to be of somewhat lower status.

In the context of interactions where there are disparities in linguistic proficiency among participants, a phenomenon common to intercultural communication, accommodative behaviours among conversational participants, motivated by participants' natural psychological orientations, play an important role in facilitating communication. Recent years have seen increasing application of accommodation theory in business communication studies. In what follows, we are going to look at two questions: What accommodation strategies do native and non-native speakers use? How are these accommodation strategies perceived by their recipients?

Task 8.1 Foreigner talk

Try the following task adapted from Ferguson (1975).

Instructions: Read the following sentences. Imagine yourself as an English speaker. You are acting as spokesperson for a group of three and addressing a group of non-English speakers who look non-European. They may have heard some English before but they are not really able to understand it or speak it. First write down the way you think the English speaker might say it or act in trying to communicate with the non-English speakers. Then answer the following questions:

- Would you use this kind of language yourself in this situation? Are you more likely to use some features than others?
- Would you make use of gestures in connection with this kind of language?

Sentences:

1   I haven't seen the man you're talking about.
2   He's my brother, he's not my father.
3   Did you understand what she said?
4   Come and see me tomorrow. Don't forget!
5   Yesterday I saw him and gave him some money.
6   He's working with me. He'll work with you too.
7   Who is that man? Is he your brother?
8   He always carries two guns.
9   Where's the money I gave you yesterday?
10   She's going tomorrow.

(Ferguson, 1975, p. 12)

The existing research literature is mainly focused on adjustments made by native speakers when interacting with non-native speakers. Early work by Ferguson (1975) cited in Task 8.1 has shown that native speakers adopt 'foreigner talk' when they talk to non-native speakers with perceived low linguistic proficiency similar to the way in which mothers talk to their babies. The simplified speech register is characterised by high frequency words, reduced syntactic complexity, clearer and exaggerated articulation, slower speech rate, and so on. The benefits and problems of using a simpler speech register in the context of second language learning and classroom teaching, especially its role in facilitating learning in the form of modified input, have been well discussed in second language research in the 1980s and 1990s (for a review, see Faerch and Kasper, 1986; Gass and Varonis, 1991). Bremer and Simonot (1996) proposed a number of options that speakers have in getting their message across and preventing misunderstanding. The main options are summarised below.

- Encouraging participation
  - encouraging self-initiated topics;
  - offering turns;
  - open questions;
  - allowing for pauses;
  - taking up and restructuring fragments or incomplete contributions.
- Raising predictability
  - meta-discourse comments and signposting;
  - clear pauses and placing topic ahead of the rest of an utterance.
- Raising transparency
  - raising accessibility
    - at perceptual level: short utterances; highlighting with volume, articulation and position in the utterance; facilitating segmentation with pauses, slower rate of delivery;
    - at level of lexical meaning: high frequency vocabulary, using another language when relevant;
    - at level of conceptual meaning: linking complex topics to the 'here and now', absolute instead of relational reference to time;
  - raising explicitness
    - full forms instead of ellipsis, pro-forms, reduced phonetic forms.
- Lexicalisation of what is encoded morphologically.
- Repetition.

A potential problem with accommodation of this kind is the risk of overdoing it, since there are 'limits on the normal applicability and extent of accommodative adaptation' (Ylänne-McEwen and Coupland 2000, p. 196). Over-accommodation takes place when speakers underestimate their recipients' receptive competence and oversimplify their speech register. For example, 'foreigner talk' may be appropriate when the recipient has low language proficiency as Ferguson (1975) originally envisaged, but it would be patronising to recipients with higher levels of language proficiency, despite the speaker's best intentions. To adjust her linguistic behaviour appropriately, a speaker needs to make an assessment of the recipient's receptive competence, drawing upon her previous experience of interacting with the recipient or the social, cultural and linguistic group with which she associates the recipient. This is where things can go wrong: the speaker's ascription of the linguistic competence to the recipient may be imprecise; there might be differences between the level of competence perceived by the speaker and the recipient's self-perceived competence; the recipient may be matched into a wrong group. Another problem with over-accommodation is that although it may be considered helpful for a particular interaction, it 'will not necessarily encourage initiative and progress and might, in the long run, beside the risk of being patronising and reinforcing power difference, be demotivating' (Vasseur et al., 1996b, p. 96).

In recent years, some studies (e.g. Rogerson-Revell, 2010; Sweeney and Zhu, 2010) have applied CAT to business communication which, different from casual conversation, has clearly defined transactional goals and requires higher communicative efficacy. The study by Sweeney and Zhu (2010) provided an opportunity to look into adjustments native speakers would make in business communication and the extent to which they would make these adjustments. In their study, participating native speakers of English were invited to fill in a discourse completion task (DCT) which prompted participants' linguistic response twice in a number of negotiation contexts. In the first round they were not told with whom they were negotiating, while in the second round they were told specifically that they were negotiating with non-native speakers. Some examples of answers given by the same speakers but for different interlocutors can be found in Table 8.1.

Their study not only found a range of accommodative strategies used by native English speakers, but also showed that these accommodative strategies came with a cost: adjustments on one level sometimes result in divergence on another level. For example, in P8NS's response to non-native speakers, he used a subjectiviser ('I'm afraid') and a mitigating supportive move ('if we are to sustain our order levels'). However, the request has become less explicit and transparent. Interestingly, despite significant variation in the use and the extent of accommodation strategies in the task, the participants

Table 8.1 Examples of accommodation strategies used by native speakers

Participant	Negotiation with native speakers	Negotiation with non-native speakers
P14NS	As I'm sure you are aware we already have a well established and successful relationship with your company. I'm looking to negotiate a contract with you today. What's your best offer? (Indirect request with two supportive moves)	What's the best offer you can give me? (Indirect request without any supportive move)
P8NS	We need to look again at pricing. (Explicit direct strategy)	I'm afraid we're going to have to revisit your terms if we are to sustain your order levels. (Indirect strategy)

Source: Sweeney and Zhu, 2010.

shared similar views when they were asked about their understanding and attitudes towards accommodation. There was a general awareness of the need to adjust one's language for non-native speakers and a relatively accurate awareness of what causes problems. One participant commented, 'shorter sentences, simpler vocabulary. Fewer fill-in words – can sound quite blunt, so tend to smile more to soften it.'

To sum up this section, we have discussed communication accommodation theory and explored why and how speakers make adjustments towards their audience. We have looked into the application of communication accommodation strategies in business communication and discussed benefits and costs associated with the use of accommodation strategies. Many of the accommodation strategies discussed in this section are in essence strategies of negotiating meaning, which will be the focus of the next section.

8.2 Negotiating misunderstanding

In this section, we will explore what participants in intercultural encounters do to manage misunderstandings and to negotiate understanding. We will draw insights mainly from the work on lingua franca communication, which has received increasing attention among researchers and practitioners in recent years.

Lingua franca communication refers to situations where all or some participants interact with each other in a language other than their native languages. It is very often the case that lingua franca participants speak the shared language with different degrees of proficiency. Two key arguments from lingua franca communication are of relevance to our discussion. One is that *communicative efficiency* rather than linguistic accuracy becomes the primary concern of lingua franca speakers (Ehrenreich, 2010). The standard and native form of the language used as the shared means of communication is no longer used as a reference point. The other argument is that despite its heterogeneous nature, lingua franca communication shows a remarkable *cooperative* feature. Meierkord's work (1998, 2000), for example, shows how participants use various non-verbal means to create a friendly and cooperative atmosphere and to build up conversation collaboratively, including using laughter to substitute verbal back-channels, using pauses to indicate topic changes and to mark the transition between different phases of a conversation, and collaborative construction of turns. Pitzl's work (2009) shows how participants creatively adapt native speakers' idioms and build on its metaphoricity to establish a sense of playfulness and in-group solidarity. In what follows, we will look into what speakers can do to signal misunderstandings and to negotiate meaning jointly in the event of misunderstandings.

Signalling misunderstanding

When misunderstandings occur, speakers apply a continuum of procedures ranging from explicitly signalling their non-understandings or difficulties to coping strategy. Explicit strategies include asking specific questions in the form of meta-linguistic queries and comments (such as 'sorry', 'pardon', or 'what does it mean', etc.) or repetition of problematic items. In Example 8.1, S1 signalled his lack of understanding in Turn 5 by using a discourse marker, '*hm*', with rising intonation. His signal was acknowledged by S3, who thought S1 did not follow his argument and subsequently elaborated his argument in Turn 6. In Turn 7, S1 resorted to an explicit strategy of using a metalinguistic question, 'What does an asset mean?' The explicit strategy worked and in Turn 8, S3 explained its lexical meaning.

Example 8.1

1   S1:   yeah well i tried to explain this by centre periphery
2   S3:   yeah you tried [yeah]
3   S1:   [but it's] i mean i'm not a Finn so i ((xx)) so much insight that's the problem
4   S3:   but that's an asset
5   S1:   hm?
6   S3:   that's an asset that you're not a Finn in this in this topic i think
7   S1:   what does an asset mean?
8   S3:   it's an advantage
9   S1:   ok yeah (.) well (.)

(Mauranen, 2006, p. 132; transcription slightly altered)

In real-life interactions, not all the mis- or non-understandings are signalled. A number of coping procedures have been identified by Vasseur et al. (1996a). These include *over-riding* practices, whereby participants ignore the utterances beyond their comprehension and carry on with their topics; *silence*, whereby participants opt out of turn-taking; *minimal feedback*, whereby participants acknowledge the other participants' utterances merely with feedback tokens such as 'yes', 'hm', 'yeah' or equivalents. While minimal feedback helps to keep the flow of interaction and to give speakers more time and contextual information to gradually formulate their hypotheses to some extent, its prolonged use often leads to confusion, since the burden rests on the other participants to interpret and piece together the limited information available. Some experienced speakers may be able to interpret these coping strategies as symptoms of mis- or non-understanding and perform a comprehension check. In Example 8.2, after Paula, a Chilean woman, gave several minimal feedback tokens, the interviewer suspected that Paula might not understand the question and initiated a comprehension check in Turn 5.

Example 8.2

X: interviewer; P: Paula

1   X: d'accord et vous avez déjà fait des études ↑ pour ça pour être secrétaire médicale? vous avez suivi
     Okay and you have had some training for that to be a medical secretary you have had

2   P: oui
     Yes

3   X: des études spéciales?
     A special training?

4   P: hm + oui:
     Hm + yes

5   X: vous avez compris ce que je vous ai demandé? est ce que vous avez compris la question (rires) non?
     You have understood what I have asked you have you understood the question (laughs) no

6   P: non non non
     No no no

7   X: non bon (.)je vais maintenant voir avec vous au chili
     No well (.) I will now check with you in Chile

8   P: hm
     hm

(Vasseur et al., 1996b, p. 79; transcription slightly altered)

Managing misunderstandings

The following list of clarification and negotiation strategies is based on Mauranen (2006) and Firth (1996).

- Confirmation checks: direct questions such as 'have you understood my question?' 'did I understand right?' 'yeah?', etc.
- Self-repair: rephrasing or elaborating one's own speech.
- Interactive-repair: jointly dealing with 'trouble' in interactions and constructing meanings collaboratively.
- Letting it pass: ignoring anomalies or ambiguities in order to focus on content rather than form.

Task 8.2 Strategies of managing misunderstandings

Read the following extract and identify the strategies speakers use in managing misunderstandings.

Context: Seminar discussion among students in a European university. It begins with S1 asking S3 a question.

1 S1: eh if you think eh that NATO has a future it doesn't [(( ))]
2 S2:   [*we need it or we don't*]
3 S1: *we need it or we don't thank you (to S1)*
4 S2: we need it or we don't (.) according to your opinion
5 S3: my country eh we came (xxx) and eh we wanted eh to access NATO because eh we felt that eh we would more secure more secure and eh i think eh now if it is transforming into this political organisation with with Russia is on i don't think that Polish people will promote it because it was eh just we wanted eh somehow protection against Russia even now eh so we m- may not approve this k- this eh direction of transformation eh but i think that still it is important for us eh to have this i don't know con- consciousness that eh (.) eh this eh idea of collective defence is works still now so i think eh it is eh it it has left eh
6 S2: *sense of security (.) feel sense of security*
7 S3: yeah *but eh on the other hand* this sense eh can be a truly a real a real *not only a sense* it should be some real eh basis for that...

(Mauranen, 2006, pp. 137–138)

8.3 Interpreting and mediating interaction

In the previous section, we looked at what people do to negotiate meaning in situations where all or some of the participants interact with each other in a language other than their native languages. In this section, we are going to explore situations where participants do not share any common language, and/or when the presence of interpreters is deemed necessary either for communication needs or out of concern for the symbolic value of languages – such as national pride and equality in specific situations.

In most cases, interpreter-mediated interactions, by their nature, are multi-party interactions in which participants take turns. Turn allocations are most likely to be straightforward on formal occasions, for example, meetings between heads of state, major business meetings, conferences, etc. In these settings, there are two main types of interpreting depending on how turns are allocated. Interpreters can either wait for a gap in conversation to interpret what a speaker has said, or speak along with the speaker. The former is called consecutive interpreting while the latter simultaneous interpreting.

On less formal occasions, interpreter-mediated interactions often contain series of dyadic sequences of turns with the third party being present. According to Baraldi and Gavioli (2010), there are broadly three types of interpreter-mediated interactions:

- After-turn translation: interpreters interpret immediately after one speaker's turn.
- After-sequence translation: interpreters interpret a series of turns by one speaker.
- Negotiation of translation: interpreters and speakers negotiate whether translation is necessary or when and how translation can be delivered.

One important factor that influences how turns are allocated is the role perceived by and assigned to interpreters by speakers. Example 8.3 shows how a doctor, a patient and an interpreter negotiated their roles in a clinical consultation. In this example, the doctor tried to find out whether and how much the patient knew about kidney transplantation. He did not start the exchange by addressing the patient directly. Instead, he started with a question to the interpreter about whether the patient knew about transplantation. The opening question, in fact, served many functions: it acknowledged the presence of the interpreter and aligned the doctor with the interpreter by referring to the patient with the third person pronoun, 'he'. For people who are familiar with doctor–patient interactions, it signposted, albeit not explicitly, what was going to be discussed next, i.e. the doctor was trying to communicate to the patient what was involved in kidney transplantation. The question could also be interpreted as an indirect request for the interpreter to check with the patient as a 'mediator'. However, the interpreter took the question at its face value and gave her answer in Turn 2 which, if ratified, would have rendered the doctor's forthcoming explanation unnecessary. The doctor subsequently disagreed with the interpreter's reply directly in Turn 3. The interpreter then realised what she was expected to do and asked the patient the question. However, in her question to the patient, she did not translate *trapianto* ('transplantation') into English for some reason. By now, the doctor decided to change his conversational strategy by asking the patient directly in English and with a second person pronoun 'you' in Turn 4. His utterance overlapped with the interpreter's. In Turn 8, the interpreter tried to negotiate with the doctor: while acknowledging the doctor's ability to speak English, she asked whether she could speak for the doctor. The negotiation of turns in this example was protracted, partly because there seemed to be a shift in the role assigned to interpreter by the doctor and partly because the interpreter failed to engage with the doctor's 'negotiation of translation' at the beginning.

Example 8.3

D: Doctor, a native speaker of Italian
M: Interpreter
P: Patient, a native speaker of English.

1   D: Luis sa qualcosa del trapianto?
            Does he know anything about transplantation?
2   M: Si, qualcosa
            Yes, something
3   D: no, perché c'è molta [gente che non sa nien [te
            No, because there are many who do know nothing
4   M: [no, infatti   [you know what is it? What
                                               trapianto?
                    Yes that's true
5   D: [Allora, you know, it is an operation
            Now
6   M: [Mhm. Because the doctor wants to kn[ow
7   P: [mhm
8   M: Io vedo che lei sa, però se vuole parlo io
            I see you can, but if you want I shall speak

(Baraldi and Gavioli, 2010, p. 157)

The role perceived by and assigned to interpreters by speakers has an impact not only on how turns are allocated, but also on what is to be interpreted or how to interpret in a culturally appropriate way. Some examples can be found in Knapp-Potthoff and Knapp (1987) and Spencer-Oatey and Xing (2009). *Kaolü kaolü* (考虑考虑) in Chinese literally means 'think it over'. It is often used as an indirect refusal to a request in the Chinese context. But how shall an interpreter interpret this utterance? Rendering it as 'well, we'll think it over' may be misleading, but specifying its underlying intention 'it is no from us, but to save face, we do not want to say it directly' may turn out to be wrong. Example 8.4 contains a problematic intervention by an interpreter despite his best intention. During a Chinese business delegation's visit to a British engineering company, the British chairman made a welcome speech and then asked his staff to introduce themselves. After this, he invited the Chinese visitors to introduce themselves. The following extract details what happened next.

Example 8.4

Context: A welcome meeting. Int: Interpreter.

1 Jack: could could I now ask if if the members (.) could each introduce themselves so that we can learn (.) um (.) who they are and what their interests are.

2 Int: *he says that is he wants you that is to introduce yourselves that is your interests or that is something about your work unit or introduce some of your interests and hobbies.*

3 Sun: (turns to colleagues and discusses with them and the interpreter in Chinese)

4 Sun: *we each introduce ourselves*

5 Shen: *it's best if you do it on our behalf*

6 Sun: (reading from a script) *first of all, to [X] Company =*

7 Int: *no no. he said first you introduce yourself (.) I am that is I am that is I am from such and such a company, I am from such and such an organization*

8 Sun: *I am [surname] from Company [name]*

9 Int: *He is from [name of Company]*

10 Chen: *say what you do*

11 Sun: *I'm involved in design*

12 Xu: *give your full name (.) full name (.) full name (.) say you're a design engineer*

13 Sun: *design engineer*

14 Int: *His name is [name] and he is a design engineer.*

(Spencer-Oatey and Xing, 2009, p. 228. English translation of the Chinese delegates' utterances is given in italics)

The interpreter, who was a Chinese PhD student in a local university and hired by the British company, stepped in at Turn 7 when the leader of the Chinese delegation decided to ignore the chairman's request and began to make his reciprocal speech in reply to the chair's welcome speech. Assuming that the leader did not understand him, the interpreter interrupted the leader and gave specific and somewhat patronising instructions on how to make self-introduction. This took the leader by surprise, but he gave in. In the next few turns, he managed to give his self-introduction with cues from his fellow businessmen. The question is: was the interpreter's intervention necessary or appropriate? At that time, for the Chinese delegation, self-introduction was not their priority. They were more concerned about saying a few words of appreciation out of courtesy. This misalignment in what they wanted to do and what they were expected to do was made worse when the interpreter attempted to 'regulate' the interaction. The example shows that although interpreters are obliged to clarify misunderstandings and to facilitate interactions, what is to be clarified and how to facilitate interactions are a matter of negotiation and discretion.

8.4 Understanding professional and institutional discourse

So far, we have focused on what we do to manage differences in linguistic competence and misunderstanding in interactions. In this section, we are going to explore how knowledge about the system, in particular, knowledge of professional and institutional discourse, can facilitate effective communication in institutional interactions. We draw insights mainly from studies on institutional discourse (e.g. Gumperz, 1999; Roberts, 2011; Sarangi and Roberts, 1999) and on healthcare communication (e.g. Collins et al., 2011; Roberts, 2009). Let us first look at the following extracts from two selection interviews. The trainees in both extracts have recently lost their jobs and were applying for paid traineeships at a publicly funded institution in the UK. The trainee in the first one was an electrician of South Asian background. He spoke fluent English and had lived in the UK for over a decade. The trainee in the second one was a bricklayer, a native speaker and from the local area.

Example 8.5

R: interviewer; T: trainee

1	R.	Have you visited the skills centre?
2	T:	Yes, I did.
3	R:	So you've had a look at the workshops?
4	T:	yes.
5	R:	You know what the training allowance is? Do you?
6	T:	Yeah.
7	R:	Do you know how much you've got to live on for the period of time.

Example 8.6

1	R:	Have you visited the skills centre?
2	T:	Yep. I've been there. Yeah.
3	R:	So you've had a chance to look around?
		And did you look in at the brick shop?
4	T:	Ah yeah. we had a look around the brick shop.
		And uhm, it look o.k. I mean its-.
5	R:	All right.
6	T:	Pretty good yeah.

(Both extracts from Gumperz, 1999, pp. 459–460)

In the two extracts, the interviewers asked more or less the same questions at the beginning (Turns 1 and 3 in both examples), but there were differences in the way the trainees responded to the questions and how the interviews went subsequently. The electrician in the first one gave minimal responses and did not offer any additional information about his visit to the skill centre. Without any content or topic to respond to, the interviewer went on to check whether the electrician was familiar with the financial implications of the training in Turn 5 and rephrased his question again in Turn 7 after getting another minimal response from the electrician in Turn 6. The bricklayer in the second extract responded to the interviewer's questions less formally and offered an evaluative comment about the brick shop in Turn 4. In the same turn, he also tried to rephrase his comment, and paused in mid-sentence as if he was trying to adjust his comments to be more appropriate to the context of the interview. After all, 'o.k.' sounded only lukewarm. In Turn 5, the bricklayer's response was 'repaired' by the interviewer who completed the utterance by supplying an evaluative phrase 'All right'. His contribution was in turn met with a positive response from the bricklayer who acknowledged the repair by rephrasing his evaluative comments once again.

The differences in the way the interviews were conducted in the two extracts could be explained from a number of perspectives. Gumperz (1999) raised the issue of 'ideology-based prejudice': the electrician of South Asian background was treated less favourably. There is also the issue of power. Seeing the interviewer as someone authoritative and with an exclusive right to allocation of turns may impede the electrician from offering any information which he thought was irrelevant to the question. But the most important issue here is that the electrician failed to understand the 'hidden' agenda behind the interviewer's questions. The questions were not aimed to find out whether the applicants have the right skills and knowledge, but to probe the applicants' interest in the course as well as their motivation. Without the knowledge of this type of institutional discourse, the electrician failed to 'display' his interest in and commitment to the course. It is precisely for this reason that Roberts and her colleagues (e.g. Roberts and Campbell, 2006) argue that there is a 'linguistic penalty' for those who are born and educated overseas and unaware of the largely hidden rules of institutional activities. The paradox is that although this group of people may speak English fluently, their English is very often regarded as 'poor' because they fail to match institutional and cultural expectations at various levels, including communicative styles, discourse organisation and rhetoric. Roberts (2011, p. 90) argued,

> it is not ethnicity per se that disadvantages minority ethnic groups in job interviews but a lack of socialisation into the norms and assumptions of this activity, since it is candidates who were born overseas, whatever their linguistic background, that fare less well...

there is a 'linguistic penalty' experienced by this group. This penalty is faced by anyone who has not developed the 'linguistic capital' of the particular institutional sub-field of the job interview.

Roberts and her colleagues (Campbell and Roberts, 2007; Roberts and Campbell, 2006; Roberts et al., 2008; Roberts, 2011) conducted a series of studies to demonstrate the depth of social-cultural knowledge and 'linguistic capital' required for the types of job interview which aim to assess competency such as teamwork, communication and problem-solving skills that are currently dominant in Britain, North America and other parts of the West. Consider the following questions in job interviews; what do you think the interviewer intends to find out through the questions?

- Why did you apply for this job?
- How does an organisation manage change?

The first question is frequently asked at the beginning of a job interview as a lead-in question. It serves many purposes, including breaking the ice, getting to know the candidate's individual circumstances and motivations, and opening up further questions. You may have many practical reasons to apply for the job (better pay, more convenient location, flexible hours, etc.), but the interviewer is more interested in finding out what you can do for the institution, how your goal fits with that of the institution and how committed you are to the application. The second question, according to Roberts and Campbell (2006), is about how flexible you may be in a job. The expectation is to demonstrate your flexibility, perhaps through narratives of your own experience of managing change.

Apart from understanding the hidden agendas of interview questions, Campbell and Roberts (2007) argue that interviewees also need to be adept at presenting a 'likeable' self, as someone who is neither too 'institutional' (i.e. giving well-rehearsed answers and only saying things that one is expected to say and hence sounding insincere) nor too 'personal' (i.e. talking about personal experiences that are not strictly work-related). The key is to synthesise the institutional and personal self by 'couching institutional discourse in informal personal vocabulary, or framing personal narratives with analytic conclusions' (p. 256). The meshing of two types of discourse requires a sophisticated level of discursive skills, but failure to get it right can lead to an undesirable outcome. In the following example, the candidate, Sara, a Maltese, applied for an internally advertised junior management position in a delivery company but failed to get the job. When replying to the question about the challenge of the job, she adopted an 'overly' institutional discourse by discussing the current situation and stating what was perhaps the common knowledge among the company in a 'matter of fact' way. The word 'obviously' in Turn 4 framed her argument as something plainly evident and rendered her interpretation of the situation to appear less original. She then moved on to talk more specifically about the challenges in Turns 6 and 8. Although she had some awareness of the issues resulting from the staff reduction, she did not mention the key term, 'communication', which the interviewer was looking for. When the interviewer, a white British male, was later probed by the research team about his impressions of Sara, he reported that Sara was 'lecturing' to him, 'saying what she'd been told to say', 'unspecific' and 'waffling'. These unfortunate impressions are partly because Sara failed to synthesise institutional and personal discourse appropriately, particularly at the beginning of the interview (Turns 2 and 4).

Example 8.7

I: interviewer; C: candidate, Sara

1 I: so what would you see as the key challenges of the job
2 C: well (.) (Office X) is er:m currently going through more major change (1) with a lot of the work from the mail centre actually being moved to (Office Y)
3 I: mhm
4 C: er:m so obviously that's going to have a hu:ge impact on (.) what (.) is actually handled by [the
5 I: [yeah
6 C: delivery office it's gonna have huge a impact (.) you know are we gonna need to reduce the number of staff are we going to have to have staff working at different times (.) are we going to have to have split shifts maybe which has happened in other offices
7 I: mhm
8 C: er:m there's a whole host of things there that might need to happen (.) so (.) there's gonna be a lot of challenges because whatever you decide on (.) you've got to put it down in a form that you can discuss not only with your your bosses but also with e:r (.) your staff and with the union

(Campbell and Roberts, 2007, pp. 256–257;
transcription slightly altered)

Evidence from available studies on medical communication (Moss and Roberts, 2005; Roberts et al., 2004) suggests that, similar to job interviews, failure to understand how professional discourse in medical encounters works may make doctors' consultations protracted, make unnecessary demands on doctors' time, and on some occasions lead to an unfortunate impression of not being 'treated' appropriately on the patient's part and 'not co-operative' on the doctor's part. For example, at the start of consultations, patients need to say why they have come to see the doctor, usually prompted by the doctor's questions such as 'How can I help you?' 'How are you?' and so on. The current medical model in a typical doctor–patient consultation in the UK expects the patient to include three aspects in their self-report: a description of symptoms, the context in which the symptoms occurred. and their stance (i.e. how they feel about the symptoms). The research by Roberts et al. (2004) shows that there are differences in the way patients present themselves and their symptoms. In Example 8.8, the patient, an elderly woman of South Asian origin, instead of organising her self-report in an orderly manner, embedded her symptoms and contexts of the symptom in her affective talk about the pain. She repeated 'I can't cope' and emphasised the overpowering impact of the pain several times in the opening. Although the severity of the pain successfully came through in the exchange, very little was said about the context of the pain and other symptoms. In Turn 17, the doctor had to direct the patient to the context of the problem to extract information about the problem.

Example 8.8

1	D:	come in come in please come in good morning
2	P:	good morning
3	D:	have a seat
4	P:	thank you
5	D:	how are you today
6	P:	oh: [creaky voice] not very good
7	D:	not very good (.) what's happening
8	P:	I pain here (.) too much (.) I can't cope you know
9	D:	right
10	P:	yesterday (.) whole day
11	D:	right
12	P:	and I eat (.) three times (.) paracetamol
13	D:	right
14	P:	two three hours it will be all right and then (.) come pain again (.) I can't cope (.) pain like
15	D:	you can't cope with this pain
16	P:	yeah very very bad (.) I don't know what's the wrong with me
17	D:	sure how long you have this

(Roberts, 2009, p. 254; re-transcribed, transcription convention as Example 8.7)

To sum up, the above examples from job interviews and doctor–patient communication show that professional and institutional discourses have their own features, agendas and expectations. The knowledge of these features would facilitate and on some occasions be critical to successful communication. When there is communication breakdown in interactions involving non-native speakers, people tend to attribute difficulties in communication to inadequate linguistic abilities on non-native speakers' part. However, sometimes it is not linguistic ability, but a lack of knowledge of how the system works that leads to the undesirable outcome of an interaction.

8.5 Chapter summary

Achieving understanding is a process of negotiation and requires joint effort by participants. In this chapter we have identified a number of practices or strategies among conversational participants to achieve the ultimate goals of communication, i.e. attaining communicative efficiency and maintaining an interpersonal relationship. In particular, we have focused on the following aspects:

- communication accommodative behaviours and practices when there are perceived differences in linguistic abilities among participants;
- strategies for signalling and managing misunderstandings;
- ways of mediating interactions among interpreters;
- the importance of understanding and meeting the expectations of professional and institutional discourse.

In the next chapter we will move beyond strategies and practices of meaning negotiation and focus on the concept of intercultural communicative competence.

9 How to develop intercultural communicative competence

Thomas Aitken, author of *The Multinational Man: The Role of the Manager Abroad*, presented humorously an impressive list of qualities to be expected from 'a global manager', multinational man. An ideal global manager should have:

> the stamina of an Olympic runner, the mental agility of an Einstein, the conversational skill of a professor of languages, the detachment of a judge, the tact of a diplomat, and the perseverance of an Egyptian pyramid builder. [And] that's not all. If they are going to measure up to the demands of living and working in a foreign country, they should also have a feeling for the culture; their moral judgement should be not too rigid; they should be able to merge with the local environment with chameleon-like ease; and they should show no signs of prejudice.
>
> (Aitken, 1973, cited in Townsend and Cairns, 2003, p. 317)

While clearly such a super-being exists only in one's imagination, the comment reflects the multi-faceted nature of competence required for intercultural encounters. In this chapter, we extend our attention beyond meaning negotiations in interactions to generic abilities and skills needed for intercultural communication. First, we explore what these generic abilities and skills are, before we talk about how to develop them through intercultural education and training.

9.1 ICC in foreign language teaching and learning

In language and intercultural communication studies and a number of adjacent fields, the term, Intercultural Communicative Competence (ICC), is a key, yet often controversial, concept. It, however, has followed a relatively clear line of development in the field of foreign language teaching and learning, which has close links and overlapping interests with intercultural education. In this section we will look at some key concepts and models in the development of ICC in foreign language teaching and learning, before a brief overview of ICC in multidisciplinary contexts in the next section.

Competence vs. performance (Chomsky, 1965)

The term 'competence' is essential to Chomsky's early work (1965), which claimed that human beings have an innate and biologically determined faculty responsible for acquisition and mental representation of language. According to Chomsky, when children acquire a language, they not only learn how to put together and interpret a string of words 'in concrete situations' (i.e. performance), but also develop implicit knowledge of what is permissible or not in a language (i.e. linguistic competence). It is the latter, i.e. knowing what is permissible or not, that allows a native speaker to create new utterances they may have never heard or to tell whether an utterance is ungrammatical.

Communicative competence (Hymes, 1972)

Dell Hymes (1972), an anthropological linguist, critiqued Chomsky's distinction between competence and performance. He argued that for a speaker to communicate effectively, she needs to have communicative competence (i.e. knowing how to use the language appropriately) in addition to grammatical knowledge as specified in Chomsky's linguistic competence.

Communicative competence is further broken down into different components (Canale and Swain, 1980; Canale, 1983; van Ek, 1986). The following component model is based on van Ek (1986):

- Linguistic competence: production and interpretation of meaningful and grammatically correct utterances.
- Sociolinguistic competence: awareness of the impact of context such as setting, relationship between communication partners, intentions, etc. on the choice of language forms.
- Discourse competence: appropriate use of strategies at discourse level.
- Strategic competence: appropriate use of communication strategies to get meaning across and to understand others' messages.
- Socio-cultural competence: familiarity with the social-cultural context of the target language.
- Social competence: both the will and the skill to interact with others, such as motivation, attitude, self-confidence, empathy and the ability to handle social situations.

Intercultural communicative competence and intercultural speakers (Byram, 1997)

The models of communicative competence outlined above give well-deserved attention to notions of contextual appropriateness, willingness, and communication strategies at various levels. However, they implicitly refer to 'the native speaker' as a model, which has three main problems. The first is, as Byram argued, 'the problem of creating an impossible target and consequently inevitable failure' (1997, p. 11). Second, it would create the wrong kind of competence, implying that 'a learner should be linguistically schizophrenic, abandoning one language in order to blend into another linguistic environment, becoming accepted as a native speaker by other native speakers' (Byram, 1997, p. 11). The third problem, as Kramsch (1998b) and Leung (2005) pointed out, is that the notion of a native speaker is only an idealised and outdated myth. Three types of privilege traditionally associated with the native speaker, i.e. entitlement by birth, right acquired through education, and prerogative membership in a speech community, are all problematic at both epistemic and operational level. Rampton (1990) also challenged the validity of the notion and proposed the terms language expertise, language inheritance, and language affiliation in place of native speaker.

To move away from the native speaker model, Byram (1997) proposed a model of intercultural communicative competence in which an 'intercultural speaker' mediates between different perspectives and cultures. In his model, Byram refined the first three dimensions of competence identified in van Ek's model and added an 'intercultural competence' which consists of the following sub-components (pp. 48–53):

- Attitudes (savoir être): curiosity and openness, readiness to suspend disbelief about other cultures and belief about one's own.
- Knowledge (savoirs): knowledge of social groups and their products and practices in one's own and in one's interlocutor's country, and of the general processes of societal and individual interaction.
- Skills of interpreting and relating (savoir comprendre): ability to interpret a document or event from another culture, to explain it and relate it to documents from one's own culture.
- Skills of discovering and interaction (savoir apprendre/faire): ability to acquire new knowledge of a culture and cultural practices and the ability to operate knowledge, attitudes and skills under the constraints of real-time communication and interaction.
- Critical cultural awareness/political education (savoir s'engager): ability to evaluate critically and on the basis of explicit criteria the perspectives, practices and products of one's own and other cultures and countries.

In the model, Byram differentiated intercultural competence from intercultural communicative competence. The former, intercultural competence, refers to the ability to interact in one's own language with people from another culture and does not necessarily require knowledge of the target language, while the latter is about interacting with people from another culture in a foreign language. Another innovative aspect of the model is that each component also interacts with other components, with intercultural competence feeding into the other three competences, as Figure 9.1 shows. He also specified the locations of learning and indicated the teacher and learner's role in each location.

From third place to symbolic competence and the multilingual subject (Kramsch, 2009a)

The concept of 'third place' was initially used by Kramsch (1993, 2009a, cf. 'third culture' in 2009b) as a spatial metaphor for 'eschewing' the traditional dualities on which language education is based: first language vs. second language, native culture vs. target culture, native speaker vs. non-native speaker, us vs. them, self vs. other. Instead of seeing the goal of language learning as replacing the learner's language and culture with another, the concept 'third place' creates a symbolic

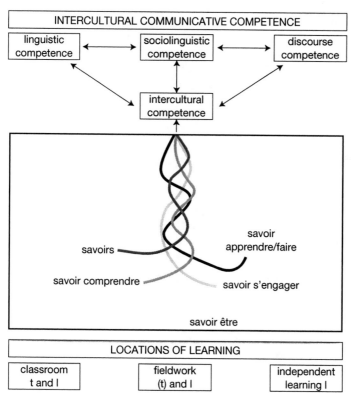

Figure 9.1 Byram's ICC model
Source: Byram, 1997, p. 73.
Note: t: teacher; l: learner

space where the learner's own and the target culture interact. It offers a dialectic solution to the traditional view of L1 and L2 as in an either/ or relationship.

Informed by research on identity and language learning in the last 20 years, in particular, the subjective nature of language learning, Kramsch (2006, 2009a) revisited the notion of 'third place'. In an admirable self-critique, Kramsch summarised the pitfalls and challenges that come with the term (2009a). First of all, the spatial metaphor suggests, problematically, that the learner knows how to navigate several systems and their cultural and historical boundaries. Second, the term has been 'romanticized' as some hybrid culture that exists along with other cultures. In fact, it was intended to reflect a relational state of mind, not to create another separate entity. Third, it does not acknowledge the symbolic power of language and symbolic nature of multilingual individuals, who are 'not just communicators and problem solvers, but whole persons with hearts, bodies, and minds, with memories, fantasies, loyalties, identities' (2006, p. 251).

Kramsch proposed reframing the term as 'symbolic competence', as an ability 'not only to approximate or appropriate for oneself someone else's language, but to shape the very context in which the language is learned and used through the learner's and other's embodied history and subjectivity' (Kramsch and Whiteside, 2008, p. 664). Symbolic competence is not meant to replace communicative competence. Rather, it complements the latter by creating a mindset that expands possibilities and opportunities for the learner. It includes:

- An ability to understand the symbolic value of symbolic forms and the different cultural memories evoked by different symbolic systems.
- An ability to draw on the semiotic diversity afforded by multiple languages to reframe ways of seeing familiar events, create alternative realities, and find an appropriate subject position 'between languages'.
- An ability to look both at and through language and to understand the challenges to the autonomy and integrity of the subject that come from unitary ideologies and a totalising networked culture.

(Kramsch, 2009a, p. 201)

Empirical examples of how symbolic competence operates in the above aspects can be found in Kramsch and Whiteside (2008).

9.2 A multidisciplinary overview of ICC

Beyond foreign language education, the term intercultural communicative competence has been defined, refined and debated across several other disciplines including intercultural education, communication studies, interpersonal communication studies, and international business and management studies. Almost without exception, each discipline has its own take on the concept. The diversity of conceptualisations of ICC across (and sometimes even within) various disciplines has led to the use of a range of related terms, some of which are outlined below in Table 9.1. It should be noted that this is not meant to be an exhaustive list.

Table 9.1 A sample of ICC and related terms

Terms and examples of works	Notes
Intercultural Communicative Competence (Byram, 1997)	One of the most influential models in foreign language teaching and learning.
Intercultural Communication Competence (Spitzberg and Cupach, 1984; Chen and Starosta 1998)	The term is widely used by experts in communication and interpersonal communication studies. The focus is very much on 'competence in communication'.
Intercultural competence (Deardorff, 2004, 2006)	A shorter version of the term.
Transcultural communication competence (Ting-Toomey, 1999)	The term refers to an approach integrating theory and practice and thus enabling a mindful application of intercultural knowledge in a sensitive manner.
Cross-cultural/trans-cultural competence (Ruben, 1989; Hampden-Turner and Trompenaars, 2000)	The term 'cross-cultural competence' is used in Ruben's review (1989) and used interchangeably with the term 'trans-cultural' competence in Hampden-Turner and Trompenaars (2000).
Cross-cultural effectiveness (Kealey, 1989)	The term emphasises the objective of intercultural communication, i.e. effectiveness.
Intercultural sensitivity (Bennett, 1986; Bhawuk and Brislin, 1992)	This term is key to Bennett's developmental model of intercultural sensitivity. It is defined as 'sensitivity to the importance of cultural differences and to the points of view of people in other cultures' (Bhawuk and Brislin,1992, p. 414).
Global competence (Hunter et al., 2006)	The term avoids the use of the word 'culture'.
International competence (World Work, an intercultural consultancy company)	The website lists 22 factors and 10 competencies under 'international competence'.
Intercultural interaction competence (ICIC) (Spencer-Oatey and Franklin, 2009)	The term is used partly as an umbrella term for reporting existing work and partly to reflect the authors' focus on interaction.

Task 9.1 Defining ICC

As the review shows, there are a number of models and definitions of ICC in the literature. Choose a model or definition and discuss the following questions: Who proposed the model/definition? To what context does it apply and for what purpose? What does it emphasise? How does the model/definition appeal to you?

Categorising ICC models

So what do we make of these different conceptualisations of ICC? There are three possible approaches.

Disciplinary context and orientation ICC is researched in a number of disciplines including foreign language education, intercultural education, communication studies, interpersonal communication studies, and international business and management studies. A main distinction can be made between those disciplines emphasising 'communicative' competence (related to foreign language education) and those centred around 'competence in communication' (frequently linked to interpersonal communication studies and communication studies). Spitzberg and Cupach's model of relational competence (1984) is an example of 'competence in communication' models.

Aims, objectives and criteria of ICC models In addition to its disciplinary context and orientation, each ICC model has its own interpretation and assumption of what constitutes a successful intercultural interaction. Two key terms, appropriateness and effectiveness, occur frequently in the definition of ICC as its purposes and criteria. In fact, as Deardorff's study (2004) showed, the top-rated definition among intercultural scholars in her study was one that defines ICC as 'the ability to communicate effectively and appropriately in intercultural situations based on one's intercultural knowledge, skills, and attitudes' (Deardorff, 2004, p. 194). Appropriateness is concerned with the propriety and suitability of behaviours in a given context, while effectiveness is about achieving desired outcomes and getting things done.

The third criterion used in measuring success of an intercultural encounter in addition to appropriateness and effectiveness is establishing and maintaining relationships. As Byram argued (1997, p. 3),

> Successful 'communication' is not judged solely in terms of the efficiency of information exchange. It is focused on establishing and maintaining relationships. In this sense, the efficacy of communication depends upon using language to demonstrate one's willingness to relate, which often involves the indirectness of

politeness rather than the direct and 'efficient' choice of language full of information.

The relationship between different elements of ICC In a recent review Spitzberg and Changnon (2009) classified five different types of ICC models on the basis of potential similarities (Table 9.2).

Table 9.2 Five types of ICC model

Type	Main features	Examples
Compositional models	The most common type of ICC model, providing lists of relevant abilities, skills and traits.	To illustrate the spectrum and diversity of competences, Spitzberg and Changnon (2009) list more than 300 concepts and skills referred to in the literature.
Co-orientational model	Primarily concerned with interactional achievements of intercultural understanding.	Intercultural communicative competence, proposed by Byram (1997).
Developmental model	Specifies stages of progression.	Developmental intercultural competence model by Bennett (1986). It proposes sequential, developmental stages of denial, defence, minimisation, acceptance, adaptation and integration.
Adaptational model	Emphasises interdependence of participants in the process of cultural learning.	Communication accommodation theory by Gallois et al. (1988) See Chapter 8, this book.
Causal process	Specifies the interrelationships among components.	Process model of intercultural competence by Deardorff (2006). The model identifies several key stages in developing intercultural competence with each stage facilitating the next one.

9.3 Intercultural learning through education and training

The multi-faceted nature of ICC, ranging from knowledge to skills and from awareness to attitudes, means that learning takes place not only inside but also outside the classroom, and not only in terms of theory and understanding, but also in application and practice.

What is unique about intercultural learning?

Intercultural learning takes various forms through a variety of means. Unlike many traditional classroom-taught subjects, intercultural learning is not confined to lectures and classrooms. Differentiation can be made in the following ways.

- Locations of learning: classroom, fieldwork (e.g. a short visit, an exchange programme) and independent learning. These three locations overlap with each other and form a continuum from structured learning to informal education.
- Degree of direct contact: The experiential learning approach (also known as learning by doing, Kolb, 1984) is based on the assumption that culture learning is best achieved when people have direct or simulated experiences, while a didactic approach assumes that cognitive understanding, which can be developed through traditional means such as lectures, reading and group discussion, is essential before individuals can effectively interact with people of another culture.
- Culture-specificity: whether and how much training is focused on one culture (culture-specific) or general principles regardless of cultures (culture-general) (Gudykunst and Hammer, 1983).
- Educational level: Many universities across the world now offer postgraduate degrees in intercultural communication, and many schools in North America and Europe incorporate global citizenship, a concept closely related to intercultural communication, in their curriculum. Modes of delivery: e.g. classroom-based learning, e-learning, work-based learning.

ICC is not something one either has or not. Rather, ICC develops incrementally over time through learning in classroom and, simultaneously, learning from the real world. As Byram (1997) rightly pointed out, while classroom learning is often seen as preparation for 'real' experience, the dichotomy of 'classroom' and 'real world' is misleading, for engagement with the 'real world' takes place in parallel to classroom learning.

Some aspects of ICC benefit more from direct contact than other aspects. Classroom-based training enables learners to acquire knowledge about another culture and the process of communication and to reflect on their own practice under the lecturer's guidance. In contrast, intercultural learning through participation in intercultural exchanges or study abroad programmes can increase participants' knowledge of the host culture, improve fluency in the host country language, reduce anxiety in interacting with people from different cultures, develop sensitivity to cultural difference and increase efficacy. Participants also develop greater intercultural networks and friendships with people from different cultural backgrounds.

To achieve optimal intercultural learning through intercultural experience, it is essential to get the right balance between challenge and support. While intercultural experience is likely to enhance participants' intercultural learning and personal development in many ways, immersion itself does not guarantee success. As discussed in Chapter 5, existing studies (e.g. Vande Berg, 2009) show that merely exposing students to the local environment is not enough. What makes a difference to the success of intercultural learning in this context is the support from their 'cultural mentors' and structured learning, which helps the learner make sense of their intercultural learning experience. The support can also take the form of facilitation and mediation, both of which promote participants' active participation and engagement in educational activities and interactions (Baraldi, 2012). Examples of how to mediate interactions and to manage conflict can be found in Baraldi (2012) and Iervese (2012) respectively.

Support, provided at the right moment at the right place, enables the learner to maximise 'affordance' and to transform from just 'being there' to participation and engagement. Affordance, a term borrowed from Gibson's work in psychology (1979), originally refers to the interrelationship between an individual's capacity/properties and the environment that allows the individual to interact with the environment. It describes learning opportunities and possibilities that a learner can perceive and exploit. In the context of intercultural learning, the term helps to differentiate exposure or immersion from the learning potential that each learner can 'afford'. Affordance can be different from one participant to another, depending on ability, past experiences, motivations, and the degree of participation and engagement.

What are the key models and approaches in intercultural learning and teaching?

A number of key models and approaches, some of which are more systematically researched than others, are available in the literature on intercultural learning and teaching.

Contact theory The earliest influential theory of intercultural learning is Allport's intergroup contact theory (1954). It postulates that prejudice between members of different groups may be reduced through intergroup contact under four key conditions, i.e. equal status; common goals; intergroup cooperation; and institutional support. This theory has received attention among policy-makers and practitioners specialising in racial integration and equality, and racial conflict resolution. Together with Kolb's experiential learning, it has often been used as the rationale for creating opportunities for intercultural experience such as study abroad, exchange programmes, overseas expeditions, etc. An up-to-date overview of studies on intergroup contact can be found in Pettigrew and Tropp (2011).

Experiential learning theory Also known as 'learning by doing', experiential learning theory is one of the most influential educational approaches in intercultural learning. It advocates that learning takes place best through direct participation in and direct encounter with the events of life. The most well-known model of experiential learning is David Kolb's learning cycle, in which the following four stages feed into each other in a loop (1984):

1 concrete experience, followed by
2 observations and reflection, followed by
3 forming abstract concepts and generalisations, followed by
4 testing concepts and generalisations in new situations, which leads to the next round of the cycle.

Transformative learning theory Originally developed for adult learning, transformative learning theory proposes that learning is a process of 'using a prior interpretation to construe a new or revised interpretation of the meaning of one's experience in order to guide future action' (Mezirow, 1996, p. 162). It believes that learning is essentially a process of perspective transformation, i.e. the change in frames of reference, which takes places through reflection on experience and engagement with new experience. It complements experiential learning theory by providing an account of how experience can transform one's belief systems and behaviours. Berwick and Whalley (2000) note that, consistent with the principles of transformative learning, several studies have suggested that cultural learning is a 'generative' and 'recursive process' that involves the changing of internal schemata about other groups. Examples include Byram et al.'s study (1991) of changing perceptions of French culture among British secondary students in the process of learning French as a foreign language.

Reflection Reflective learning, experiential learning and transformative learning theory are not mutually exclusive. In fact, Kolb's model of experiential learning embraces reflective practices and incorporates them into the learning cycle. For Boud et al. (1985), reflection is the key to turning experience into learning. They believe that reflection is both a self-organised learning activity and has to be done with intent and be goal-oriented. At the same time, it is a complex process intertwined with feelings and emotions which can be barriers or incentives.

Reflection is also the key to many pedagogical toolkits such as critical incidents, reflective journals and ethnographic participation, which are outlined below. Reflection is essential to assessment tools such as Autobiography of Intercultural Encounters (AIE, 2009) designed by Michael Byram, Martyn Barrett, Julia Ipgrave and their colleagues for the Language Policy Division of the Council of Europe's assessment of intercultural experience. As a way to encourage intercultural learners to reflect critically, AIE takes the form of a series of questions and prompts carefully designed to guide the learner's reflections on her intercultural encounter (such as: What happened when you met this person/these people? Where did it happen? What were you doing there? Why have you chosen this experience?). It provides the learner with a structure by which to analyse the incident and consider what they learnt from the encounter.

Critical incidents Critical incidents are brief descriptions of significant events in interactions involving people from different cultures, in which there is a problem of misunderstanding, conflict, or an inappropriate or ineffective act. Critical incidents can be used for a variety of purposes:

- Written and generated by learners themselves as a learning tool. Given appropriate guidance, recording critical incidents encourages learners to reflect on what has happened. Examples of critical incidents written by students during their study abroad experience can be found in an on-line database (at www.lancs.ac.uk/users/interculture/index.htm) as part of the Interculture Project, a joint project of Lancaster University, Sheffield University, the University of Central Lancashire, St Martin's College, Lancaster, Homerton College, Cambridge, the Centre for Information on Language Teaching and Research (CiLT), and the Central Bureau for Educational Visits and Exchanges (CBEVE).
- Prepared by trainers and educators in the form of *cultural assimilators* as a pedagogical tool for raising awareness and encouraging reflection. Cultural assimilators typically include a description of a scenario followed by a question. A number of solutions or options are sometimes made available to readers. Cultural assimilators frame intercultural issues in contexts similar to real-life situations and add a human dimension by telling a story about characters either constructed or based on real persons. They can make the issues appear relevant to readers and are particularly effective for identifying cultural differences.
- Used by researchers in the form of a self-report as a data collection instrument. It is a useful method for capturing incidents that are difficult to predict and observe. An example can be found in Arthur (2001) in which self-reports of critical incidents were collected at six points from a group of Canadian students during their 7-week study abroad in Vietnam.
- As an assessment tool to measure one's sensitivity to significant events. The AIE assessment described earlier in this section is such an example.

Reflective learning journals Known by various names (e.g. diaries, culture learning journals, learning log, etc.), reflective learning journals have been deemed essential to reflective and experiential learning, since they provide a tool to connect thoughts, feelings and action and to turn experience into explicit learning (Moon, 1999). They can be used to record critical incidents as part of intercultural training or research. Berwick and Whalley's study (2000) of a group of Canadian students of Japanese during their 3-month stay in Japan demonstrates that learning journals can encourage individual reflection on a number of fronts: linking current experience with prior learning; reviewing events that are not supported by prior knowledge; re-examining culture-learning approaches; and debating intercultural differences. The authors also argued that in their study, learning journals enabled the researchers to work empirically and analytically and at a distance from learners' encounters with another culture.

Elsewhere, it is argued that the use of reflective learning journals can facilitate language learning, particularly with regard to aspects of language learning and teaching experiences which are normally hidden or largely inaccessible to external observers, such as affective factors, language learning strategies and learners' own perceptions. Examples of language learning studies that use teachers' and learners' journals as their primary data source can be found in the third section of Bailey and Nunan's edited volume (1996).

Task 9.2 A reflective journal entry: a domestic dad in a Japanese host family

> Yesterday I was watching TV with my sister and brother (host siblings) and we had rented a video to watch. So I said, 'Can we watch it now?' And they said, 'No, wait until your mom and dad have finished washing the dishes.' I was stunned. The father was washing the dishes? The other day, he made dinner, too. I was so impressed. The attitude that had been conveyed to me before was one of extreme chauvinism, and I had a few problems putting up with it, but the father must be really liberated. My interpretation is all Japanese should not be stereotyped.

The above journal entry was selected from Berwick and Whalley's data (2000, p. 334). It recorded a critical incident which challenged the learner's prior knowledge. Do you have a moment like this in your experience of living abroad or in your encounters with people from different backgrounds? Can you write up the experience as an entry for a reflective journal? You may consider the following questions when writing:

- What has happened?
- What is the issue/event/topic?
- How do you feel about it?
- What is the significance of this issue to you?
- What are the implications?
- Has the event subsequently made you think or act differently?

And finally, what do you think may be the potential problems of writing a journal?

The learner as ethnographer The ethnography of speaking, as a discipline that brings language and cultural practices together, offers a set of toolkits and guidance to intercultural learners. It encourages the learner to actively participate in day-to-day practices as a field ethnographer who gathers and records data about practices through observation and participation, an idea captured in the term 'thick description' proposed by Geertz (1973). It offers the learner a holistic approach in observing an action in its context and analysing a practice in its entirety. Other benefits include a 'palpable' sense of being with a group and the habit of 'thick comparison':

> differences are not simply read off from behaviour and compared within one's own surface memory of a similar event in one's home country, but as far as possible are interpreted thickly and then compared with a detailed analysis of one's own cultural world.
>
> (Barro et al., 1998, p. 81)

The Ealing Ethnography project, carried out at Thames Valley University in London in the 1990s, provides an excellent example of how a learner develops ICC ethnographically (Roberts et al., 2001). The project had three phases. In phase one, students were introduced to ethnographic methods in classrooms through lectures and exercises including 'home ethnography' (meaning ethnography carried out in one's own country in contrast to ethnography abroad) in which students were encouraged to select a community and carry out participant observation. In the second phase, students undertook extensive field study during their residence abroad. The third phase was the writing-up stage. A student's ethnographic project is given in Example 9.1.

Example 9.1 The *cumplido* compliments in Las Palmas.

A student whose placement was in Las Palmas chose the speech act of the *cumplido* (compliment) as a topic for her ethnographic study, following a series of misunderstandings when she first arrived. She documented and analysed the use of the term for compliment, *cumplido*, in Spanish. Some of the *cumplido* categories that emerged included:

a) about an object
b) about a person
c) to affirm belonging to a group
d) to seek reassurance
e) gender differences
f) power differences
g) as a courting skill.

She also noted the local's interpretations of the speech act as cultural insiders. Many of her informants accepted that *cumplido* compliments are important for social relationships, for example, when the daughter-in-law gave *cumplido* to her mother-in-law, but they were also aware that *cumplido* compliments are essentially insincere or hypothetical (Barro et al., 1998, p. 95).

9.4 Intercultural learning from a language socialisation perspective

Intercultural learning not only takes place in educational settings, but also is embedded in many everyday opportunities and challenges that face those novices or newer members of communities.

What is language socialisation?

Read the following extract from a dinner table conversation. What do you think the mother was trying to do and how?

Example 9.2

(Jordan: 8 years old; Sandra: 4 years old)

Father:	Jordan, would you like some more meat?
Sandra:	Meat!
Mother:	How do you ask, dear?
Jordan:	xxx (inaudible utterance)
Sandra:	Please

(Blum-Kulka, 1997, p. 203)

The above example is typical of dinner table conversations in many Western families where parents attempt to *socialise* children into politeness routines *through* and *into* language at mealtimes. Socialisation refers to the process whereby younger or newer members of a community become aware of norms, practices, values and beliefs of the community and develop skills and knowledge required to become competent members of that community. Among many types of socialisation (values, morals, religious, gender, etc.), language socialisation as shown in the above example is the most relevant to our discussion here. It refers to the process in which children, adolescents or newer members of communities learn to speak a language in a manner appropriate to the community and to adapt to the norms and values associated with speaking the language. Unlike other types of socialisation, language socialisation is a dual process: socialisation *through* language and socialisation *into* language (Ochs and Schieffelin, 2008).

Language socialisation takes place both explicitly and implicitly. While explicit learning on what to say and how to say it in a manner acceptable to the community is an important part of the process of developing communicative competence, language socialisation also takes place implicitly through observation and other less explicit means such as small talk or jokes. As Scollon et al. (2012, p. 163) commented, when starting a new job a person might receive specific training through the organisation's handbooks and manuals. At the same time, she is also expected to observe the general practices of older and more experienced employees and to follow their behaviour. The following comment by a student learner and user of WebCT (an on-line learning tool) shows how the learner was socialised into a more causal writing style through 'seeing other people'.

Example 9.3

I noticed in myself, at first my answers were very formal, very similar to term papers, very academic. Now it's becoming more conversational. Because, I think, I saw other people. Their writing was more conversational. So then I didn't want to appear unfriendly or cold. And I thought it's true, because we're communicating. It's not live, however it is to your colleagues and everything. So, I think it's become more casual now.

(Dana, English L1 student, novice WebCT user; Yim, 2011, p. 15)

Language socialisation is pervasive. 'It is both a lifelong and a "life-wide" process across communities and activities' (Duff, 2012, p. 564). It takes place at different stages of life such as infancy, childhood, adolescence, adulthood and later stages of life. It is also life-wide where the context is concerned. It can take place at home, in school, in the community, amongst a peer group, at work, in academic contexts, in vocational training, and so on.

How can a language socialisation perspective help with our understanding of intercultural learning?

Language socialisation as a field of study was initially developed for the purpose of investigating how children develop their language, communication and literacy skills in specific cultural contexts. In recent years it has expanded to include studies of second language learners and newer members of communities, who are also the main concerns of the field of intercultural communication. Although the application of language socialisation to studies of intercultural communication is only emerging, the perspective has much to offer for understanding intercultural learning.

First, a language socialisation perspective highlights the role of language in the process of intercultural learning. Through the use of language, 'younger or newer members of communities are socialized to the beliefs and socio-cultural and linguistic practices of their communities, both explicitly and implicitly,...while also being socialized to community-specific ways of using language' (Baquedano-López and Kattan, 2007, p. 74). Language socialisation in this sense fulfils a dual purpose: learning to speak the language in a way appropriate to the community, and adapting to the beliefs and norms of the community. In Li and Zhu's work (in press) on Chinese complementary schools in the UK, they found that the language teacher constantly made reference to traditional Chinese cultural values, including family values, work ethics and the sense of belonging (Example 9.4).

Example 9.4

The teacher asked a boy to read out a sample sentence and then asked them what the key word 应该, 'should, must' means. After a short pause, a girl answered (in English) 'Must.' Teacher then asked the pupils to make sentences using the key word. Cues and encouragement were given to the pupils to make the following sentences:

'我们应该尊敬长辈。' (We must respect members of the older generation.)
'我们今年应该回中国。' (We must go back to China this year.)
'我们应该写我们的作文。' (We must write our compositions.)
'你应该好好学习。' (You must learn well.)
'弟弟应该好好睡觉。' (Younger brother must have a good sleep.)
'我应该做作业了。' (I must do homework.)

(Li and Zhu, in press)

Second, a language socialisation perspective brings to the fore shared practices and ways of doing things in communities, in schools, at the workplace, etc., which can be best learned through observation and, crucially, through participation. These 'ways of doing things' are, more often than not, unwritten and therefore either neglected or simplified in guidebooks. The discussion we had about the necessity of learning about the system and institutional discourse among newcomers in Section 8.4 is relevant here. While many newcomers are prepared to 'do as the Romans do', the task of socialising into a new culture is challenging when one is not aware of the existence of these hidden rules or when these practices are very different from those of one's home culture. It is even more so for new immigrants, many of whom either have little autonomy over their lives or do not have adequate linguistic competency. In Duanduan Li's study (2000), she reported how Ming, a Chinese immigrant in America, learned 'the American way'. The first excerpt from Ming's interview in the following case study shows how Ming began to realise that the preferred way of communication in her new workplace was different but useful ('it's good for work'). However, she found it difficult to talk and to explain what she wanted ('I had a little trouble to talk'), despite her co-workers' explicit socialisation ('don't be afraid to talk'). Excerpt 2 shows how Ming used her newly socialised style of communication to make an effective request for workspace, and its impact on her ('I feel free'). 'The American way', according to her, was 'directly, truthful and things a little bit sweet, so it won't be so complicated'.

Case study: the American way

Ming was a 29-year-old, newly arrived Chinese immigrant woman in America. She got her first job in a filing department at an American medical equipment company. The following two excerpts were selected from her interviews a few months after she had settled into the job.

Excerpt 1: 'Just talk, talk, talk'

But here…at the beginning I had a little trouble to talk. The people [co-workers] always encourage me, 'Don't be afraid to talk! It's nothing wrong. If you feel there is something, talk!'…The co-workers…because you know, they talk so much. Sometimes I just don't know why you guy, I mean the people who live in the American a long time, *they talk so free! And so – confident.* They just talk so much. Just talk, talk, talk, and then…

Excerpt 2: 'Directly, truthful, and things a little bit sweet'

They sometimes, I think, they occupies too much…So one day, I just encouraged me and I TALK! And then I feel free! …You know, it's funny, I LEARNED THE AMERICAN WAY! 'Honey, [in a

> mimicking tone, laugh] *could you please put that away, because I need more room.*' And she was like – [making a shocked face] 'All right.' If you are not directly, they'll think maybe they guess wrong, misunderstand. So I think in America, in America, best way is *Directly, truthful, and things a little bit sweet*, so it won't be so complicated.
>
> (Li, 2000, pp. 72–75, original emphasis)

Third, a language socialisation perspective ratifies newcomers' (peripheral) 'participation' in intercultural learning. Drawing on Lave and Wenger's (1991) notion of 'legitimate peripheral participation', Scollon et al. (2012) suggested that in socialisation, newcomers' participation is often peripheral since they are not yet fully qualified. Despite this, however, their participation is legitimate and serves as the (only) means of becoming a competent member of the community. Scollon et al. further argued that the concept of participation is important in that it indexes the social nature of the process of socialisation, which is very often overlooked. It also reminds us of the 'unfinished' and ongoing nature of learning and socialisation. In the case study cited above, Ming became socialised into her workplace and adopted a new communication style through being part of it, not through the ESL training programme in which she was enrolled prior to the job, or any guidebook.

Fourth, a language socialisation perspective also provides an opportunity to examine the relationship between cultural insiders or experts and learners. In the process of socialisation, the role of cultural insiders or experts can be taken by parents, siblings, peers, co-workers, mentors, team leaders, managers or employers. However, these have different interests and agendas in socialisation and some of them may act as gatekeepers. Failure to align with the practice of the community or failure to show one's potential to fit in can have undesirable consequences for newcomers. Sarangi and Roberts (2002) recorded how a candidate, a native speaker of Spanish, failed an oral interview for membership of the Royal College of General Practitioners in the UK, partly because she was unfamiliar with the type of questions and partly because the hesitations in her reply, often found in second language speakers' speech, were attributed to uncertainty about the answer.

Some other studies revealed that in some cases, novices are not just passive recipients of socialisation, adapting to and accepting the existing norms of communication and values and beliefs. They can resist and negotiate what they are being socialised into through a variety of means and resources. One such resource is language creativity and language play, something demonstrated by many language learners in the process of learning a new language (Cook, 2000). In Example 9.5, the Chinese complementary school teacher gave some examples of collocations with the phrase 期待 (meaning 'longing for'). She made reference to a united motherland, family reunion, peace and friendship. However, the pupils used this opportunity to make fun of each other as well as to make light of the learning task. In reply, B changed the subject matter from social and moral ideals (a united motherland, family reunion, etc.) to a trivial matter (moon-bathing) and a real person (in fact, one of his mates). He also transliterated his classmate's girlfriend's name, Jennifer, into an amusing Chinese phrase literally meaning 'real clay Buddha'. In doing so, he inadvertently showed resistance to the teacher's attempt to socialise him and his classmates into the culture and ideals connected with the language (in this case, the Chinese language and its culture).

Example 9.5

Context: a Mandarin class of 13-year-olds in Newcastle. T: female teacher in her forties. B: a boy.

T: "期待"可以说什么？期待祖国统一, 期待家人团聚, 期待和平友好。
    What can you say with qidai *(longing for)? Longing for a united motherland;*
    longing for family reunion; longing for peace and friendship.
B: xxx (name of another boy in the class) 期待真泥佛跟他晒月光。
    xxx is longing for Jennifer to moon bathe with him.
    (All laugh)

(Li and Zhu, in press)

As the above discussion shows, a language socialisation perspective offers a new analytical stance for the study of intercultural learning. Recent advances in the application of language socialisation in second language acquisition (e.g. Duff, 2012; Watson-Gegeo, 2004), heritage language learning (He, 2012), immigrants (e.g. Baquedano-López and Figueroa, 2012), academic discourse (e.g. Duff, 2010) and workplace (e.g. Roberts, 2010) also help with our understanding of intercultural learning.

9.5 Chapter summary

In this last chapter of the second part of the book, we have reviewed and compared various ICC models in a range of disciplines, with a focus on ICC models in foreign language teaching and learning. We have also discussed the uniqueness of intercultural learning, and proposed that:

- Intercultural learning takes various forms through a variety of means.
- ICC develops incrementally over time through learning in the classroom and learning from the real world.
- Some aspects of ICC benefit from direct contact more than others.
- It is essential to get the right balance between challenge and support.
- It is also essential to maximise affordance and to transform from just 'being there' into participation and engagement.

A number of key models and approaches in intercultural learning are reviewed briefly. These include:

- contact theory
- experiential learning theory
- transformative learning theory
- reflection
- critical incidents and cultural assimilators
- reflective learning journals
- the learner as ethnographer
- a language socialisation perspective.

To conclude, in Part II we have focused on 'how to communicate effectively, appropriately and at the same time, to build relationships', the three main goals of intercultural communication. We have looked at a number of factors and skills that lead to successful intercultural communication and intercultural learning that facilitates the development of ICC. In Part III we will introduce some major theories and models in the study of intercultural communication which have implications for our understanding of intercultural issues in everyday life and the development of competence in intercultural encounters.

Part III

Studying and researching intercultural communication

While Part I of this book focuses on practical concerns in the field of intercultural communication and Part II on how to communicate effectively and appropriately, Part III now aims to go behind the questions of what and how by looking at major theories, models and methodological considerations in the study of intercultural communication. It centres on three questions:

- The classical question: what is the relation between language, culture and thought?
- The fundamental question: how to define culture?
- A paradigm-shifting research question that emerged in recent years: how does language practice contribute to the construction of intercultural identities?

Each chapter in this last part has a section, 'Thinking back', which revisits issues discussed in Parts I and II of the book. It completes the cycle which starts with practice, engages with theory and returns to practice.

10 The relation between language, culture and thought

The classical question

> The differences between languages are not those of sounds and signs but those of differing world views.
>
> (Humboldt, 1836, translation in Humboldt, 1963, p. 246)

> The limits of my language mean the limits of my world.
>
> (Wittgenstein, 1922)

In this chapter, we are going to discuss the 'classical' question which can be traced back to as early as the eighteenth century, i.e. the relation between language, culture and thought. We start with an overview of the Sapir–Whorf hypothesis, followed by a selective review of influential arguments and lines of enquiry. The last section examines relevant issues from previous chapters in light of the classical question.

10.1 The Sapir–Whorf hypothesis: language controls or influences thought

Task 10.1 Languages differ from each other

Translate the following sentences into the languages you speak and then compare the original and translated sentences. Discuss the questions next to each sentence.

1 *Cats eat mice.*
   Question: are there changes in word order?
2 *Her grandma gave her two books.*
   Question: do the language(s) mark tense, plurality or gender and if so, how?
3 *The bird flew down from out of the hole in the tree.*
   Question: how do the language(s) express the manner and directionality of the motion, i.e. 'down-from-out-of'?

Many differences between languages surface through the above task. Some languages (e.g. English, Chinese and Swahili) follow the word order of SVO, while other languages (e.g. Classical Arabic, Welsh and Samoan) follow that of VSO. In some languages (e.g. French and German), most nouns have either a feminine or masculine gender, whereas in other languages (e.g. Chinese), gender is not marked. Some languages (e.g. English) classify nouns into singular or plural, whereas Arabic has an additional category, i.e. dual (two), to represent two people or objects. Some languages mark the status difference and the degree of intimacy between the speaker and audience with the use of honorific inflections in address terms. For example, *nim* is used as an honorific suffix in Korean to mark the status difference between speaker and audience: *halmeoni* for one's own grandmother, and *helmeonim* for someone else's grandmother. In some languages (e.g. English, German or Dutch), the motion path or the manner of action is 'bundled up' with the verb (as *out of* in the phrase *fly out of*) while, in some other languages (e.g. French, Spanish or Turkish), the motion path is indicated by the main verb in a clause such as *enter*, *exit* or *cross* and the manner is expressed by adding an element or phrase to the sentence.

How do we account for these variations? Can these linguistic variations be explained in terms of cultural differences? If yes, to what extent? Does the existence (or lack) of a particular feature make a difference to the way we perceive reality? In other words, what is the relation between language, culture and thought? This is a classical question that many researchers from anthropology, cognitive science, neurology, psychology, sociology, etc., have attempted to answer since the beginning of the twentieth century.

The most often cited hypothesis, among various speculations and arguments, is perhaps the Sapir–Whorf hypothesis. As an influential linguistic anthropologist at that time, Edward Sapir believed that no two languages were similar. He speculated that there was a close relation between language, thought and the real world which he referred to as culture:

> Language is a guide to 'social reality'…it powerfully conditions all our thinking about social problems and processes. Human beings do not live in the objective world alone, nor alone in the world of social activity as ordinarily understood, but are very much at the mercy of the particular language which has become the medium of expression for their society…The fact of the matter is that the 'real world' is to a large extent unconsciously built up on the language habits of the group. No two languages are ever sufficiently similar to be considered as representing the same social reality. The worlds

in which different societies live are distinct worlds, not merely the same world with different labels attached.

> (Sapir, 1929, reprinted in 1949/1985, p. 162)

Sapir's view was taken up by his student, Benjamin Whorf, a full-time fire prevention engineer and part-time linguist. In his series of publications (e.g. Whorf, 1956), Whorf used examples from the Hopi language to demonstrate how language impacts on habitual thinking processes. For example, he compared the way the concept of time was expressed in the Hopi language (a language spoken by Native Americans in northeastern Arizona) and standard American English and found some substantial differences. According to Whorf, in the Hopi language, there is no plural form for nouns referring to time, such as days and years. Instead of saying 'they stayed ten days', the equivalent in Hopi is 'they stayed until the eleventh day' or 'they left after the tenth day'. In addition, all phase terms, such as summer, morning, etc., are not nouns, but function as adverbs. The equivalent of 'this summer' is 'summer now', or 'summer recently' in Hopi. There is no 'tense' in the language either. Whorf proposed a 'linguistic relativity principle' on the basis of these examples together with others which he explained as follows:

> From this fact proceeds what I have called the 'linguistic relativity principle,' which means, in informal terms, that users of markedly different grammars are pointed by their grammars toward different types of observations and different evaluations of externally similar acts of observation, and hence are not equivalent as observers but must arrive at somewhat different views of the world.
>
> (Whorf, 1956, p. 221)

Although the Sapir–Whorf hypothesis is well cited and considered a classical proposition question in many fields, there are a number of myths and controversies associated with it.

First, the rigour of the linguistic examples used by Whorf in his argument is called into question. One example is Eskimo snow. Whorf argued that while English has few terms for snow, Eskimos use a large number of words for different types of snow such as falling snow, snow on the ground, snow packed hard like ice, slushy snow, wind-driven flying snow and so on, presumably because of their living environment and lifestyle. However, Martin (1986) and Pullum (1991) both pointed out that this was a misconception. We now know that the number of Eskimo snow words does not differ significantly from English. It was suggested by an expert on Eskimo language that in fact there are only a dozen words for snow in the Central Alaskan Yupik Eskimo language, not as many as some fervent followers of Whorf's argument originally thought (Pullum, 1991). English also offers a range of words describing snow such as slush, sleet, blizzard, avalanche, in addition to some descriptive words such as flurry or dusting. Elsewhere, the rich and detailed description of the expressions related to Hopi terms for time and space offered by Malotki (1983) also challenges some of the claims on Hopi words for time made by Whorf.

Second, differing interpretations of the Sapir–Whorf hypothesis exist in the literature, centring on the strength of the relation between language, culture and thought, partly due to ambiguity that emerged from both Sapir and Whorf's own arguments. Note the qualifying word 'somewhat' in Whorf's formulation and the words 'guide', 'powerfully conditions' and 'to a large extent' in Sapir's speculation in the earlier quotes. It is ironic that the very idea about the relation between language, culture and thought itself is a victim of ambiguity of language. A dichotomy between linguistic determinism and relativity was often drawn upon. These are also known as strong vs. weak versions of the Sapir–Whorf hypothesis and, according to Pavlenko (2011a), appeared in Brown (1958) for the first time.

- Linguistic determinism: language *controls* thought and culture.
- Linguistic relativity: language *influences* thought and worldviews, and therefore differences among languages *cause* differences in the thought of their speakers.

Out of these two versions, linguistic determinism has received strong criticism in the literature, even though it is not clear who has ever supported it (Gumperz and Levinson, 1996) or whether this is indeed what Sapir or Whorf had in mind. Kramsch (2004) listed three reasons why it should be discarded. First, it is possible to translate the essence of meaning from one language to another. Second, bi/multilingual speakers can speak two or more languages and sometimes code-switch among languages in ways 'not dictated by the habits of any one speech community' (p. 239). Third, growing sociolinguistic variation and diversity within one language makes it implausible to maintain that all the speakers of one language think the same way.

In contrast, linguistic relativity received much attention among scholars and members of the general public during the 1950s and 1960s, since it has fundamental implications for the understanding of linguistic and cultural differences. However, interest in the hypothesis came to an abrupt halt at the end of the 1960s when evidence from the cognitive sciences strongly argued for a commonality in human cognition (see colour terms in the next section), and the view that language is innate and biologically determined prevailed. The debate about linguistic relativity was renewed in the 1990s, triggered by new evidence from linguistics and psychology, the social turn in applied linguistics and the growing prominence of bilingual and multilingual studies. Recent publications from Daniel Everett (e.g. 2008, 2012), which argue that language is a tool developed to solve problems, just like the bow and arrow, have added to the momentum. In the next few sections, we focus on five influential arguments or topics in the debate.

10.2 Colour terms: language influences, but does not determine perception

Studies of language effect on colour categorisation have produced interesting insight into the linguistic relativity hypothesis. One of the key studies was Berlin and Kay (1969). In this study, the researchers first elicited colour terms from native speakers of twenty different languages and then asked the informants to map each colour term in their native languages with all the possible colours on a colour board, as well as identifying one prototypical colour. In the second phase of the research, the researchers analysed a pool of ninety-eight languages using the colour categories derived in the first phase. The study concluded that there were a limited number of 'basic colour terms' such as white, brown, red, in world languages and these colour terms appeared to follow an evolutionary sequence in world languages. Despite some strong criticism of its research design, in particular, the inclusion of bilingual speakers as informants, Berlin and Kay's proposal of colour term universals and commonality in human cognition was generally regarded as a substantial counter-argument against linguistic determinism.

But how about linguistic relativity, the moderate claim on the relation between language, culture and thought? A growing number of studies on colour terms suggested language effects on perception (e.g. Kay and Kempton, 1984) and memory (e.g. Brown and Lenneberg, 1954; Lucy and Shweder, 1979, 1988). These studies often make use of a cross-linguistic design to compare whether different language speakers perform differently in colour perception or recall tasks. However, these studies often face a validity problem of controlling linguistic influence when testing perception if language is assumed to impact on perception.

Kay and Kempton came up with an excellent solution in their study (1984) which aimed to test language effect on colour perception among English and Tarahumara speakers (a language spoken by Native American people of northwestern Mexico). There is a crucial difference in colour terms between these two languages: while English has two different colour terms for green and blue, only one single word, i.e. *siyóname*, is used in Tarahumara. But what effect does the existence of linguistic categories have on English speakers? Does the lack of colour terms mean that Tarahumara speakers cannot perceive differences between green and blue? To test this, Kay and Kempton designed two experiments.

In the first, they showed the speakers of two languages three similar colours in the blue–green colour range and asked them to choose the one that was most different from the other two. Not surprisingly, English speakers showed a tendency to group together two colours which could be described by the same word, even if the colours concerned were not as close as they were to the third one technically. Tarahumara speakers, on the other hand, showed very little language effect and grouped the colours together according to their distance in colour range. The difference in grouping results could be easily interpreted as evidence of 'Sapir–Whorfian effect', i.e. language determines thought. However, Kay and Kempton argued that the grouping results among English speakers might be influenced by their naming strategy, i.e. unconsciously resorting to linguistic categories when the speakers found the discrimination task difficult. To control the linguistic influence, Kay and Kempton designed the second experiment, in which English speakers were asked to judge whether the difference in greenness between Colour A and Colour B was bigger than the difference in blueness between Colour B and Colour C. When tested this way, English speakers showed comparable results to Tarahumara speakers because their focus was directed to the perception task itself without the influence of the language. Combining the results from the two experiments, the study showed that perception was indeed subject to the influence of language. However, when the linguistic influence was controlled, speakers of different language backgrounds showed similarities in their perception, suggesting that *language has some effect on perception, but it does not determine perception.*

In addition to colour terms, recent years have seen further empirical evidence of the relation between language and cognition from other domains such as number (e.g. Gordon, 2004; Pica et al., 2004), space (e.g. Levinson, 2003; Levinson and Wilkins, 2006), shape and material-based classification (e.g. Gentner and Boroditsky, 2001) and motion (e.g. Slobin, 1996, 2000). Evidence from bilingual or multilingual populations with regard to these cognitive domains is summarised in Pavlenko (2005b).

10.3 'The geography of thought': culture influences thought independent of language

In his book *The Geography of Thought*, Richard Nisbett, a cultural psychologist and cognitive scientist, used a number of examples and research findings to argue that mind has social origins and people from contrasting cultures such as Asians and Westerners think and see the world differently (Nisbett, 2003). One of the research questions that epitomises the geography of thought is whether a culture prefers grouping by categories or by relationship. Try the following activity adapted from Chiu (1972) by Nisbett (2003).

> *Activity: chicken, cow and grass*
> There are three objects: chicken, cow and grass.
> If you were to choose one object that goes with cow, which would you choose, chicken or grass?

Chiu found that American children preferred grouping chicken and cow together because they think of both as animals, in other words, these two objects belong to the same taxonomic group. In contrast, Chinese children preferred grouping grass and cow together because cows eat grass. Based on the results of a series of picture grouping tasks, Chiu concluded that American children tended to categorise by identifying similarities among objects while Chinese children are likely to be guided by relationships among objects. Chiu's findings on the existence of cultural differences in categorisation were further confirmed by other studies (e.g. Ji et al., 2004; Norenzayan et al., 2002; cf. Unsworth et al., 2005).

How can we explain cultural differences in cognitive style? Could they be caused by linguistic differences as the Sapir–Whorf hypothesis suggests? Ji et al. (2004) put this to test among bilingual speakers of Chinese and English. Using *word triplets* (panda, monkey, banana) instead of pictures, they administered the grouping task in different languages among two groups of bilingual speakers of Chinese and English who differed in their age and context of English learning. One group was from Mainland China and Taiwan and learned to speak English as a foreign language, the other group was from Hong Kong and Singapore and learned English either early in childhood or simultaneously with Chinese. The results showed that

- Both bilingual groups tended to categorise objects according to relationship rather than similarities irrespective of the language in which they were tested.
- Bilingual Chinese from Mainland China and Taiwan showed greater tendency to group by relationship when tested in Chinese than when tested in English.
- For bilingual Chinese from Hong Kong and Singapore, the language of testing did not make a difference: they showed a similar tendency to group objects by relationship when tested in English and Chinese. Compared with the bilingual group from Mainland China and Taiwan, however, the degree of the preference among bilingual

speakers from Hong Kong and Singapore was weaker, suggesting that there was a shift towards the 'Western' direction.

The first finding, according to the authors, suggested an effect of culture on thought independent of language. The differences between the two groups of bilinguals indicated that although there was an effect of language on thought, it became insignificant compared with the effect of culture on thought. While these interpretations seem plausible, the study assumed that for bilingual populations, the language of testing activates different thinking processes. Is this really the case for bilingual speakers? We will explore this issue further in Section 10.6.

10.4 Cultural key words: vocabulary as index of a culture

The importance of vocabulary in relation to culture is central to Sapir's argument. He once commented that

> Vocabulary is a very sensitive index of the culture of a people... Languages differ widely in the nature of their vocabularies. Distinctions which seem inevitable to us may be utterly ignored in languages which reflect an entirely different type of culture, while these in turn insist on distinctions which are all but unintelligible to us.
>
> (Sapir, 1933, p. 166)

One area connecting vocabulary and culture concerns cultural key words. These words, common to the language concerned and frequently used in semantic domains such as emotions or moral judgement, can be studied as focal points of a culture. Through these key words, we can untangle core cultural values, beliefs and expectations. This argument is well echoed in publications on cultural key words including Raymond Williams' *Keywords: A Vocabulary of Culture and Society* (1983), Tony Bennett and his colleagues' *New Keywords: A Revised Vocabulary of Culture and Society* (2005) and Burgett and Hendler's *Keywords for American Cultural Studies* (2007).

Some examples of cultural key words include *duša*, *sud'ba*, and *toska*, Russian terms roughly meaning 'soul', 'fate' and 'yearning/ melancholy' respectively (Wierzbicka, 1997b); *wakimae*, a Japanese term roughly meaning 'discernment', describing the expectation to observe social norms in society (Ide, 2005; also discussed in Chapter 6); *Ubuntu*, a Nguni term meaning 'personhood, humanness' and representing a value frequently found in various cultures across the African continent (Kamwangamalu, 2008); *Li* (礼), *he* (和), Chinese terms meaning politeness and harmony (Cortazzi and Shen, 2001).

While these cultural key words reflect the degree of importance of a concept or an idea in the culture concerned, caution should be taken against the risk of essentialising the culture under study, a problem we will turn to in the 'Thinking back' section in this chapter and again in the next chapter.

In describing and analysing these culture-specific terms, Wierzbicka (1997b) developed an analytical framework, i.e. 'cultural scripts', to overcome cultural and language bias in translation while at the same time being clear, precise and accessible. It uses a set of simple, indefinable and universally lexicalised concepts such as *I*, *you*, *do*, *good*, *bad*, etc., to describe a culture-specific word.

An example of cultural script for the Japanese cultural key word *amae*, roughly meaning 'trustful relationship', is provided below.

Amae
a) X thinks something like this about someone (Y)
b) When Y thinks about me, Y feels something good
c) Y wants do good things for me
d) Y can do good things for me
e) When I am with Y nothing bad can happen to me
f) I don't have to do anything because of this
g) I want to be with Y
h) X feels something good because of this.

(Wierzbicka, 1997b, pp. 278–279)

> **Task 10.2 Cultural key words**   (TC)
>
> Each culture has its own cultural key words. Give three examples of cultural key words for the culture(s) with which you are familiar. Explain (1) what the selected cultural key words mean approximately; and (2) what they tell about the culture(s).

10.5 The language of thought: language as a window into human nature; and thought exists independently of language

Contrary to many anthropologists' claim of cultural and linguistic relativity, some scholars, influenced by evolutionary psychology, argue for cultural universals. Brown (1991) once constructed a list of hundreds of human universals, incorporating categories such as language and content, such as having colour terms. Taking a similar view on cultural universalism, Steven Pinker criticised linguistic determinism unequivocally in a series of publications, in particular *The Language Instinct* (1994) and *The Stuff of Thought* (2007). Although Pinker accepts that the Sapir–Whorf hypothesis comes in many different interpretations (as seen in his summary of ten different versions of interpretation of the hypothesis in Pinker, 2007), his criticism seems to be aimed at the argument that language was the only means of thought, drifting away from the main tenets of the hypothesis. He argues that 'the idea that thought is the same thing as language is an example of what can be called a conventional absurdity'. The thrust of his main argument is that it is possible to think without language. In fact, people think not in any particular language, but in a language of thought known as 'mentalese', a representation of concepts and propositions in the brain. This is evident among adults with aphasia, people who grow up without language (a 'languageless' man is reported in Susan Schaller's case study (1991, cited in Pinker, 2007)), babies before they learn language, primates who are capable of recognising kinships among new members of the group, and people who self-report that they think through other means such as mental images or shapes, rather than verbally.

10.6 The bilingual mind: thinking and speaking in two languages

The arguments in the previous sections, with the exception of geography of thought, have mainly built on evidence from monolingual speakers or cross-linguistic comparison. What insights can studies on bilingual speakers offer to the debate on the relation between language, culture and thought? Some of the answers can be found in the volume *Thinking and Speaking in Two Languages*, edited by Aneta Pavlenko (2011a), and a review on bilingualism and thought also by Pavlenko (2005a).

Pavlenko (2005a) provided an overview of findings from bilingual studies which have either direct or indirect bearing on the debate in a number of areas including colour, categorisation of objects and substances, number, space, motion, time, emotions, personhood and discourse. She added another three areas to the list in her publication (2011a), i.e. inner speech (silent self-talk), autobiographical memory and written narratives. The expansion into new areas through bilingual studies has brought some interesting insights into the relation between language, thought and culture. For example,

- At discourse level, bilinguals are able to draw on different linguistic repertoires, stances and interpretations and to construct different identities when describing personal experiences in different languages.
- In autobiography, narratives expressed in the language of the event seem to be more efficient, accurate, detailed and emotional.
- With regard to emotions, evidence has shown that bilinguals may form two distinct emotion repertoires and conceptualisations in their two different languages.

Based on her review of empirical data available in the literature, Pavlenko (2011b) identified seven processes of conceptual restructuring in bilingual minds. These are:

1 co-existence of L1 and L2 categories
2 the influence of L1 on L2 categories
3 convergence of L1 and L2 categories
4 restructuring in the direction of L2 categories
5 internalisation of new categories absent in L1
6 the influence of L2 on L1
7 attribution of L1 categories.

Pavlenko further suggested that the processes of conceptual restructuring in bilingual minds may be domain-specific and conditioned by age of acquisition of L2 (early bilinguals show strong influence of L2), context of acquisition and length of exposure (immersion and residence in the L2 context facilitates conceptual restructuring), language proficiency and frequency of language use (advanced and frequent L2 speakers are more susceptible to conceptual restructuring).

Bilingual studies not only provide an exceptional opportunity to test the Sapir–Whorf hypothesis, but also to broaden the scope of investigation. Pavlenko argued that

> the time has come, at least in the fields of bilingualism and second language acquisition, to discard the narrow search for evidence for or against Linguistic Relativity and to engage in broad explorations of thinking and speaking in two or more languages.
>
> (2011b, p. 252)

10.7 Thinking back: relevance to intercultural communication

This review of the historical and current debate on the interrelationship between language, thought and culture shows that there is a connection between language, culture and thought, although how they are connected and what role cognition plays in the mix are controversial. The debate has direct implications for the field of intercultural communication in a number of areas, in particular, approaches to language and culture learning and the rationale behind the search for culture-specific ways of communication.

Approaches to language and culture learning The interplay of language and culture manifests itself in that languages spread across cultures and cultures spread across languages (Risager, 2006).

Therefore, when it comes to language and culture learning, it makes sense to take culture as an essential and integrated component of language learning and to rely on language as a means of understanding culture and developing intercultural understanding. We have followed this line of argument in the current book. In Chapter 1 we reviewed three approaches used in the language classroom (i.e. teaching culture-as-content, integrated language-and-culture, and intercultural approaches), with each approach reflecting the growing presence of culture in language learning. In Chapter 9 we investigated what a language socialisation perspective can offer to intercultural learning, and highlighted the role of language in learning about another culture.

Culture-specific ways of communication The relation between language, culture and thought has been used as an explanatory factor or justification in the search for culture-specific ways of communication. In Chapter 6 we examined a number of culture-specific ways of communication, including high vs. low context; high involvement; directness vs. indirectness; and cultural variations in turn-taking and space management. We also discussed some key concepts that have direct bearing on communication: i.e. politeness, face, rapport and solidarity, and some culture-specific terms such as *wakimae* and *dugri*. Some of the studies behind these culture-specific ways of communication assume that culture (in whatever way it is defined) influences or determines (for those with a more radical view) our ways of interaction. In these studies, cultural variations and specificity in ways of interacting are explained in terms of differences in cultural values, beliefs, history and expectations.

A number of issues, however, need to be raised with regard to this approach. Attributing differences and variations in ways of communication to cultural values may be convenient at some times or convincing at other times, but this approach carries with it the risk of stereotyping and essentialism. As an example, Kramsch (2004) referred to Robert Kaplan's cross-cultural rhetorical 'doodles'. Kaplan (1966) argued that there are culture-specific thought patterns in second language learners' writing in English, depending on learners' cultural backgrounds. The following diagram (Figure 10.1) shows different types of argument structure among five groups of speakers. English is a straight line, Oriental is a spiral cycle, Semitic is a zigzag and Romance and Russian digress at various points. Kaplan's model, as one of the first studies on culture-specific patterns of organisation in writing, is intuitively appealing, but at the same time simplistic and dangerous. We now know it is not justifiable to subsume many differing cultural groups under one label. Neither is it feasible to assume that members of a cultural group can be treated as the same.

English   Semitic   Oriental   Romance   Russian

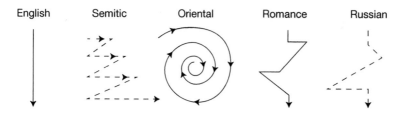

Figure 10.1 Representations of development of arguments in second language learners' writing
Source: Kaplan, 1966.

Second is the logical issue of equating correlation with causality. While the debate on the relation between language and culture so far accepts and agrees that language and culture are inseparable and interrelated, how language and culture influence each other and in which direction are still matters of disagreement. To identify communication patterns that frequently occur in a culture is one thing. Going one step further to say that culture determines communication patterns is another. A cultural account needs to be offered cautiously, and justified at an empirical level rather than used as a 'convenient' explanation. Going back to Kaplan's cultural rhetoric as an example, we now know that differences in writing conventions are directly or indirectly influenced by the wider social context, in particular, the pedagogical approach dominant in a culture. Culture is only one of the factors.

And the final caveat as we conclude this chapter: the problematic and changing conceptualisations of culture. The term 'culture' has been used as a synonym for 'social reality' and 'the (real) world' in Sapir and Whorf's original argument (see the quotations at the beginning of this chapter). It is unclear when and how the term 'culture' in the debate began to be interpreted in the way it is presented in contemporary literature. We will leave the discussion on what culture is to the next chapter.

To conclude this chapter, here is a quote from Gumperz and Levinson (1996) which well articulated the challenge in correlating communication patterns with a specific, yet loosely defined and cross-cutting culture:

Communication relies on shared meanings and strategies of interpretation. However, this common ground is distributed in a complex way through social networks. Such networks may constitute effective 'sub-culture,' nested communities within communities; but they can also cross-cut linguistic and social boundaries of all sorts, creating regional and even global patterns of shared, similar communicative strategies in specialist networks.

(Gumperz and Levinson, 1996, p. 12)

11 Theories of culture
A fundamental question

'I don't know how many times I've wished that I'd never heard the damned word', wrote Raymond Williams (1979), one of the founders of cultural studies. It is perhaps not a surprise to many that 'the damned word' is *culture*. The scale of multiplicity in the contexts where the word occurs is unrivalled. In addition to '*national* culture', the English lexicon now has *regional, ethnic, diasporic, transnational, gay, lesbian, black, club, street, drug, body, consumer, material, sports, media, visual, cyber, nano, techno* culture(s), etc., and many more can be found in Bennett (2005). The word also means different things to different people. When Alfred Kroeber et al. reviewed definitions of culture in the literature in 1952, they already found no less than 160 different definitions.

In this chapter we first review four dominant approaches to the concept of culture relevant to the field of intercultural communication. We ask the following questions:

- Who are the researchers?
- What is culture and what isn't culture?
- What is the goal of intellectual work?
- What is the disciplinary root?
- What are the challenges?

This will be followed by an overview which aims to identify similarities and differences between these different approaches, to explore tensions within the field and, most importantly, to suggest a way forward. In the last section, we reflect on implications these diverse approaches may have for the study of intercultural communication.

11.1 Compositional approach: culture as a collection of things shared by a group of people

The first approach is to see culture as a whole, embodied in a number of *things* and *shared* by a *group* of people. Since this approach mirrors the 'compositional' approach in the discussion of ICC models in Chapter 9, we will call this approach 'compositional'. Here is a selection of definitions from several disciplines.

- Culture is *that complex whole which includes knowledge, belief, art, morals, law, custom, and any other capabilities and habits acquired by man as a member of society* (Anthropologist: Edward Burnett Tylor, 1871, p. 1).
- Culture is *the deposit of knowledge, experience, beliefs, values, actions, attitudes, meanings, hierarchies, religion, notions of time, roles, spatial relations, concepts of the universe, and artefacts acquired by a group of people...*(Communication experts: Samovar et al., 1998, p. 36).
- *The collective programming of the mind which distinguishes the members of one human group from another...The 'mind' stands for the head, heart, and hands – that is, for thinking, feeling, and acting, with consequences for beliefs, attitudes, and skills... culture in this sense includes values; systems of values are a core element of culture* (Psychologist: Hofstede, 2001, pp. 9–10).
- *The culture of a group can now be defined as a pattern of shared basic assumptions that was learned by a group as it solved its problems of external adaptation and internal integration, that has worked well enough to be considered valid and, therefore, to be taught to new members as the correct way to perceive, think, and feel in relation to those problems* (Business management expert: Schein, 2004, p. 17).
- *Culture is a fuzzy set of basic assumptions and values, orientations to life, beliefs, policies, procedures and behavioural conventions that are shared by a group of people, and that influence (but do not determine) each member's behaviour and his/her interpretations of the 'meaning' of other people's behaviour* (Applied linguist: Spencer-Oatey, 2008, p. 3).

As seen in the selection above, there are two key words in this approach: 'things', and 'group'. Let us look at each in turn.

What counts as 'things' and how they are related to each other

Nowadays, among those who adopt a compositional approach to theories of culture, the consensus is that culture manifests itself in every aspect of life and is not confined to art, music, literature, food, fashion, festivals and folklore (see earlier discussion in Chapter 1). Second, among various components of culture, the invisible ones such as values, beliefs, attitudes, assumptions, etc., are at the core and thus more fundamental than those visible, tangible or audible ones such as behaviours, appearances or ways of doing things. In this regard, there are two well-known metaphors: culture as an onion and culture as an iceberg.

- Culture as an onion: each culture component is enveloped by another layer of culture components, just as onion peels, with values at the centre. One version of an onion diagram can be found in Hofstede (2001, p. 11).
- Culture as an iceberg: culture components are compared to an iceberg, with values, beliefs, etc., hidden beneath the surface. They are there but you cannot see them. What you can see is only 'the tip of the iceberg', a small proportion of what culture is. The origin of this metaphor is often attributed to Hall (1976).

The centrality of cultural values in defining a cultural group, particularly a national culture, underlines the work of many scholars who dedicated themselves to categorising national cultures in terms of values and belief systems. Below are some examples of influential works:

- Geert Hofstede's cultural dimensions: individualism vs. collectivism; high vs. low power distance; masculinity vs. femininity; high vs. low uncertainty avoidance; and long- vs. short-term orientation (Hofstede, 2001).
- Shalom Schwartz's basic human values: self-direction, stimulation, hedonism, achievement, power, security, conformity, tradition, benevolence and universalism (Schwartz, 1992, 1994).
- Edward Hall's cultural theories: high vs. low context; polychronic vs. monochronic time; and proxemics (how personal space differs between cultures) (Hall, 1976).

Who are the 'groups'?

Culture is shared by a group of people, but what are these groups and where do we draw the lines between groups?

Historically, cultural differences were often interpreted in terms of gender, race, ethnicity and social class in the 1970s, and nationalities in the 1980s (Moon, 2002). Nowadays, although culture is still predominantly associated with ethnicity and national membership in the public discourse and among researchers, it is defined more broadly – at the conceptual level at least – and thus independently of any of the above groups. Spencer-Oatey and Franklin (2009) list several other groups, including:

- Religious groups: religious beliefs such as Christianity, Islam, Hinduism, Buddhism, Judaism, etc., can have a fundamental impact on members' worldview, ethics and lifestyle.
- Organisations: each organisation has a culture of its own depending on its management structure, leadership style, goals, size, history, etc. In Chapter 3, we talked about how internal and external

communication strategies of an international corporation, such as choice of language and lines of communication, are very often decided by, as well as contributing to, the formation of an organisation's culture.

- Professional groups: each profession has a culture of its own. As discussed in Chapter 8, healthcare professional culture, as an example, is different in many ways from that of other professionals such as diplomats, financiers, academics, teachers, politicians, lawyers, etc.

Although Spencer-Oatey and Franklin also list 'communities of practice' as a separate group, in essence, the concept of communities of practice is an all-encompassing *grouping principle* rather than a fixed group. Originating in Lave and Wenger's work about learning theory (1991), the concept describes 'an aggregate of people who, united by common enterprises, develop and share ways of doing things, ways of talking, beliefs, and values – in short, practices' (Eckert and McConnell-Ginet, 1999, p. 186). Wenger (2006) further points out that for a community to become a community of practice, it is crucial for its members to have a shared domain of interest and engage in joint activities and practice. Examples of communities of practice include nurses who meet regularly for lunch in a hospital cafeteria, a youth gang who survive on the street and have their own identity, or an on-line group, such as mumsnet, in which parents share advice and exchange information. Communities of practice help us to see that a cultural group does not have to be one of those fixed and pre-defined ones. It can be of different sizes: some are large while some small; it can have different structures: some operate a strict membership scheme while some go for a loosely defined membership structure.

The above list of groups, together with the notion of 'communities of practice', has important implications for conceptualising culture. It shows that

- Cultural groups exist at many different levels, in different sizes and for different purposes.
- A cultural group can co-exist with another group (i.e. co-culture), be embedded in another culture (i.e. sub-culture) or overlap with another group.
- A person can belong to several different cultures at the same time.

Critiques of the compositional approach

The taxonomies of cultures that have emerged through culture categorisation reveal some salient cultural differences in values and beliefs and therefore can be used as a starting point when formulating hypotheses. The cross-cultural comparative paradigm, on which the compositional approach relies, also has a certain degree of clarity and consistency. However, this approach attracts criticism and often runs into difficulties at both operational and conceptual levels.

At the operational level, there are a number of 'cultural paradoxes'. These are behaviours which seemingly contradict a dominant value associated with the culture. Some examples of cultural paradoxes are given in Task 11.1.

(TC)
Task 11.1 Cultural paradoxes

The following three paradoxes are selected from Osland and Bird (2000, p. 65). How do you explain these seemingly contradictory behaviours?

1 Charitable behaviour in the USA: The USA is regarded as having an individualistic culture and is oriented to self-reliance and individual achievement. But why do Americans have the highest percentage of charitable donation and readily volunteer their help for community projects and emergencies?

2 Simpatía in Costa Rica: Simpatía is a cultural key word for Spanish culture and represents a feeling of community, harmony and warmth in interpersonal relationships. Yet, Costa Rica is not known for its service. In a survey carried out in 1991, cited in Osland and Bird, many Costa Rican customers allegedly preferred working with automatic bank services on the phone rather than with 'human' customer advisers. But what happens to Simpatía?

3 Ambiguous clauses in Japanese: According to Hofstede's cultural dimension (2001), the Japanese have considerably lower tolerance for uncertainty (ranked seventh out of fifty countries in an uncertainty avoidance index) compared with the Americans (ranked forty-third). But why do the Japanese often use ambiguous clauses in their business contracts, while Americans 'dot every i, cross every t, and painstakingly spell out every possible contingency'?

Sources of cultural paradoxes, according to Osland and Bird (2000), are several. One is the way cultural dimensions are often framed as dichotomies or represented on a continuum. In fact, it is probable that both ends of such dimensions can be found in one culture. For example, the Chinese culture promotes harmony, but at the same time respects hierarchy. The other source of cultural paradoxes is that values do not simply co-exist with each other. Instead they relate to each other and are context-dependent. In some contexts, some values take precedence over others.

At the conceptual level, many questions have been asked about the practice of *categorising and describing* national cultures in terms of core values. These include:

- Can we 'lump' people into one culture (Scollon et al., 2012)?
- Can we emphasise cultural regularity over variability (Kesckes's interview question reported in Spencer-Oatey, 2005b, cf. Spencer-Oatey and Franklin, 2009)?
- Do nations have cultures (McSweeney, 2002)?

These three questions are the main reasons behind the view that there is inherent essentialism (i.e. regarding a cultural group as having definable 'essences') and reductionism (i.e. describing a complex phenomenon, event or structure in terms of a simpler counterpart) in the way cultural value studies attempt to categorise and describe national cultures. This is indeed a problem that faces not only many cultural value studies but also those who attempt to describe the norms of a culture. For those who are against categorising national cultures, they believe that 'national norms' or 'tendencies' are only a statistical myth and can lead to over-generalisation and stereotypes. After all, the average number of legs per capita is under two but most of us have exactly two legs. They also believe that cultural value studies fail to recognise the national heterogeneity and superdiversity that exist in many parts of the world as the result of globalisation and migration. The predominant practice of equating 'culture' with national or ethnic cultures is also problematic. While a national culture does impact on an individual's way of thinking and behaviour, we now know that groups can be of many levels, sizes and purposes and that different 'cultures' may cross-cut and overlap. A workplace culture can be influenced by national culture, organisational culture, professional culture and local cultures. These different cultures interact with each other and lead to a set of unique characteristics. One source of culture may feature more prominently at some times than other times. In Chapter 8, we looked at how job interviews and patients' self-report in doctor–patient consultations are permeated by institutional and professional cultures.

The problems of cultural value studies are further exacerbated by the practice found in the work of its many followers. These works often assume that there is a one-to-one causal relationship between cultural values and behaviours, and therefore attribute observed differences in behaviours and styles of communication to differences in cultural values. As our discussion in Chapter 10 shows, a cultural account needs to be offered cautiously rather than used as a 'convenient' explanation.

Transcending dichotomies: the dialectical approach

Some alternative approaches or perspectives have been proposed to transcend dichotomies or polarised categories. One is the dialectical approach proposed by Martin et al. (2002). Moving away from deciphering what culture is, this approach is designed to reflect the 'processual, relational, and contradictory' nature of intercultural communication: 'processual' because cultures change; 'relational' because aspects of intercultural communication interplay with each other; and 'contradictory' because intercultural communication is about simultaneously holding two contradictory views. The following summary of six dialectics is based on Martin and Nakayama (2010, pp. 67–68).

- Cultural–individual dialectic: some behaviours are idiosyncratic and others reflect cultural trends. People belong to cultural groups, but at the same time, it is important to think of them as individuals.
- Personal–contextual dialectic: some aspects of communication remain relatively constant over a range of contexts, while others are context-dependent.
- Differences–similarities dialectic: group difference and similarity co-exist with each other.
- Static–dynamic dialectic: some aspects of culture remain relatively constant while others are subject to constant change.
- Present–future/history–past dialectic: the past is seen through the lens of the present and what happens currently cannot be fully understood without knowledge of what is in the past.
- Privilege–disadvantage dialectic: privileges can be disadvantages at the same time.

In essence, the approach offers a methodology to recognise the interdependent and complementary aspects of the seemingly opposite characteristics of culture. It suggests a way to reconcile cultural and individual behaviour, individual and contextual variations, difference and similarity, and the static and dynamic natures of culture as well as past and present. The same approach can also be applied in interpreting regularity and variability.

11.2 Interpretive approach: culture as semiotic

Clifford Geertz (1973) raised two issues regarding the way cultural analysis was done. One is the intrinsic incompleteness in trying to pin down what culture is. For Geertz, 'turning culture into folklore and collecting it, turning it into traits and counting it, turning it into institutions and classifying it, turning it into structures and toying with it' (p. 5) are merely escapes, not solutions. The other issue is 'thinness' in description, i.e. relatively undetailed and closed observation of what is happening. To solve these issues, Geertz proposed conceptualising culture as semiotic:

Believing…that man is an animal suspended in webs of significance he himself has spun, I take culture to be those webs, and the analysis of it to be therefore not an experimental science in search of law but an interpretative one in search of meaning. It is explication I am after, construing social expression on their surface enigmatical.

(p. 5)

Geertz named his approach as interpretative and distinguished it from the then dominant cultural analysis in terms of goals and methods. He was not concerned with identifying coherence of a culture, or 'arranging abstracted entities into unified patterns', but was keen to 'inspect' events. To achieve this goal, he proposed 'thick description', a method of describing and observing behaviours in detail and in their contexts as opposed to the practice of merely recording what happened. An example is the practice of leaving the dinner table. Instead of simply saying that French children are not allowed to leave the dinner table early, observers need to provide a description that answers questions such as 'How do meals end?', 'Do meals at different times of the day end in different ways?', 'What is the home context?', etc. (see Barro et al., 1998).

The value of the 'culture as semiotic' approach lies in that it moves away from a causality model which, often found in the compositional approach, attributes observed unique behaviours and events to culture. Since it focuses on uncovering the meaning of actions in their contexts, it exposes a culture's 'normalness without reducing particularity' (Geertz, 1973, p. 14). It has helped to develop a unique intercultural learning method referred to as 'the learner as ethnographer' (Chapter 9). It also has a strong influence on the other two conceptualisations of culture to be discussed in the next two sections.

11.3 Action approach: culture as a process

For some scholars, culture is not an entity, but a process. Here is a selection of views and arguments.

Small culture

'Small culture' was proposed by Adrian Holliday. It refers to 'a dynamic, ongoing group process to enable group members to make sense of and operate meaningfully within those circumstances' (2011 [1999], p. 205). The term is also used at the same time to refer to cultures shared by members of the same generation, occupation, education or similar prior experience, which can be metaphorically speaking smaller than national cultures (2005). The notion emphasises the dynamic and changing nature of culture, recognises the role of people in culture-making and acknowledges commonalities that can be identified among people of the same age, occupation, ability, common experience, other than nationalities and ethnicities. An example of small culture in operation is that when a new class is formed, each student will use their culture-making ability to negotiate new rules of interaction and bring in 'small culture residues from other educational, classroom, collegial and peer experience' (2011 [1999], p. 206).

Culture as a verb

Using the above phrase as the title of his paper, Street (1993, p. 25) argued that instead of trying to define what culture is, we need to treat culture as a verb, i.e. as an active process of meaning-making and discovering what culture does. Using examples from the South African context, Street argued that the very identities of ethnic groups are indexed by a range of cultural artefacts such as traditional costumes, Zulu dance, local languages (see the discussion of Zulu dance in Chapter 5). 'Culture' accentuates differences and boundaries between different groups in the following manner:

> One thing that culture does is create boundaries of class, ethnicity (identification with a larger historical group), race, gender, neighbourhood, generation, and territory within which we all live. Boundaries are created and maintained when people observe, learn and finally internalise the rituals and habits of speech, the disposition and dress of their bodies and modes of thought to the extent that they become entirely automatic and unconscious.
>
> (Thornton, 1988, cited in Street, 1993, p. 33)

Culture as 'an evolving connected activity, not a thing' (Fay 1996, pp. 62–63)

For Brian Fay, culture was not a text to be read, because it gave a misleading impression that culture is static, closed and given. In his opinion, comparing it to a conversation as Burke (1957, cited in Fay, 1996) suggested was an improvement, since the metaphor captures the dynamic and ongoing nature of culture: conversation involves active participation and perspective-taking in an open and fluid structure. But this was not sufficient. For Fay, it is crucial to see culture as an evolving connected activity reflecting the 'interplay between, on the one hand, the activity of its members as they appropriate and alter cultural meanings and, on the other, the enabling and limiting role of culture as it shapes these agents and their activity' (p. 63). The power struggle and resultant (in)equality in participation among members requires an approach that acknowledges that culture both allows and limits the agency of participants.

11.4 Critical approach: culture as power and ideological struggle

The critical approach borrows its name from critical theory (see Held, 1980). Similar to the action approach, it advocates the agency of participants and believes that through 'doing' culture, people create and are limited by culture as well. However, different from the action approach, it positions culture as a part of macro social practice, contributing to and influenced by power and ideological struggle. In interpreting human activities, it takes into account relationships, in particular, power differences between and within groups, as well as other aspects of society such as economy, history, politics, education, media, etc. It believes that these aspects of society are interconnected and jointly exert influence on human activities. In the *Handbook of Critical Intercultural Communication*, Halualani and Nakayama specify the relationship between culture and power structure in the following way:

> Culture is therefore an assemblage of meanings and representations, that are vested with or are reified and spoken via different power interests, most notably by dominant structure and culture groups themselves.
>
> (Halualani and Nakayama, 2010, p. 6)

For Halualani and Nakayama, culture differences can be reified by either those in power (i.e. ascribed cultural differences) or subordinate cultural groups themselves (i.e. (re)claimed cultural differences). This brings a critical perspective to understanding generalisations about a cultural group. The practice of generalisation about a cultural group has frequently been criticised as cultural essentialism in the literature as well as in practice and training (recall the task about stereotypes in Chapter 5). But interestingly, as Holliday (2005) pointed out, having been essentialised in various ways by the dominant West, people from the East and the South sometimes seek to confirm their essentialised identities, for example, through cultural artefacts such as traditional dress, dances, rituals and playing the 'culture card' to either appeal to a Western market or to gain access to power. Task 11.2 gives some examples of 'self-imposed' essentialising discourse.

Task 11.2 Why choose a Filipina?

In her book *Intercultural Communication: A Critical Introduction*, Ingrid Piller (2011) compared the cultural generalisations that are frequently found on websites advertising Filipina and Russian 'mail-order brides'. Read the following examples (pp. 123–125) and discuss what generalisations the discourse attempts to confirm, resist or create, and why.

(a)   Why choose a Filipina? Women from the Philippines are noted for their beauty, grace, charm and loyalty. With their sweet nature and shy smiles, Filipina ladies possess an inner beauty that most men find irresistible. Filipina women are by their nature family-oriented, resourceful and devoted. What's more, English is one of the official languages of the Philippines, so communication is straightforward, and as the majority of Filipina ladies are Christian, cultural compatibility is easier than some other Asian countries.

(b)   We [Filipinas] are different from most Asian cultures. We are loyal to family unit more than country. We are comfortable loving and marrying men of other race, while most Asians 'lose face' if marry outside their own cultures. [...] Marry a Filipina, and you not have to eat with chopsticks or bow all time.

11.5 Overview: complexity of culture

We have presented four approaches to culture so far. The compositional approach sees culture as a collection of things; the interpretive approach regards culture as symbols that can only be captured through thick description; the action approach views culture as a meaning-making process; and the critical approach places culture as a site of power and ideological structure. Each approach has its own lines of enquiry and methodologies as well as its own arguments on what is and is not culture. Given these diverse conceptualisations of culture, *how do we deal with complexity of culture in the study of intercultural communication?*

A possible way forward is to use culture as a tool, or using Scollon et al.'s words, to consider culture 'not as one thing or another, not as a thing at all, but rather as a heuristic...a "tool for thinking"'. This solution was suggested by Scollon et al. (2012, p. 3) when they noted that under the compositional approach alone, there was a variety of (competing) definitions of culture in the literature, each focusing on one or a set of behaviours and patterns which constitute culture. Scollon et al. argued that these definitions of what culture is are useful to some extent, in the sense that they each draw attention to a different aspect of human behaviour.

Seeing culture as a set of rules…leads us to ask how people learn these rules and how they display competence in them to other members of their culture. Seeing culture as a set of traditions leads us to ask why some aspects of behaviour survive to be passed on to later generations and some do not. Seeing culture as a particular way of thinking forces us to consider how the human mind is shaped and the relationship between individual cognition and collective cognition.

(Scollon et al., 2012, p. 3)

Following this, we can add that seeing culture as a web of symbols leads to the question: how do these symbols invoke meaning in contexts? Seeing culture as a process invites us to reflect on the role of agency of participants in human activities; and seeing culture as power and ideological struggle helps us to view the role of an individual in relation to the rest of society. We can use categories, ideas and meanings rising from definitions of culture to interpret human activity and social practice with the knowledge that what is represented by categories, ideas and meanings is in fact far more fluid, complex and open.

At an operational level, a possible way forward is to engage with the practical nature of the field and to take a problem-solving approach, using culture as a resource, but not limited to it. The field of intercultural communication was founded by Edward Hall (e.g. Hall, 1976) many years ago to solve a practical challenge of preparing American diplomats before they were posted overseas. Nowadays, as we discussed in Part I of this volume, intercultural communication issues are relevant to everyday life and exist across a range of sites. The practical nature of the field of intercultural communication makes it imperative for intercultural scholars, consultants, educators and students to ground academic discussions in the context of practical concerns, to balance conceptual complexity and applicability in real life and to embrace a problem-solving approach in dealing with real-life issues.

Admittedly, this is perhaps easier said than done. My own experience suggests that the task of bridging theories and practice in the field of intercultural communication is more challenging than in some other fields. A few years ago, I presented a paper at a SIETAR conference with the topic 'I write therefore I am', looking into how presentation of self in application letters is influenced by learners' social-cultural backgrounds. The first question after my presentation was not about my theoretical orientations, analytical stance or implications for teaching and learning in a second language, but about its application – 'How shall we apply what you have told us in selection and recruitment?' I was struck by the gap between the objective of academic research and the practical concerns and expectations from people 'on the ground' who are keen to solve problems in their professional and personal experience.

While we may be acutely aware of cultural influences on the way we behave or think, there is not a one-to-one causal relationship. What this means is that when solving a 'cultural' problem in real life, we need to be realistic, as well as innovative, about what we do. *We can use culture as a resource, but at the same time should not be restricted or limited by a cultural analytical lens.* During the course of preparing for this volume, I was approached by a local government officer who would like to look into the poor practice of recycling household waste among some ethnic groups in several boroughs of London. In my subsequent conversations with him, it transpired that there were many contributing factors behind poor performance in addition to 'cultural' factors: the communication barrier (many of the residents do not speak English); the highly transitory nature of communities due to internal and international migration; and the lack of incentives or accountability (recycling facilities are usually shared among those living in flats). The challenge was to understand the extent of cultural impact on residents' participation in recycling and to unpack what is and is not culture.

11.6 Thinking back: from what culture is to what intercultural communication is

As a field of enquiry, intercultural communication is often defined as the study of how people from different cultural backgrounds communicate with each other, and is used as an umbrella term to refer to both the study of interaction between people of different cultures and comparative studies of communication patterns across cultures. While this definition seems to set the boundaries and scope of the field clearly, there are a number of questions that need to be asked.

First, with whom is the field concerned? We now know that cultural groupings are not given or pre-defined. They can be of different levels or sizes; overlap with or be subsumed within another; come into existence, rejuvenate, retract, or disassemble through interaction. However, in many studies and in the public discourse, the default position is to associate culture with ethnicity or nationality. A predominant number of studies in the field of intercultural com-munication, as we cited in our earlier discussion of learning style, advertising and international business negotiation in Part I, are carried out either in an etic paradigm (comparing one culture with another using cultural-general constructs) or an emic paradigm (using local cultural terms to interpret a cultural phenomenon) over many decades with the aim of identifying intercultural differences and intercultural factors that impede communication. These studies have been either criticised for or warned about over generalisation or stereotyping in their observations. But what shall we do about this growing body of evidence? Despite the risk of over-generalisation, these studies provide a valuable source of information and draw our attention to both salient and subtle differences between different cultural groups when intercultural differences are systematically examined and cautiously interpreted. If we reject these research findings, we will be effectively 'throwing out the baby with the bath water', or in Wierzbicka's term (1997b), carrying theoretical extremism to the point of absurdity.

Second, if the field starts with people from different cultural groups, is it at risk of circularity or reification? This problem is well articulated in the form of questions raised by Scollon et al. (2012):

> How does a researcher isolate a situation to study as 'intercultural communication' in the first place? If you start by picking a conversation between an 'American' and a 'Chinese', you have started by presupposing that 'Americans' and 'Chinese' will be different from each other, that this difference will be significant, and that this difference is the most important and defining aspect of that social situation.
>
> (p. 4)

As scholars of intercultural communication, we are not alone in our struggle to get to grips with a concept that is fundamental to the field, yet has diverse and sometimes conflicting conceptualisations. Elsewhere, debates also take place concerning the notion of 'language' in sociolinguistics, 'native speakers' in TESOL, 'gender' in gender studies, 'politeness' in politeness studies, etc. These debates challenge our ways of thinking. Through problematising key notions, they create new perspectives and analytical lenses and enable us to develop a richer understanding of the issues involved. At the same time, we also need to take care not to confuse the need to problematise the notion of culture at a conceptual level with the need for a working definition of culture for those disciplines and studies which investigate group variation. For some disciplines such as cross-cultural psychology (e.g. Richard Nisbett's work (2003), discussed in Chapter 10), their primary goals are to discover similarities and differences in behaviours and cognition in different cultures, and they can only do so, at least at the moment, by treating culture as given and as a variable that differentiates groups of people who share certain ways of living. The same applies to language socialisation studies (Chapter 9), which examines the dual processes of learning to speak in a way appropriate to a community and adapting to the beliefs and norms associated with speaking that language; and arguably, cross-cultural pragmatics (Chapter 7), which studies patterns of communication in different cultures.

To avoid the issue of reification and to minimise potential bias, it is important to bear in mind that while we accept there are cultural ways of speaking and communication and that culture impacts on behaviour and thinking, not all the problems of intercultural interactions are due to or should be attributed to cultural differences. Intercultural interaction is subject to an array of influential factors: some factors may definitely be cultural; some are not cultural themselves, but interplay with cultural factors, and some may have nothing to do with culture. Take intercultural couples for example. As discussed in Chapter 4, although it is intuitively appealing to see intercultural marriage as a meeting place of two cultures, cultural differences between intercultural partners are not relevant all the time. They may become less prominent over time. They may be in the background and negligible at some times, but at other times present themselves in an in-your-face manner. To complicate matters, couples tend to see themselves as individuals but their partners as representative of a different culture (Piller, 2011). In examples provided in Chapter 8, we demonstrated that it is not *ethnicity per se* that leads to failure or breakdown in intercultural communication. Sometimes it is the lack of knowledge about professional and institutional discourse that puts ethnic groups or outsiders in a disadvantaged position.

So, what is the field of intercultural communication really about? Suffice it to say that the field of intercultural communication is primarily concerned with how individuals, in order to achieve their communication goals, negotiate cultural or linguistic differences which may be perceived relevant by at least one party in the interaction. In effect, intercultural communication serves as a specific case of interpersonal interaction. It shares the same goals as interpersonal interaction: effectiveness, appropriateness and relationship-building. At the same time, it provides an opportunity to examine what we do when the other party in the interaction, either by ascription or self-orientation or a combination of both, appears, sounds or interacts differently from ourselves, and thus helps us to appreciate and understand differences we encounter in everyday life.

12 Language, identity and interculturality

A paradigm-shifting question

'Where are you from?'

As someone who was born and grew up in China, who has spent the last 15 years working in British higher education and lived in Newcastle and London, I have often found it difficult to answer the above question in small talk. I can never get it right. If I say that I'm from London, I can guarantee that the next question will be 'But where are you really from?'. People expect to hear that I am from China or somewhere in Asia. But I feel that I am misleading them if I just give them what they want to hear. I am Chinese, but that is not all. I am a Chinese living in London, a professor in a British university and have two children of school age who were born and grew up in England. I have a good idea of who I am, but I need to do a lot of work to explain it to other people, or be selective in presenting myself with some element of audience design. This is because I am an 'outlier', living away from my ethnic place of origin.

Identity is multiple and complex. As my own case shows, who you think you are is not necessarily the same as how other people think of you. It is perhaps not surprising to many that identity is a heavily researched concept in a number of disciplines and fields including applied linguistics, philosophy, psychoanalysis, social psychology, politics, anthropology and cultural studies, to name but a few. In this chapter, we start with a brief overview of the multiplicity of the concept of identity and then focus on the relationship between cultural identity and ethnicity. In the third section, we explore interculturality, a line of enquiry that investigates how people employ interactional resources in identification.

12.1 Identity: multiplicity and types

Identity is a difficult term to define, since it is rich with (contradictory) meanings and implicatures both in its ordinary sense and in academic discourse. The paradoxical nature of the term is well demonstrated in Karen Tracy's attempt to define it as a unitary yet contradictory concept. For her, identities

Are best thought of as stable features of persons that exist prior to any particular situation, and are dynamic and situated accomplishments, enacted through talk, changing from one occasion to the next. Similarly, identities are social categories and are personal and unique.

(Tracy, 2002, pp. 17–18, emphasis in original)

Task 12.1 Who am I?

Complete the following 'I am' sentence up to twenty times, each time using a different word or phrase to describe yourself. After you have completed, please read the task commentary to analyse your description.

I am: _____

As an alternative way of interpreting the depth and scope that come with the term, some scholars have looked into different types of identity. A selection of different varieties of identity is given below.

Master, interactional, relational and personal identities   These four types of identity proposed by Tracy (2002) differ from each other on two dimensions: stable vs. situated and social vs. personal.

- Master identities refer to those aspects of personhood (e.g. gender, ethnicity, age, nationality) which are relatively stable and do not change from situation to situation.
- Interactional identities refer to specific and situational roles people enact in a communicative context. A person can be a college student, a volunteer for Oxfam, a passenger and a mother.
- Relational identities refer to interpersonal relationships such as power difference or social distance between people involved in a given situation. They are negotiable and context-specific. For example, in an appraisal meeting, there is power difference between a manager and an employer whose work-related performance is assessed. If they meet in a lift, however, the power difference is less an issue.
- Personal identities refer to personality, attitudes and character which are relatively stable and unique.

Discourse, situated and transportable identities   This classification by Zimmerman (1998) differentiates contexts created and invoked by different types of identity in interaction.

- Discourse identities are those that people assume and project in the various sequentially organised activities of talk, e.g. speaker, listener, story teller, story recipient, questioner, respondent, etc. They can shift turn by turn. For example, a person who asks a question may need to respond to some questions first and a story recipient may become a story teller in subsequent turns.
- Situated identities are those that come into play in a particular situation. As an interviewee, where you find yourself, e.g. in a news interview, police interview, or job interview, makes a difference to your expectations. Compared with discourse identities which change constantly, situated identities remain relatively stable.
- Transportable identities are latent identities that 'tag along' with individuals as they move through their daily routines, and may or may not be relevant to interactions. Examples include 'male', 'young' or 'white'. Participants may be aware of these identities, but they may not orient to identities in interactions.

Imposed, assumed and negotiable identities   This classification by Pavlenko and Blackledge (2003) differentiates identities in terms of acceptance and negotiability.

- Imposed identities are those which one cannot contest or resist at a particular time and place. Pavlenko and Blackledge gave two examples of imposed identities. One was the identification of Jews in Nazi Germany and the other was citizenship-related language testing required from immigrants who apply for a British passport.
- Assumed identities are those accepted and not negotiated by many at a given time. Examples of assumed identities include heterosexual white middle-class males or monolingual speakers of the majority language.
- Negotiable identities are those contested by groups and individuals through their agency and choice. A wide range of negotiable identities were included in the collection edited by Pavlenko and Blackledge, e.g. ethnicity and nationality, gender, race, class and social status, able-bodiedness, sexuality, religious affiliation, linguistic competence and ability.

The multiplicity of identity as highlighted in these classifications is a reflection of three broad paradigms in theorisation of identities in scholars' quest (Benwell and Stokoe, 2006). These paradigms are:

- identity as a project of the self;
- identity as a product of the social; and
- identity as constituted in discourse.

Historically, identity was regarded as a project of the self (a concept equally difficult to define) and as something to do with 'the mind/body/soul/brain' and therefore subjective, internal and unique (Riley, 2007). It has roots in philosophy and flourished in the fields of psychology and psychoanalysis. The recognition by scholars in the nineteenth century (e.g. Hegel, 1807/1977) that self cannot exist without the other paved the way for the second paradigm, which emphasises the social and collective nature of identities as embodied in a range of social variables and group labels such as middle class, elderly, northerners. Examples of scholarly approaches that build on the social nature of identities include variationist sociolinguistic theory, which explores the link between linguistic variables and social factors such as gender, age or social class. The third paradigm, identity as constituted in discourse, has two parallel lines of enquiry. One focuses on the process of identification and treats identity as a discursive performance, constructed and negotiated through interactions. This line of enquiry provides a backdrop to the interculturality approach which will be explored in Section 12.3. The other is to examine dominant discourse and ideology that impact and reproduce identity. A fairly detailed review of these three paradigms can be found in Benwell and Stokoe (2006).

In the next section, we shall look at a specific case of identity, i.e. 'cultural identity', which people often refer to in intercultural communication.

12.2 Cultural identity

Cultural identity is very often described as a collection of multiple identities, consisting of predominantly ethnic identities along with other intersecting identities such as race, nationality, gender, class and religious affiliation. One possible take on the relationship between cultural identity and other types of identity can be found in Orbe and Harris (2001), who took a more dynamic view of the multi-faceted nature of cultural identity. They proposed that while race and ethnicity are a part of cultural identity, other variables such as abilities, age, gender, nationality, sexual orientation, spirituality and socio-economic status interact with these two and act as cultural identity 'markers'. Some markers can become more salient and intense than others in the process of communication.

Although cultural identity is not only about ethnicity and race, ethnicity and race are central to cultural identity to the extent that ethnic or racial identities are often conflated with cultural identity in practice. This raises the question, why do ethnicity and race play such a prominent role in cultural identity? The answer partly lies in habit and the need to categorise others' ethnicity and race, as observed by Omi and Winant (1994, p. 59):

> One of the first things we notice about people when we meet them (along with their sex) is their race…This fact is made painfully obvious when we encounter someone whom we cannot conveniently racially categorize – someone who is, for example, racially 'mixed'.

There are plenty of examples in everyday life when a person has been assigned ethnic or racial identity that either conforms to or differs from what the person considers him or herself to be. One of the interesting anecdotes I have heard was a colleague's experience as a visiting teacher on an exchange programme in Australia. When she was introduced to the children in an Australian primary school, they asked her where she came from. She duly confessed that she was from Germany. However, one child was quick to point out that it could not be true, since she was not wearing a scarf like all the other previous visiting teachers from Germany!

The fact is that when we categorise others' ethnicity and race, we use a range of *audible, visible* and *readable* cues and rely on our prior experience and knowledge of the salient features of a species – in other words, schemata, the idea we discussed earlier in Chapter 6.

You are how you sound   An example of audible cues is the way we speak language(s), in particular, accent and fluency. There have been some interesting and fruitful studies linking perception of dialectal accent and identification of ethnicity. Linguistic profiling studies by John Baugh and other scholars (Baugh, 1999, Purnell et al., 1999) are such an example. In these studies, the researcher called the same landlord for an appointment but used three different varieties of English: Standard English, AAVE (African-American Vernacular English) and Chicano English. The results were that in areas where the population was predominantly white, a much higher percentage of the requests made with the Standard English were successful, while those with non-standard varieties achieved a lower success rate. Other studies (e.g. Anisfeld et al., 1962; Fayer and Krasinski, 1987) have shown that, similar to dialectal variations, 'foreign' accents or accents of second language users were often judged to be less educated, less intelligent or poorer.

Fluency in a heritage language is often used as a marker of the strength of one's orientation towards ethnicity of the community. According to Fought (2006), speaking the language of the community may be a way of asserting ethnic identity amongst members of the community; those members who do not speak the language of the community may find their ethnicity called into question.

You are how you look   The visible cues we use in categorisation of ethnicity include one's appearance. Much anecdotal evidence can be found in the literature documenting how people ascribe ethnicity according to one's appearance. Ien Ang, the author of *On Not Speaking Chinese* (2001), was born into a family of Chinese descent in Indonesia and grew up in the Netherlands. She wrote about her predicaments of Chineseness: 'In Taiwan I was different because I couldn't speak Chinese; in the West I was different because I looked Chinese' (p. vii). Fought (2006, p. 6) also reported a Panamanian girl of African descent who was told by her teacher to check 'black' on the form because, in the teacher's words, 'that is what people see when they look at you'.

Some studies (e.g. Rubin, 1992, reported by Lippi-Green, 1997/2012; Williams, F., 1983) identified the link between visual and audio cues, in particular, how we hear and 'imagine' accent through someone's appearance (e.g. whiteness, blackness, Asianness, etc.). In Williams's study (1983), a group of European-American students were shown three videos which used the same audio file, but with three speakers of different ethnicity: European-American, African-American and Mexican-American. Despite using the same audio file, the last two videos were rated as of significantly lower standard than the first. These studies revealed how one's prior knowledge of ethnicity and categorisation of ethnicity through racial phenotype (e.g. skin colour, hair, facial features, etc.) can lead to bias in perception and result in 'linguistic discrimination'.

You are what you are on paper   Categorisation of ethnicity also takes place through written, hence, readable cues. One such cue is name. Those who carry 'foreign' names may find themselves at a disadvantage when it comes to applying for jobs. Shahid Iqbal, as reported by Sangita Myska (2012) in the *BBC News Magazine*, adopted a British name, Richard Brown, when he realised at the age of 18 that his name proved problematic in getting a job. He then found the vacancies for which he had previously applied but which, allegedly, were 'filled', were now available. He is now the owner of an engineering company in Birmingham and has decided to keep the name of Richard Brown.

Apart from names, how you write tells others about yourself. Studies have shown that second language speakers' texts differ from native speakers' in a variety of linguistic and rhetorical aspects (e.g. Hinkel, 2002) and in the degree of flexibility (e.g. Biesenbach-Lucas, 2007, discussed previously in connection with an email request in Chapter 1). My study on presentation of self in application letters (Zhu, 2007) also found that when it comes to presenting themselves as desirable, there were salient differences in several aspects between

British students and those 'international' students from China in a postgraduate course in a UK university.

Crossing and passing

Some studies in sociolinguistics have identified a phenomena described as *crossing*, in which speakers use the language varieties of social and ethnic groups to which they do not normally belong. Classic studies on crossing have examined the use of an English-based Caribbean Creole among white teenagers in South London (Hewitt, 1982) and the use of Panjabi, stylised Asian English and Creole, among three groups of white, Afro-Caribbean and Panjabi teenagers in the southern Midlands of England (Rampton, 1995, 1999). In the following example, Asif and Salim switched from Panjabi to stylised Asian English in their response to Miss Jameson's first use of 'after you'.

Example 12.1

Asif and Alan were in detention under the supervision of a teacher, Mr Chambers. Miss Jameson, who came to swap with Mr Chambers, arrived at the room at the same time as Kazim and Salim, two of Asif's friends. SAE: stylised Asian English.

Kazim and Salim arrive at the door.

1	Asif:	Kaz [in Panjabi] stay here stay here.
2	Mr C:	(see you messing around)
3	Alan:	(.....)
4	Asif:	[chants, in Panjabi] your [obscenity] nonsense
5	Miss J:	after you
6	Asif:	[in SAE] after you::
7	Salim:	[higher pitch, in SAE] after you::

(Rampton, 1995, p. 72, transcription slightly altered.

[ ] = notes on language)

Crossing occurs very often among adolescents who borrow phonology, syntax or lexicon from another language variety for a variety of reasons. In a review by Fought (2006), she identified some common themes. For example, crossing can be used to undermine parents' or teachers' authority as a form of rebellion; to disguise the use of taboo and offensive language; to achieve humorous effect in verbal play; and to signal a desire to affiliate with the values of the borrowed code, such as 'tough, cool and good to use', which may or may not be directly attributed to ethnicity. In the above example, Asif and Salim's dramatised switch to SAE in replying to Miss Jameson's 'polite' formulaic expression in Lines

6 and 7 could be interpreted as a part of 'verbal duelling', and a way of marking their resistance and undermining the teacher's authority.

In contrast to crossing, passing refers to 'the ability to be taken for a member of a social category other than one's own' (Bucholtz, 1995, p. 351). Riley (2007, p. 233) cited a case of a call centre in India where young people were trained to 'pass' for Americans. Part of the call centre training course was designed to erase all traces of their Indian accent in English and to acquire a 'pleasant middle American (not educated American) accent'. They were given names such as Nancy, Sally Jane, Bill, Jim, etc., and biographies of their American identities: place and date of birth, parents' occupation, etc., while few of them had ever been to America. In Bucholtz's study (1995), she documented several cases in which people affiliated with ethnicity that was not a part of their biological origin. In the following extract, a light-skinned Black woman described how she found 'a kind of psychological shelter' in being a Spaniard.

> *Due to a complex combination of socio-economic circumstances, I happened to find a kind of psychological shelter in Latino heritage and even grew to identify more with it than with my own culture(s)... It wasn't until years later I realised why I had such an obsessive drive to learn Spanish and why I felt so at ease, relaxed and at home in Spain, a country whose people had the exact same skin color I did. I had simply been searching for a kind of psychic shelter, wherever I could find it.*
>
> (Zook, 1990, cited in Bucholtz, 1995, p. 357, emphasis in original)

To sum up, in this section we have looked at some possible definitions of cultural identities. Through the discussion of audible, visible and readable cues of cultural identities, I hope to illustrate that the categorisation of cultural identities is subject to both self-selection and ascription-by-others. In the next section, we explore the role of self-orientation and discuss how the battle of self-orientation and ascription-by-others plays out in interactional practices.

12.3 Interculturality: from being to doing cultural identities

Recent years have seen growing use of the term 'interculturality' in public discourse, intercultural learning and education, and other related fields. In public discourse, interculturality, derived from the adjective 'intercultural', is used largely to refer to interaction and active engagement between different cultural groups and communities, in contrast to multiculturalism, which concerns organic co-existence of cultural groups and communities. In the field of intercultural learning and education, interculturality represents a language-and-culture learning pedagogy which believes that the goal of language learning is to become intercultural speakers, mediating between different perspectives and cultures, rather than to replace one's native language and culture with 'target' ones (see Chapter 1 for further discussion of the intercultural approach).

As an emerging research paradigm, interculturality represents a line of investigation that departs from traditions of seeing cultural memberships or cultural differences, largely, if not always, as something 'given', 'static', or as something 'one either has or does not have'. Instead, it problematises the notion of cultural identities and emphasises the *emergent*, *discursive* and *inter-* nature of interactions. By examining interactional practices, particularly sequences of talk, interculturality seeks to interpret how participants make (aspects of) cultural identities relevant or irrelevant to interactions through *interplay* of self-orientation and ascription-by-others and interplay of language use and identities. This theoretical perspective originates in Nishizaka's seminal work (1995), extended by Mori's work on Japanese and American students' talk (2003). Two journal special issues (Higgins, 2007; Sercombe and Young, 2010) present some recent, concerted efforts by scholars to develop the approach theoretically and methodologically. The main agenda and contributions can be summarised through the following six questions:

1 Are cultural memberships always relevant to intercultural interactions?
2 What do participants do with cultural memberships?
3 How do participants do cultural identities?
4 What interactional resources are available for doing cultural identities?
5 Why do people bother with interculturality?
6 How far can participants go when doing interculturality?

We shall look at each question in turn.

Are cultural memberships always relevant to intercultural interactions?

This is the starting point for the interculturality approach. Echoing the arguments of many scholars who advocate multiplicity of social identities (e.g. Antaki and Widdicombe, 1998), the interculturality perspective argues that an individual has a number of identities and belongs to many membership categories, but not all identities are equally salient or relevant at a given point in differing social interactions. Cultural memberships such as 'being Japanese, American,

Jamaican, Spanish, etc.' cannot be taken for granted. Instead, they are contingent on participants' self-orientation and ascription-by-others, and brought about in interactions as a situated, practical accomplishment (Higgins, 2007). Example 12.2 is an extract from an interview about foreigners' experience in Japan on a radio programme, from Nishizaka (1995, p. 304). Read the extract first. What could you say about A's cultural membership? Is he a non-Japanese just like B?

Example 12.2

A: interviewer; B: interviewee. The interview was conducted in Japanese, transcribed broadly and then translated into English.

1	A:	One thing I want to ask you is: when Japanese people talk in
2		Japanese, they are sometimes only diplomatic,
3	B:	Yes.
4	A:	[they] are just apparently sociable,
5	B:	Yes.
6	A:	[they] are sometimes so, aren't [they]?
7	B:	Yes.
8	A:	For example, 'Well, Shiri-san, come to my home uh next holiday,' say [they] very easily.
9	B:	Yes.
10	A:	If you actually go there on the next holiday, [they] will say, 'Oh? For what have you come here,' may be. hhhh
11	B:	hhhhhhhhhhhh Yes.
12	A:	I mean, what [they] say and
13	B:	Yes.
14	A:	what [they] mean seem different,
15	B:	Yes
16	A:	this way Japanese often
17	B:	Yes.
18	A:	talk, don't [they]. [they] often talk so.
19	B:	Yes. Yes.
20	A:	How about this.
21	B:	This is a little troublesome to foreigners, [they]
22	A:	It's troublesome, isn't it.
23	B:	Yes, wrongly, [they] will take what is said for what is meant,

(Nishizaka, 1995, p. 304, transcription slightly altered:
[ ] = text added in translation)

In fact, the interviewer A was Japanese and the interviewee B was a Sri Lankan living in Japan. The point Nishizaka was trying to make is that a speaker could make their cultural membership irrelevant through interactive work. During the interview, the interviewer, a Japanese himself, deliberately distanced himself from 'being a Japanese' by repeatedly referring to Japanese as 'Japanese people' or 'they'. In doing so, the interviewer oriented to his interactional role as an interviewer rather than his Japaneseness. The interviewee accepted his alignment and tried to establish himself as a representative of foreigners living in Japan. He confirmed the interviewer's assertions in almost every turn by saying 'yes' and elaborating occasionally (e.g. Turns 21, 23, etc.). In Turn 21, he used the word 'foreigners' as if he was talking about other people, not about himself.

In arguing that cultural memberships of participants are not *a priori*, interculturality studies distance themselves from those approaches to intercultural communication research which assume cultural differences as default, and attribute mis- or non-understandings in interactions to cultural differences. In fact, interculturality studies have demonstrated that cultural memberships may not be the source of breakdown in intercultural interactions, in that

- Cultural memberships are not always salient or relevant in interactions; participants can make cultural memberships irrelevant.
- Cultural memberships, when relevant to interactions, do not always lead to problems of talk.

What do participants do with cultural memberships?

As Antaki and Widdicombe (1998, p. 2) eloquently put it, cultural memberships can be 'ascribed (and rejected), avowed (and disavowed), displayed (and ignored)'. Participants can do a number of things with cultural membership. They can make their cultural membership irrelevant as shown in Example 12.2, above. They can ascribe membership to others in social activities. They can claim memberships of groups to which they do not normally belong (recall the discussion we had earlier on crossing and passing). They can resist cultural membership assigned by others. Day (1998) identified some ways in which resistance occurs. These include:

- dismissing the relevance of the category;
- minimising the supposed 'difference' between categories;
- reconstituting the category;
- ethnifying the ethnifier, i.e. turning the table by assigning cultural memberships to those who assign memberships in the first place;
- actively avoiding it.

In Example 12.3, Lars suggested Chinese food for the party they were planning. Rita took the next turn and made a comment about Chinese food. Since it was not clear from the data how the following turn was allocated, we could only speculate that Xi, an ethnic Chinese, felt obliged to take the floor when her cultural expertise was made relevant. She faced two choices: either dismissing the potential relevance of the category of being a Chinese or continuing the flow of the discussion by commenting on Chinese food as a cultural insider. She opted for the first by suggesting that she was fine with any type of food, thus presenting herself as an individual rather than a cultural expert on Chinese food. Her subtle resistance to making her Chinese background salient in the conversation, however, encountered admonishment from Lars, who was quick to point out that this was not just about Xi herself.

Example 12.3

Participants were workers in a Swedish factory. They were planning a party.

```
51  Lars:   don't we have something that, one can eat
52          that, China or
53  Rita:   Chinese food is really pretty good
54  Xi:     haha (( )) it doesn't matter, I'll eat anything
55  Rita:   ah ((that's [what I that))
56  Lars:              [yeah, but this concerns everyone
57          doesn't it?
```

(Day, 1998, p. 162; transcription slightly altered)

How do participants do cultural identities?

Participants 'do' cultural identities through a range of interactional work and discursive practice. The key mechanism of interculturality can be summarised in the following points.

1 membership categorisation as a prerequisite;
2 whether a person's cultural membership is relevant or operative is achieved locally through moments of identification by participants of interaction;
3 the paradox of identification on the spur of the moment and control;
4 indexical and symbolic cues of relevant category-bound activities and features.

Membership categorisation as a prerequisite The prerequisite for a person to 'have an identity' is that the person is cast into a category with associated characteristics or features (Antaki and Widdicombe,

1998, p. 3). This principle draws on the concept of the Membership Categorization Device (MCD, Sacks, 1972). Sacks observed that people use language to order objects of the world into categories such as family, Londoner, Mexican, student, etc. There are conventional expectations about what constitutes a category's normative behaviour. If someone displays a certain set of features or carries out particular actions usually associated with a category (category-bound activities, in Sacks' terms), she would be cast as a member of the category. For example, if you take lectures, are registered on a course or have a student ID card, you may be categorised as a student. A person can belong to several categories. For example, a student could also carry the categories of female, mother, stamp collector, Irish, musician, tourist, shopper, etc.

Making cultural membership relevant locally through moments of identification by participants of interaction   A person can belong to several categories at the same time, but not all of them will be relevant to a social activity or practice at a given time. Omoniyi (2006) proposed a model of 'hierarchy of identity', arguing that a person's various identities are allocated in a hierarchy based on the degree of salience it claims through 'moment of identification'. Moments of identification are specific points in interactions or social activities for participants to signal their identity work through various means and resources.

The paradox of identification on the spur of the moment and control   On one hand, identification appears to occur on the spur of the moment during interactions; on the other hand, it is a controlled decision made by participants. Participants need to pick up 'cues' of identification, assess options of identification available at that particular moment, take into account their prior knowledge about and experience of a membership category, or do a quick calculation of costs and benefits that may come with each option, e.g. desirability of resistance and ascription of categorisation to them and their interactional partners.

Indexical and symbolic cues of relevant category-bound activities and features   Participants in interactions, at moments of identification, rely on the combination of symbolic and indexical cues that evoke the relevance of particular category-bound features and activities associated with cultural identities. This principle draws upon Gumperz's idea of 'contextualisation cues', which refer to 'any feature of linguistic form that contributes to the signalling of contextual presuppositions' (1982, p. 131). Examples of symbolic and indexical cues include accent, code-switching, address terms and culture-specific terms, among other things. The audible, visible or readable cues of ethnicity as discussed in the previous section are all indexical and symbolic in nature. It is through these indexical and symbolic cues that participants make demonstrably relevant certain aspects of their own cultural identities or those of others, intentionally or inadvertently. Their recipients may choose to align with, avow, resist, or ignore cultural identities evoked by these cues. In some cases they may misread or fail to pick up the cues, which leads to misunderstanding.

What interactional resources are available for doing cultural identities?

As our discussion about indexical and symbolic cues shows, participants have a range of linguistic forms and interactional resources at their disposal to do identity work. The following list represents some of the areas and analytical focuses reported in interculturality studies.

- Topical talk related to cultural expertise and practice. In Zimmerman's study (2007), she examined how topics about two traditional cultural foods, *kimuchi* (pickled spicy vegetables in Korea) and *tsukemono* (pickled vegetables in Japan), were used to evoke relevant cultural identities and as a conversation strategy for establishing and demonstrating solidarity among conversation participants. She also found that cultural expertise was often claimed by non-members of the culture and that presumed cultural experts did not always enact their cultural memberships. One type of topical talk on cultural practice is comment about the degree of appropriacy of social, cultural and linguistic behaviour in specific contexts, which is termed as 'talk about social, cultural and linguistic practices' in my work (Zhu, 2008, 2010; an example can be found in Chapter 9).
- Cultural references by names and address terms. Ryoo (2007) reported a conversation in which a Korean shop owner introduced himself as Jackie Chan, a Hong Kong movie star, in his attempt to avoid the hassle of dealing with a salesperson. In my study of Chinese diasporic families (Zhu, 2008), the choice and avoidance of a particular address term as well as the choice of Chinese or English names were found to function as indexical and symbolic cues of Chinese cultural values and identities.
- Use of the language or a code normally associated with a group. Cutler (2007) examined the practice of a white teenager who marked himself linguistically as white by overemphasising his pronunciation of /r/. Day (1998) gave several examples of how linguistic expertise is often used as an index of cultural identity. In

one example, a participant challenged another participant's self-orientation to Swedish by questioning whether a presumably Swedish word spoken by him is Finnish.

Why do people bother with interculturality?

There are various reasons for and consequences of 'doing cultural identities'. My own study on interculturality (Zhu, 2010) showed that interculturality plays an important part in reinforcing and negotiating social relationships among different generations of diasporic families who, more often than not, face the tension between cultural values of diasporic communities and those of the local communities, and the need to deal with different language ideologies and discrepancies in linguistic abilities. Elsewhere, Higgins argued that interculturality can be used as 'a source for comity, affiliative positioning and mutual understanding' (2007, p. 3). Interculturality also helps participants to organise their participation in conversations by selecting possible respondents for category-bound activities or features evoked by indexical and symbolic cues (Mori, 2003). References to cultural memberships are frequently employed as a strategy in the context of tandem language learning, a language exchange activity in which each learner is a native speaker in the language which the other learner wants to learn (Woodin, 2010).

How far can participants go when doing interculturality?

This is perhaps the most challenging question for scholars working on identity. Interculturality studies have argued that cultural identities cannot be taken for granted and therefore, in this sense, they are neither given nor fixed. Few of them, however, have gone further to argue that cultural identities are socially constructed and *entirely* up to participants' orientation and negotiation, a position advocated by many studies following a poststructuralist approach in recent years. As Block (2006) commented, the poststructuralist approach, which seeks to frame identity as 'socially constructed, a self-conscious, ongoing narrative an individual performs, interprets and projects in dress, bodily movements, actions and language', has become dominant among theorists and researchers interested in how individuals do identity work. In some studies following the poststructuralist approach, agency of participants in doing identity has been taken to an extreme to imply that all choices become possible (cf. May, 2001) and identity has become a 'free-floating' concept (Dervin, 2012).

This reluctance on interculturality scholars' part to adopt a poststructuralist stance on cultural identities, in my opinion, is justifiable. As May (2001) argued, although negotiation is the key to construction of cultural identity, there are limits to it. The limitation partly comes from the fact that certain parts of cultural identity, such as how we look and how we use language, are visible, audible and readable, and is partly due to the fact that some national and ethnic categories such as Chinese, European American, Jewish, black, etc., are socially and politically defined and reiterated through public discourse and social practices. In what follows, Matthews (2000) used a cultural supermarket metaphor to vividly highlight the limitations of choices as a consequence of social structures and (unequal) power relationships between individuals.

> just as the modern supermarket offers foods from all over the world, in all shapes and sizes, so the international media and advanced technology together make available to individuals around the world a range of identities to be assumed. However, the cultural supermarket is not a completely free market where any self identity under the sun can be assumed; nor is it a reality in an equal way for all of the inhabitants of this planet. In the former case there are social structures within which individuals exist (be these state governments, peer groups or educational systems) which constrain the amount and scope of choice available to individuals. In the latter case, there are individuals living within social structures that do not allow them to make as many choices (e.g. societies where the role of men and women are circumscribed by tradition).
>
> (Matthews, 2000, cited in Block, 2006, p. 36)

For interculturality studies, what can be negotiated by participants is the extent of alignment or misalignment between ascription-by-others and self-orientation and the relevance of cultural memberships at a specific time in interactions (see Figure 12.1). Interculturality studies have shown that participants can use a range of interactional resources to acknowledge, uphold or avow others' ascription on the one hand, or to resist, challenge, rebut or ignore others' ascription on the other.

In interpreting the relevance of cultural memberships and understanding the nature of negotiation between participants, interculturality studies benefit from Conversation Analysis (CA), a theoretical and analytical approach to social interaction with the purpose of understanding how meaning is produced, interpreted and negotiated in conversation through an analysis of linguistic features. Two ideas are of relevance to our current discussion: the role of context and the issue of 'demonstrable' relevance. In CA, no references are made to participants' internal states (e.g. goals, expectancies, motives, etc.). The sociolinguistic variables such as power relations, gender and formality only become relevant when participants themselves publicly display some orientation to them. The issues of

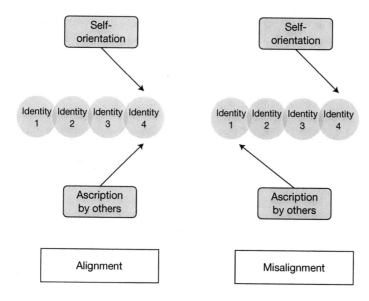

Figure 12.1 Alignment and misalignment between self-oriented and ascribed identities

demonstrable relevance also help analysts to focus on what is really relevant at a given time rather than what can be *assumed* to be relevant. As Schegloff explained:

> Showing that some orientation to context is demonstrably relevant to the participants is important...in order to ensure that what informs the analysis is what is relevant to the participants in its target event, and not what is relevant in the first instance to its academic analysts by virtue of the set of analytic and theoretical commitments which they bring to their work.
>
> (Schegloff, 1992, cited in Benwell and Stokoe, 2006, p. 37)

Task 12.2 'This is for the UK passport holder'   (TC)

Read the following conversation that took place at Heathrow airport border control. B was waiting at the head of the queue for UK nationals. She did not realise that a desk was available until A, a 'Chinese'-looking man standing behind her, alerted her in Line 1. Discuss what happened in Lines 2 and 3.

1   A: Excuse me, would you like to go to the next one over there?
2   B: (turning around) This is for the UK passport holder.
3   A: I <u>know</u>, but do you want to go to the next one?

In sum, interculturality, as a new and emerging research paradigm, provides an analytical stance that focuses on the role of interactions and discursive practice in negotiating relevance of cultural identities. It examines whether and to what extent participants bring about, align with each other, or resist cultural memberships oriented to by themselves or ascribed by others in interactions. It takes cultural identities as a process and outcome of negotiation, rather than something *a priori*. By doing so, it restores the central role of language practice in intercultural communication.

12.4 Thinking back and looking forward

We explored how language and culture are interrelated in Chapter 10 and how the boundaries and scope of the field reflect diverse conceptualisations of culture in Chapter 11. In this chapter, we revisited these issues from another route through a closer look at the link between cultural identities and language practice. The issue of cultural identities and language practices cross-cuts many key issues of intercultural communication. It concerns language learners/users, multilingual speakers, lingua franca speakers, immigrants and transnational populations, and people in general in everyday life. Through the discussion about interculturality and the relevant issues in various chapters, we have come to the view that language practices and identity are mutually dependent and interconnected. Language practices index and symbolise identities, which in turn impact on and feed back into language practices.

Some of the issues which have been discussed in relation to cultural identity and language practice in the previous chapters are:

- the notion of third culture or third place as the goal of culture and language learning (Chapter 1);
- learner identity as a contributing factor in classroom participation (Chapter 1);
- the use of a foreign language or multilingualism in advertising as a strategy of invoking cultural or national images associated with the language (Chapter 3);
- the development of cultural identity among 'third culture kids' or transnational populations who are exposed to possibly conflicting sets of cultural values and practices (Chapter 4);
- the issues of identity, language ideologies and language choice of intercultural couples and of children in transnational families (Chapter 4);
- the issue of 'staged' cultural identity and the potential risk of reducing culture to commodity at cultural heritage sites (Chapter 5);

- communication accommodative behaviours motivated by the need to maintain one's own group identity (Chapter 8);
- the issue of synthesising personal and institutional self in professional and institutional discourse (Chapter 8);
- the notion of symbolic competence as an alternative to the notion of third place (Chapter 9).

The range and diversity of these issues not only demonstrates the centrality of the issue of language and identity in the field of intercultural communication, but also reminds us of the highly multidisciplinary and interdisciplinary nature of the field. Intercultural communication draws insights from a number of different perspectives. Three broad types of intercultural communication studies can be identified as follows, together with their connections with other disciplines or field of studies.

1 Studies that are concerned with the identification and interpretation of cultural differences, applying theories and methods from sociology, social psychology, (cross-)cultural psychology, education, race and ethnic studies, anthropology, cultural studies, communication studies and business management.
2 Studies that focus specifically on interplay between cultural differences and language use. These studies draw insights from disciplines such as linguistic anthropology, sociolinguistics, discourse and conversation analysis, language learning and teaching, and pragmatics. Some have developed into their own sub-fields, such as interlanguage pragmatics and cross-cultural pragmatics.
3 Studies that examine the impact of structures of power, socio-economic relations and ideologies on communication among people of different cultural backgrounds. These are the key issues of a newly emerging field of critical intercultural communication. It benefits from many discussions in critical discourse analysis, cultural studies, gender studies and politics.

Following my earlier argument (Zhu, 2011) that *language is key to understanding culture, and culture is an indispensible part of studying language*, the present book explores the role of language in intercultural communication, paying particular attention to the interplay between cultural differences and language use. By examining how intercultural communication permeates our everyday life in Part I, what we can do to achieve effective and appropriate intercultural communication in Part II, and why we bother to study language, culture and identity together (Part III), I hope that this book can bring together different, either current or emerging, strands and themes in the field of language and intercultural communication. The book focuses on intercultural interactions in which people from different cultural and linguistic backgrounds interact with each other, and regards intercultural communication as a process of negotiating meaning, relevance of cultural identities and above all, differences between ourselves and others.

Intercultural communication as a field was founded in the 1950s to address the need among American diplomats to 'familarise' themselves with the 'cultures of their enemies'. It has yet to convince many of its critics of its theoretical coherence and practical value. There are still many misconceptions about the field. Toby Miller wrote in his endorsement for *The Handbook of Critical Intercultural Communication* (Nakayama and Halualani, 2010) that 'for too long intercultural communication was derided as a means of selling things to people who weren't the same as you'. As we have discussed in this book, intercultural communication issues may have an increasingly strong and visible presence in the business world because of the trend of globalisation and the international nature of many businesses. But there are many other sites in our everyday lives where intercultural communication issues are relevant, such as education, family, travel, study abroad, the workplace, politics, the media, law, medical communication and service encounters, some of which this book only touches upon. Another misconception is the belief that the field aims to pursue and promote 'communion' rather than acknowledge difference (Scherle and Nonnenmann, 2008). The truth, I believe, is that intercultural communication provides an analytical lens to differences we see and experience in our interactions with other people who may look different from us, speak a different language, or speak the same language in a different way. I hope this book goes some way to redress these misconceptions.

Task commentaries

1.1 'It will be just a bunch of facts to memorize'

The student's comment articulated the following concerns:

1 Teaching culture takes away time from teaching grammar, which is more important for language learning.
2 Teaching and learning culture, if not managed well, could become a matter of memorising a bunch of historical facts. And above all,
3 Language and culture are separate 'things'.

As discussed in Chapter 1, there are different interpretations of what culture is and related teaching methodologies. The student made an analogy between 'learning culture' and 'learning history'. The student's comments also contradicted the growing consensus that language and culture are inseparable, a view strongly endorsed by those advocating teaching language-and-culture as an integrated whole, those promoting an intercultural approach and those arguing for a more dynamic and hybrid view of culture as the section suggested. A good argument for not treating language and culture as separate entities can be found in Kramsch (1993, 1998a). In the introduction to her seminal book *Context and Culture in Language Teaching* (1993), Kramsch writes:

> Culture in language learning is not an expendable fifth skill, tacked on, so to speak, to the teaching of speaking, listening, reading, and writing. It is always in the background, right from day one, ready to unsettle the good language learners when they expect it least, making evident the limitations of their hard-won communicative competence, challenging their ability to make sense of the world around them.

1.2 A little boy

The poem tells the story of how a child's creativity is lost due to (over)-control by the first teacher. It raises a general question about the role of the teacher in children's learning and the development of creativity, and shows the undesirable consequence of telling children what they should do; and how they should be encouraged to create, explore and discover. Debate and discussion about roles of the teacher is widely available in the literature. As an example, Hampden-Turner (2003) mapped out three scenarios using two dimensions: 'teacher as authority' vs. 'teacher as resource'. The first scenario is an authoritative, sage-like teacher who provides no real resources and fails to relate what he does to students. The second scenario occurs when a teacher is regarded as resource, but not authority. In this case, the teacher ends up guiding on the side, with students pursuing their own agendas. In the third scenario, the teacher becomes 'conductor of talents' when he is regarded as both authority and resource.

2.1 'OK just going back over the previous minutes'

Lines 1–4 constitute the pre-meeting stage prior to the start of the meeting. The main purpose of the sequence is to check whether everyone is ready to open the meeting. Line 5 signals the transition from pre-meeting to the stage of opening of the meeting. Jaeson takes up the role of chair and officially opens the meeting with a discourse marker 'OK', a directive 'get into it', an acknowledgement, and a welcome to a new member.

Jaeson has the most turns, due to his status as the nominated chair. Many of his turns are pre-allocated in the sense that he fulfils the function of a chair by opening the meeting, acknowledging everyone's presence, introducing the new member, making evaluative comments (Lines 16, 34), and moving the meeting to the main agenda (Lines 17, 28, and 30).

2.2 'Waiting for my mother to tell me what to do!'

In the extract in Task 2.1, Lines 11–12 are witty comments from Jaeson and Harry on why IS (Information Systems) rather than IT (Information Technology) is used, following Paul's request for clarification in Line 10. Humour can be interpreted as a face-saving strategy by Jaeson in his response to Paul's question, which could give a 'not quite with it' impression. The quip from Harry gently challenged Jaeson's authority and made light of the potentially face-threatening situation facing Paul.

In the extract in the hospital, the patient made a self-denigrating joke by comparing the role of herself and the technician as child and mother. The use of humour has an added value of alleviating anxiety and defusing embarrassment often experienced in the procedure.

3.1 My Tempus does that

The two different versions of the advertisement are designed as part of Hoeken et al.'s study, which aims to investigate whether differences in uncertainty avoidance impact on the persuasiveness of advertisements. The text on the left appeals to those with high uncertainty values who regard uncertain or unknown situations as threatening, while that on the right appeals to those with opposite values, i.e. low uncertainty avoidance. In Hoeken et al.'s study (2003), they found that people tend to think those advertisements conforming to their values more appealing, but the association between value preferences and persuasive language remains at an individual level. No cross-cultural differences among the cultures in the study (i.e. Belgium, France, the Netherlands and Spain) were found.

3.2 Price or quantity first?

Let us look at differences first before revealing the cultural backgrounds of the seller and buyers.

In the three extracts, the potential conflict arises when the seller weighs up unit price against quantity in the negotiations. There are clear differences in the buyers' response to the seller's tactics. In the first extract, the conflict is resolved smoothly. The buyer seems to understand the seller's approach after two turns and makes a compromise by stating the quantity while making a firm commitment. The buyer also uses '*we*', a collective pronoun, in his response, which helps to diffuse responsibilities from himself to his company. In the second extract, the buyer starts with a comment on a difference between the seller and other sellers. It may be seen as a negotiating tactic. The seller skilfully 'dodges' the threat. However, the buyer in this extract does not give in easily. He uses the singular personal reference '*I*, in *my* case' several times, perhaps to emphasise that the negotiation needs to be done on his own terms. In the third extract, similar to the second extract, the arguments on price vs. quantity are recycled over the turns. The buyer stresses that he needs to know the 'real' prices. Both sides are very blunt in their negotiation, with only occasional phrases from the buyer such as 'I'm afraid...', showing some face concerns to the other party.

The seller in the three extracts is an Urdu speaker from Pakistan. The buyers in the three extracts are Iranian, Italian and German respectively. Now, does the knowledge of cultural backgrounds change the way you read the extracts? Gimenez (2001) argues that cultural factors may lie behind the differences observed. In his view, the Iranian and Pakistani negotiators may share similar national characteristics and organisational culture and therefore could reach agreement more smoothly. In my opinion, it is rather problematic to attribute differences to cultural factors without other information. We need to take a cautious approach in making a link between national characteristics and one's behaviour. In this case, three buyers seem to have different expectations with regard to what is negotiable and how to negotiate and to make concessions. We simply do not know whether this expectation is cultural.

4.1 Language migrant

Learning the language of the host community you are settling into can be emotionally and linguistically challenging. The rules or norms are not written down and most of them are context-sensitive (i.e. depending where, when and with whom you are speaking). You learn through mistakes and perhaps most importantly, through self-reflection. An unexpected outcome of this process is that you will become more aware of some special features of your native language/dialects. The following story is told by a former postgraduate student of mine studying in a UK university. Born and grown up in Japan, she has studied Spanish and lived in Mexico for approximately 6 years. She commented on her experience of adapting her voice to the local culture:

> First thing I noticed in Mexico is the difference in the types of voice we use. In Japanese society, especially young women, use a relatively high pitch voice and tend to speak somehow 'childish'. 'Childish' behaviour of a woman, not only the type of voice but also her behaviour itself, is considered as something 'cute' or 'favourable', and very widely accepted in our society. In Mexican society, however, they use a lower and deeper tone of voice than in Japan; it is required for both men and women as to speak and act as 'adult person', in every setting of life and naturally in business setting. In Mexican society, to use a childish voice, as many Japanese women do, could be a disadvantage, not something 'favourable', and doing so it is possible that you will not be treated properly. After a couple of month[s] of my living in Mexico I noticed about this fact and started to try using a different kind of voice, deeper and softer one, so that I am treated as an adult person (especially because an Asian woman looks much younger than a Latin American woman!).

4.2 Language choices and practice in an intercultural and multilingual family

Many issues come up in the case. First of all, the language choice: the couple. Fernando and Hiroko have chosen English as the main language of communication between themselves, probably because

English is their only shared language. Second, the language learning environment and choices available to Diego: along with the choice of English as the language of communication between them, Fernando and Hiroko have adopted the One Parent One Language policy with Diego. They speak to Diego in their own heritage languages respectively. Diego is exposed to Spanish primarily from his dad, and Japanese from his mum, and English from his parents' conversations, the television, and the general environment. But this is not all. Diego is also exposed to language mixing of all sorts in his parents' conversation, perhaps more mixing of Spanish and English than that of Japanese and English. Diego's language ability at the age of three seems to suggest that his parents' efforts have paid off. He is able to speak Japanese and Spanish fluently, with some knowledge of English.

There are many challenges facing children growing up with multiple languages. The issue of language mixing, for example. It requires a lot of effort and commitment from the parents to adjust language choices according to with whom they are speaking. It is still under debate whether parents should police the mixing of languages in their own speech or whether they should simply speak 'naturally'. Other challenges include how to keep up a particular language and motivate the child to learn it, especially when the language is not the majority language. Sometimes changing circumstances can lead to changes in language choices altogether. Other challenging issues include literacy in the minority language, socialisation into the cultures of different languages, and related identity matters such as connections with the community.

5.1 Curvy culture shock

We all have own stories to tell about a time when we relocate to a new culture and upon returning home. The process of cultural adaptation is often depicted as a U curve or W curve upon returning home. You can google the term *culture shock* and click on images to see different shapes and diagrams used by people in describing the process. The essence of these curves or shapes is that cultural adaptation is a process whereby your satisfaction level goes up and down.

5.2 Tourist websites and guidebooks: guidance or stereotypes?

In a small collection of *DK Eyewitness* travel guidebooks at home, I found only the guidebooks on Tokyo and Thailand have a separate section on etiquette under the heading of Practical Information. No etiquette is mentioned in the guidebooks for Singapore (surprisingly), Greece, Australia, Britain, Washington, etc.

Both guidebooks comment on culturally appropriate ways of greeting, as well as how to greet and return greetings as a foreigner.

> The Thai Greeting is known as the wai...The wai is layered with intricacies of class, gender, and age: each of these dictates a certain height at which the two hands must be held. The inferior party indicates the wai and holds it higher and for longer than the superior, who returns it according to his or her social standing.
>
> (*DK Eyewitness Travel Guide: Thailand*, p. 454,
> Harlow: Dorling Kindersley, 1997)

> The traditional greeting in Tokyo is a bow, its depth reflecting the relative status of participants. Visitors, however, rarely need to bow – a handshake is fine.
>
> (*DK Eyewitness Travel Guide: Tokyo*, p. 164,
> Harlow: Dorling Kindersley, 1997)

While advice like the above helps to bring attention to cross-cultural differences, some advice or comments on norms of interaction readily offered in guidebooks and websites do not stand up to scrutiny. Some of them ignore regional or individual differences and changes a country has undergone as the result of globalisation and modernisation. To give an example, a website offering advice on touring in China (www. chinaodysseytours.com/travel-guide-book/proper-protocol-etiquette. html) comments on Chinese people's modesty: 'Chinese people are inherently shy and modest. They do not display emotion and feelings in public and find speaking bluntly unnerving.'

As someone who was born and grew up in Northeastern China and has spent a good number of years living in the UK, I found these comments unfounded, misleading and irritatingly simplistic. It is true that some Chinese people may be reserved and do not like to show their emotions openly. But not all Chinese people are like this. 'Reserved' people can be found in every culture. There is nothing inherently Chinese about it. The British 'stiff upper lip', Japanese 'stoic' facial expressions and 'silent' Finns are similar stereotypes. On speaking their mind, yes, some Chinese will do everything to avoid giving a negative response directly to their friends, colleagues or acquaintances and there seems to be general preference for indirectness rather than directness, both culturally loaded concepts. But whether one can say 'no' directly depends on to whom one is speaking and in what context. For some people, saying 'no' to a stranger, someone from 'out-group' may be more forthcoming than saying 'no' to someone you know already, someone from 'in-group'. Things are also changing rapidly in China with the open door policy and economic reforms implemented since the 1980s. These changes have cascading effects on the way people behave and interact.

6.1 Performing 'high involvement'

The conversation can be turned into high involvement style by employing some linguistic devices associated with, but not specific to, high involvement style. The conversation was originally used by Jennifer Coates (1994) to demonstrate the unique turn-taking patterns (i.e. no gaps, lots of overlaps, as the title of her article shows) among female friends. Mercer (2000) called this kind of conversation 'cumulative talk', because 'speakers build on each other's contributions, add information of their own and in a mutually supportive, uncritical way construct shared knowledge and understanding' (p. 31).

6.2 Where would you stand/sit?

Please see the main text for the suggested answer regarding elevator behaviour.

Seating in a train: this is a question about how comfortable you find yourself sitting next to someone in a train. Does gender influence your choice of seats?

There is a video clip that shows how people react when you break these silent rules, e.g. choosing to sit very close to someone when there is plenty of space around. The clip, entitled 'KLM Personal Space Experiment', can be accessed at www.break.com/surfacevideo/klm-personal-space-experiment/family-off/.

7.1 Please answer me as soon as possible

Some features suggest that the sender may not be a native speaker, while other features suggest that the sender might have assessed the staff's obligations and duties differently and breached 'unwritten rules' of e-politeness.

1 It starts with the lecturer's first name.
2 The text in general lacks downgraders or politeness markers such as 'could', 'just', 'maybe', 'please'.
3 It is composed from the sender's perspective rather than the recipient's perspective. See the discussion about different perspectives associated with different types of requests in Biesenbach-Lucas (2007).
4 There are a number of requests in the email: asking the lecturer to read through some study notes, making an assessment on the

relevance of the key points and seeking advice on references. They are different in the weight of imposition and the degree of obligation.

5 The requests are made in a tone of urgency: 'please answer me as soon as possible', 'I will write tomorrow'. The number of the requests made and the amount of time these requests require make it very unlikely for them to be responded to by tomorrow.

Do these differences impact on how staff members perceive email requests? Hendriks (2010) found that the under-use of request modifications in emails had a negative effect on evaluation of the personality of the sender of the email. Similarly, Econonmidou-Kogetsidis (2011) found that lack of lexical modification can cause 'pragmatic failure'. However, Vignovic's study (2010) suggests that non-native speakers may not always be penalised for their language mistakes: once recipients discover that the sender is a non-native speaker, their negative perception of the appropriateness of emails will be significantly reduced. However, the same does not apply to breach of etiquette. In the words of Hartford and Bardovi-Harlig (1996): 'teachers tend to think less favourably of those email requests that either assess staff obligations and duties inappropriately or incur greater cost than staff can afford in terms of time and commitment'.

7.2 What brings you here?

Donal Carbaugh's recounting of his experience has a subtle sense of humour. In the stranger's attempt to identify the author, he activated his various schemas on the idea of visiting an Oxford college: 'a student' (Line 5) or 'a member of a college' (Line 9). However, none of these labels seemed to fit. Donal Carbaugh, as a visiting fellow, considered himself as a student only 'in a broad sense' (Line 6). Nor did he think himself as a member of a college in its strict sense. He was there 'at the invitation' (Line 10). He rejected the label of 'anthropologist' straight-away and revealed 'communication processes' as his subject area.

8.1 Foreigner talk

Ferguson was interested to test the hypothesis that there was a conventional 'Foreigner Talk' for English. He gave the task to a group of sociolinguistics students and collected a corpus. Despite some individual differences, some common grammatical features of Foreigner Talk are noted. These are:

Omissions   Omission of the article 'the' (e.g. 'where's the money' → 'where money'), plural and possessive markers of nouns (e.g. 'guns'), the third singular present suffix ('carries'), past tense markers (e.g. 'saw'), progressive tense marker (e.g. 'going'), future tense marker (e.g. 'will') and perfect tense (e.g. *have* seen), conjunctions (e.g. 'and'), and the auxiliary verb (e.g. *'did* you understand' → 'you understand').

Expansions   Adding the subject 'you' to imperatives ('come and see me tomorrow' → 'you come, see me tomorrow') and tag questions (e.g. Yes? OK? See? No?) as comprehension checks.

Replacement Replacing negative constructions with a 'no' (e.g. 'don't forget' → 'no forget').

In addition to these grammatical features, some speakers also paraphrased or replaced some lexical items. E.g. tomorrow → next day; always → all (the) time; father → papa; gun → bang-bang.

8.2 Strategies of managing misunderstandings

The conversation is an example of interactive repair. S1 was rephrasing S3's argument, but he seemed to struggle with the choice of words, although it is not clear from the extract whether he signalled the problem. S2 joined in and 'repaired' S1's trouble with a suggestion of a possible expression in Turn 2. His repair was well recieved by S1, who repeated the phrase and acknowledged it in Turn 3. Towards the end of S3's reply to S1's initial question in Turn 5, she used the phrase 'I don't know', which could be interpreted either as a device to hedge her argument or an indication of her uncertainty with the word 'consciousness'. This time S2 stepped in again and offered an alternative phrase 'sense of security'. S3 recognised his help ('yeah'), but made it clear that this was not exactly what she was looking for ('but eh on the other hand').

9.1 Defining ICC

As an example, Spencer-Oatey and Franklin (2009) proposed a term, InterCultural Interaction Competence (ICIC), to 'refer to the competence not only to communicate (verbally and non-verbally) and behave effectively and appropriately with people from other cultural groups, but also to handle the psychological demands and dynamic outcomes that result from such interchange' (p. 51). The term is coined partly as an umbrella term for the purpose of reviewing existing literature and partly to reflect the authors' focus on interactions. The authors further list three key skills, i.e. affective, behavioural and cognitive components, which are in short, the ABCs of ICIC. The model is multidimensional and easy to remember, but it does not seem to include any skill specific to interactions.

9.2 A reflective journal entry

A simple format for a learning journal would be to:

- Briefly describe the task, event or experience for reflection.
- Make note of your feelings at the time and now.
- Note any interpretations, analysis, conclusions and actions you had at the time.

Potential problems in journal writing:

- It can be time-consuming to keep a journal along with other activities/events taking place.
- Entries may be descriptive and emotional. Capturing what has happened is one thing; taking one step further to analyse and interpret what has happened is another.
- Reflection may be superficial and biased with the best intention. One common mistake is that learners generalise from a single and isolated event.
- There are also ethical implications. Writing a journal for one's own purposes is different from writing as part of an assignment and with the knowledge that another party will read it.

10.1 Languages differ from each other

The first sentence was provided by Jandt (2001, p. 128), who cited examples of different word order from a variety of languages from *The Atlas of Languages* (London: Quarto, 1996). These are (S: subject; V: verb; O: object):

SVO   cats eat mice; e.g. English, Chinese, Swahili
SOV   cats mice eat; e.g. Japanese, Korean
VSO   eat cats mice; e.g. Classical Arabic, Welsh, Samoan
VOS   eat mice cats; e.g. Tzotzil (a Mayan language)
OSV   mice cats eat; e.g. Kabardian (a language of the northern Caucasus)
OVS   mice eat cats; e.g. Hixkaryana (a language of Brazil).

The second sentence was made up by myself. A Chinese translation with gloss is:

她奶奶/姥姥给了她两本书。
(Gloss: she paternal grandma/maternal grandma give (了/le particle indicating past tense) she two volume book)

Putonghua Chinese differentiates paternal from maternal grandma. There are no plural semantic markers for nouns. Plurality is instead indicated by numbers and/or lexical words.

The third example is from Slobin (1996, p.83). The closest Spanish translation with gloss is:

El pájaro salió del agujero del árbol volando hacia abajo.
(The bird exited of the hole of the tree flying towards below)

10.2 Cultural key words

Wierzbicka (1997b) discussed some criteria for selecting cultural key words. These include: whether the word in question is a common word, whether the word is frequently used in domains such as emotions or moral judgements, and whether the word is at the centre of a cluster of phrases or words (e.g. *duša* in Russian is related to *na duše* (on the soul), *v duše* (in the soul) *pod duše* (after/to the soul), etc.).

The challenge in explaining what the cultural key words mean and what core cultural values they reflect is well demonstrated in Cortazzi and Shen's study (2001), in which the researchers identified considerable differences in the understanding of six Chinese key words between Chinese university students and British university students who are learning Chinese.

11.1 Cultural paradoxes

The three examples are from Osland and Bird (2000), where the authors argued for a model of 'cultural sensemaking' (taking into account contexts, schema, the influence of cultural values and cultural history in making sense of cultural paradoxes). To account for the paradoxical individualistic vs. charitable behaviour among Americans, they argued that American society has long possessed an extensive network of associations and regarded the act of giving as prestigious. Financial arrangements such as tax relief also encourage philanthropy. In the case of missing *simpatía* among Costa Ricans, they argued that *simpatía* is applicable among in-group members, i.e. family members or friends. Customers are considered to be out-group members and therefore *simpatía* does not apply to interactions between bank employees and customers. In the third example, they suggested that when signing a contract, Japanese business people are guided by collectivism, a different value, taking precedence over uncertainty avoidance (a phenomenon they called 'value trumping'). Another possibility is that many Japanese recognise the limits of contracts and the difficulties of foreseeing all contingencies.

These paradoxes, in my view, illustrate some major problems if one tries to provide a cultural account of behaviours and patterns identified among a group of people. While culture influences ways of thinking and behaviour, not everything is accountable in terms of cultural values. In the case of Japanese contracts, ambiguity may result simply from the lack of technical knowledge and resources in drawing up contracts. Resorting to value trumping can only weaken the general applicability of cultural values. See further discussion on problems with a cultural account in the main text of Chapter 11.

11.2 Why choose a Filipina?

Written in English, the extracts pitch themselves at an English-speaking audience through a spin on generalisations and stereotypes associated with the cultural groups.

The first text 'sells' Filipinas as being beautiful, family-oriented, and easy with regard to communication. Interestingly, it talks about cultural compatibility. It assumes that sharing the same religion leads to greater compatibility. It also positions Filipinas against other Asian groups.

In the second text, a comparison is made between Filipinas and other Asian groups, especially the groups who eat with 'chopsticks' (Chinese) or bow all the time (Japanese). It refers to frequently cited 'face' in Asian cultures. The colloquial style and occasional grammatical mistakes, whether or not by design, help to create a sense of informality and casualness and, most importantly, a sense of otherness.

12.1 Who am I?

The Twenty Statement Test (TST), designed by Kuhn and McPartland (1954), is a test about one's sense of self and identity. One way to analyse your own description is to classify your answers in two groups, for example, whether you are talking about your *social roles* (such as son, teacher and friend) or *personal traits* (such as happy, funny and big). There are age- and gender-related differences in self-statement. Younger persons are likely to describe themselves more in terms of personal traits while older people more in terms of social roles. Cross-cultural differences in the frequency of categories used for self-statements were reported in Bond and Cheung (1983).

12.2 'This is for the UK passport holder'

In the conversation, B did not respond to A's request in the subsequent turn. Instead, she made a statement, assuming A, who looked like a Chinese, was queuing in the wrong place, since there was a separate area for non-British nationals. However, A ignored the ascription of 'foreigner' by saying 'I know' and reinstated his previous request.

Glossary of key terms

(An extended glossary can be found on the accompanying website at www.routledge.com/cw/rial)

Assimilation
the process by which an ethnic group or migrant community adopts the characteristics of the dominant group.

Audience design
a sociolinguistic model proposed by Allan Bell (1984, 2001) to account for the fact that speakers adjust their speech styles in response to their audience.

Autonomy
a term to refer to one's ability to take charge of one's own learning.

BELF
Business English Lingua Franca. It is the study of situations where English is used as a shared language of communication and where at least one interaction participant does not speak English as their native language.

Co-culture
a term describing the co-existence of cultural groups.

Collectivism
a cultural orientation that promotes interdependence between members of groups and emphasises priority of group goals over those of individuals.

Communication Accommodation Theory
a psychological model originating from Howard Giles's work (Street and Giles, 1982) which proposes that one adjusts ways of speaking (including accent, speech rate, patterns of pausing, utterance length, gesture, posture, smiling, gaze, etc.) to either converge to or diverge from those of one's conversation partner(s).

Communicative competence
a term proposed by Dell Hymes (1972) to describe knowledge of how to use and interpret a language according to the social and linguistic norms of the speech community.

Community of practice
originating in Lave and Wenger's work about learning theory (1991), the concept describes an aggregate of people who have a shared domain of interest and engage in joint activities and practice.

Contact theory
the theory proposed by Allport (1954) which suggests that prejudice between members of different groups may be reduced through intergroup contact under four conditions: equal group status, common goals, intergroup cooperation and institutional support.

Contextualisation cue
a term developed by Gumperz (1982, 1992) to refer to the verbal and non-verbal signs in interactions that help conversation participants to evoke the relevance of particular contextual features.

Conversation analysis
abbreviated as CA, a theoretical and analytical approach to natural conversations with the purpose of understanding how meaning is produced, interpreted and negotiated in conversation through an analysis of linguistic or non-linguistic features, such as turn-taking, sequences, pauses, and how 'trouble' in conversation is solved, etc.

Critical incidents
brief descriptions of significant events in encounters with people from various backgrounds.

Crossing
a phenomenon where speakers use the language varieties of social and ethnic groups to which they do not normally belong.

Cultural acculturation
a term developed by John Berry (Berry et al., 2006) to describe cultural and psychological changes as the result of contact between cultural groups.

Cultural adaptation
a process of adjusting to a new culture over a period of time.

Cultural assimilators
a pedagogical tool in intercultural education and language learning. It typically includes a critical incident followed by a question. It is used to raise awareness about cultural differences.

Cultural dimensions
the key features or characteristics that differentiate various cultural groups.

Cultural iceberg model
an analogy of what culture is by comparing visible and invisible aspects of culture, as well as the interrelationship between these two parts, to an iceberg.

Cultural identity
referring to a set of qualities attributed to or shared by a given population. It can include ethnicity, race, nationality, gender, abilities, age, spirituality and socio-economic status.

Cultural onion model
an analogy of what culture is by comparing the various internal levels and layers of culture to that of an onion.

Cultural schema
a term used by Sharifian (2005) to refer to a subtype of schemas about norms and patterns of interactions which emerge from a cultural group's collective knowledge and are shared by members of a cultural group.

Cultural script
an analytical framework used by Anna Wierzbicka and her colleagues (e.g. Wierzbicka, 1997b) to describe a cultural key word or practice using a metalanguage which consists of a set of simple, indefinable and universally lexicalised concepts such as *I*, *you*, *do*, *good*, *bad*, etc.

Cultural tourism
a type of tourism emphasising visits to historical or architectural landmarks, museums, galleries, heritage sites, artistic performances, festivals, etc.

Culture shock
a term developed by Kalvero Oberg (1960) to describe the anxiety one may experience when moving to a new culture.

Culture with a capital C
a term to describe the artistic aspects or refinement of culture such as art, music, literature, etc.

Culture with a small c
a term to describe the behaviour and practice of everyday life.

Deep learning
a type of learning approach which focuses on understanding and developing knowledge rather than gathering information. It also sees reflection as the key component of learning.

Deficit model
a way of thinking which regards anything different from main, dominant practices as less adequate and in need of improvement.

Dugri talk
Dugri talk refers to a communication style of straight talk, originally found among Israelis. *Dugri* means 'straightforward, direct'.

Emic
an approach in studies of human behaviour across cultures whereby a researcher uses local cultural terms to interpret a cultural phenomenon.

Essentialist view of culture
an approach that believes that people from a cultural group share the same characteristics, and that misunderstandings in intercultural interactions can largely, if not wholly, be attributed to group differences.

Ethnicity
referring to a set of qualities attributed to a given population who are perceived by themselves and/or others to share history, descent, belief systems, practices, language, religion, etc. It is a term often conflated with cultural identity or race.

Ethnography of speaking
the field of study concerned with the way speech communities communicate. It can be used as a methodology, referring to the use of fieldwork and observation as a data collection method.

Etic
an approach in studies of human behaviour across cultures which involves comparing one culture with another using culture-general constructs.

Experiential learning
also known as learning by doing. It is a pedagogical approach that believes that learning is best achieved when people have direct or simulated experiences.

Face
a term used in politeness theory to refer to the public self-image a person affectively claims for himself.

Face-threatening acts
a term used in politeness theory to refer to acts that challenge the face of conversation participants.

Femininity
a cultural orientation in which caring and nurturing behaviours are preferred.

Foreigner Talk
a concept proposed by Charles Ferguson (1975) to describe the simplified speech register native speakers often adopt when speaking to non-native speakers with low linguistic proficiency.

Global citizenship
a term to describe a social ideal which calls for commitment to humanist principles and respect for human equality and diversity. Also known as cosmopolitan citizenship.

High involvement style
a type of spoken discourse style in which speakers try to show connectedness through active participation in interaction. It was first proposed by Tannen (1984). The linguistic features of high involvement include faster rate of speech, faster turn-taking, avoidance of inter-turn pauses, cooperative overlap, and participatory listenership.

High uncertainty avoidance
a cultural orientation in which people try to avoid uncertainty and ambiguity in communication and practice.

Hofstede's value dimensions
the model proposed by Geert Hofstede to differentiate between various cultures. It includes individualism vs. collectivism, high vs. low uncertainty avoidance, high vs. low power distance, masculinity vs. femininity and long-term vs. short-term orientation.

Illocutionary act
according to Austin (1962), a speech act consists of three acts: the locutionary act, the illocutionary act and the perlocutionary act. The illocutionary act is what is intended by the speaker.

Individualism
a cultural orientation that emphasises personal independence and priority of individuals' goals over those of the group.

In-group
the group with whom one feels emotionally close and a sense of belonging such as family or friends (cf. out-group).

Intercultural Communicative Competence
ICC for short, the term, broadly speaking, refers to the ability to communicate effectively and appropriately in intercultural encounters. The term is referred to by various names in different models. Although what constitutes ICC precisely varies across different models, they tend to draw on components of awareness, knowledge, attitude and skills.

Language broker
the term to describe the function of children or younger members of migrants' families who often act as translators or interpreters for their families.

Language dominance
the fact that among the languages used by a speaker, one language may be stronger than others in some, if not all, aspects of language use, such as speaking, listening, etc.

Language ideology
speakers' views or beliefs about the socio-cultural values of different languages.

Language socialisation
the process by which children or new members of a community learn to speak the language of the host community in an appropriate way and adapt to social-cultural values associated with various ways of speaking.

Legitimate Peripheral Participation
a concept proposed by Lave and Wenger (1991) to describe their view that individuals acquire skills and become competent members through participation with experts in an activity. Novices must be allowed to be part of the activity even if their participation is peripheral.

Linguistic determinism
a (strong) version of the Sapir–Whorf hypothesis of the relation between language, culture and thought, which asserts that language controls thought and culture.

Linguistic penalty
a term proposed by Celia Roberts and her colleagues (Roberts, 2011; Roberts and Campbell, 2006) to describe the fact that first generation ethnic minority candidates tend to fare poorly in job interviews, not from their lack of fluency in English, but from the largely hidden demands on candidates to talk in institutionally credible ways and from a mismatch of implicit cultural expectations.

Linguistic relativity
a (weak) version and a moderate claim of the Sapir–Whorf hypothesis of the relation between language, culture and thought, which argues that language influences thought and worldviews and, therefore, differences among languages cause differences in the thoughts of their speakers.

Locutionary act
according to Austin (1962), a speech act consists of three acts: the locutionary act, the illocutionary act and the perlocutionary act. The locutionary act is the actual utterance and its ostensible meaning.

Long-term orientation
a cultural orientation that focuses on traditions (cf. short-term orientation).

Low uncertainty avoidance
a cultural orientation in which people accept uncertainty and ambiguity.

Masculinity
a cultural orientation in which ambition, achievement and money are favoured.

Membership Categorisation Device
abbreviated as MCA, a term proposed by Sacks (1972) as an analytical concept to describe how people use language to order the objects of the world into categories such as family, mother, student, etc.

Monochronic time
a cultural orientation in which people prefer one thing at one time.

Out-group
a group with whom one feels few emotional ties or little sense of belonging (cf. in-group).

Passing
a phenomenon in which speakers use the language varieties of social and ethnic groups to which they do not normally belong in order to be perceived as one of them.

Perlocutionary act
according to Austin (1962), a speech act consists of three acts: the locutionary act, the illocutionary act and the perlocutionary act. The perlocutionary act is the consequence of what has been said.

Phatic communion
a term, usually attributed to Malinowski (1923), that refers to the type of speech in which the bonds among the speakers concerned are maintained or created through

a mere exchange of words. It is often used in contrast with other types of speech which have clear transactional goals.

Point-making style
a rhetorical style referring to how speakers state and support their communicative intent such as wishes, demands, etc.

Politeness theory
the study of linguistic behaviours that address each other's face wants in conversation. It was proposed first by Brown and Levinson (1978).

Polychronic time
a cultural orientation in which people prefer multi-tasking.

Pragmatic failure
a term used by Thomas (1983) to refer to the phenomenon of misunderstanding in interactions with second language users. There are two types of pragmatic failure: pragmalinguistic and sociopragmatic failure. The former is the type of pragmatic failure in which pragmatic force in an utterance by a second language user does not match that by a native speaker. The latter occurs when second language users make inappropriate assessment of the degree of imposition, cost/benefit, social distance, relative rights and obligations, etc.

Proxemics
the term proposed by Edward Hall to describe the study of personal space.

Race
when used in contrast with ethnicity, it refers to the biological and genetic make-up of a given population. In some contemporary academic discussions, race is regarded as a social and cultural construction instead of biological.

Rapport
a notion proposed by Spencer-Oatey (2002) to take motivational concerns of participants such as face wants and relationship building into account in interpreting interactions.

Re-entry shock
the feeling of being lost and disappointed when one returns home after being away for a while.

Sapir–Whorf hypothesis
the observations by Edward Sapir and Benjamin Whorf on the interrelationship between language, culture and thought. There are different versions of the hypothesis. The most well known are linguistic determinism and linguistic relativity.

Schema
the collection of knowledge of past experiences which is stored in the memory and retrieved when prompted to guide our behaviour and sense-making.

Schwarz's value orientations
the classification scheme of human values proposed by Shalom Schwarz. It includes benevolence, tradition, conformity, security, power, achievement,

hedonism (the need or motivation for pleasure), stimulation, self-direction and universalism.

Short-term orientation
a cultural orientation which emphasises the present (cf. long-term orientation).

Small culture
the term used by Holliday (2011) to refer to an approach which emphasises the process of establishing commonalities shared by a small social grouping through activities rather than prescribing groupings at the start.

Small talk
non-task-oriented conversation in which speakers have no explicit transactional goals.

Stereotyping
over-generalisation about the characteristics of a cultural group.

Study abroad
the type of educational activity which involves students studying and living away from their home countries.

Subculture
a group which is different from the dominant group, or a small group within a large group.

Superdiversity
the term describes a high level of social, cultural and linguistic complexity and diversity in a society.

Surface learning
a type of learning approach which focuses on memorising information rather than developing a good understanding of the subject under study.

Symbolic competence
proposed by Kramsch (2006, 2009a; Kramsch and Whiteside, 2008), the term refers to the learner's ability to approximate or appropriate someone else's language and to shape the very context in which the language is learned through the learner's and other's embodied history and subjectivity.

Talk about social, cultural and linguistic practices
an analytical tool kit proposed by Zhu (2008) to describe linguistic practice between parents and children, in which parents and children make comments about ways of speaking and associated social and cultural values explicitly or implicitly.

Thick description
a method of describing events and behaviours in detail and in their contexts as opposed to bare facts. It was proposed by Geertz (1973).

Third culture kids
a term referring to children who accompany their parents during their stay in a foreign country. The word 'third' is used to reflect the feelings experienced by the children, i.e. despite their experience in a number of cultures, they do not feel that they belong to any culture.

Third culture/place
terms used by Kramsch (2009b) to describe a symbolic place where one's own and target culture interact with each other.

Tourist gaze
a term used by John Urry (2002) to describe tourists' practices in searching for differences. It includes the way tourists gaze upon extraordinary things, as well as how the gaze is constructed, anticipated and fulfilled.

U-curve
The process and various stages of culture adaption have been described as U-shaped, with satisfaction level highest upon arrival, then lowest when experiencing culture shock, followed by a recovery.

Wakimae
a Japanese cultural key term, referring to the fact that people are expected to observe social norms in society.

W-curve
The process of relocating to another culture and then returning to one's home culture is often described as a W-shaped curve. When relocating to another culture, one's level of satisfaction is highest upon arrival, goes down very soon and rises again during recovery. A similar process applies when one returns home: highest satisfaction when arriving at home, then a feeling of loss and disappointment, followed by recovery.

Annotated further reading

Chapter 1

On culture and language learning and teaching

Risager, K. (2007). *Language and Culture Pedagogy: From a National to a Transnational Paradigm*. Clevedon: Mutilingual Matters.

An overview of national and international trends in culture pedagogy as well as detailed reviews of key literature over a span of 50 years.

Atkinson, D. (1999). TESOL and culture. *TESOL Quarterly*, 33(4), 625–654.

A 'provocative' article on the issues of culture in language teaching.

On culture of learning

Palfreyman, D. and Smith, R. C. (eds) (2003). *Learner Autonomy across Cultures*. Basingstoke: Palgrave.

The volume critically interprets what learner autonomy means in different cultural contexts and how both wider and local cultural contexts offer various types of constraint while simultaneously serving as resources for learner autonomy.

On multicultural classrooms

Boxer, D. (2002). *Applying Sociolinguistics: Domains and Face-to-face Interaction*. Amsterdam: John Benjamins.

Chapters 4 (education) and 7 (cross-cultural interaction) are relevant.

Breen, M. (ed.) (2001). *Learner Contributions to Language Learning: New Directions in Research*. Harlow: Pearson.

Chapter 6 on overt participation and covert acquisition in the language classroom (by Michael Breen) and chapter 8 on non-participation, imagined communities and the language classroom (by Bonny Norton) are relevant.

Chapter 2

On meetings

Handford, M. (2010). *The Language of Business Meetings.* Cambridge: Cambridge University Press.
  An in-depth study of language use in business meetings.

On small talk

Coupland, J. (2000). *Small Talk.* Harlow: Longman.
  A collection of essays on small talk. Chapter 1 by Holmes, chapter 4 by Jaworski and chapter 10 by Ragan are of relevance.

On humour

Holmes, J. and Marra, M. (2002). Having a laugh at work: How humour contributes to workplace culture. *Journal of Pragmatics,* 34, 1683–1710.

Rogerson-Revell, P. (2007). Humour in business: A double-edged sword: A study of humour and style shifting in intercultural business meetings. *Journal of Pragmatics,* 39(1), 4–28.
  Two articles providing an overview of the use of humour in the workplace and in intercultural business meetings.

Chapter 3

On advertising

Cook, G. (2001). *The Discourse of Advertising.* London: Routledge.
  An advanced textbook on the language of advertising from a variety of individual and combined angles including semantics, paralanguage, stylistics and narratives.

Piller, I. (2011). *Intercultural Communication: A Critical Introduction.* Edinburgh: Edinburgh University Press.
  Chapter 7, 'Intercultural communication for sale', gives an overview of language and intercultural communication issues in commercial discourse.

On negotiation

Bargiela-Chiappini, F. (ed.) (2009). *The Handbook of Business Discourse.* Edinburgh: Edinburgh University Press.
  Chapter 11, 'Negotiation studies', by Anne Marie Bulow, provides the most up-to-date review of negotiation studies.

On business discourse

Bargiela-Chiappini, F., Nickerson, C. and Planken, B. (2007). *Business Discourse*. Basingstoke: Palgrave.
  The book showcases research methods and latest findings in business discourse.

Trosborg, A. (ed.) (2010). *Pragmatics across Languages and Cultures*. Berlin: Mouton De Gruyter.
  The last section reviews the main issues in corporate communication (chapter 17), credibility in corporate discourse (chapter 18), crisis communication across cultures (chapter 19) and corporate social responsibility (chapters 20 and 21).

Chapter 4

On the impact of learning a new language on the development of identities and self

Lvovich, N. (1997). *The Multilingual Self: An Inquiry into Language Learning*. Mahwah, NJ: Lawrence Erlbaum.
  The author, brought up in a Jewish family in Moscow, tells her stories of learning French as part of her life in the former Soviet Union, Italian during her temporary stay in Italy, and English as an immigrant in the United States.

On living abroad in general

Bond, M. (ed.) (1997). *Working at the Interface of Cultures: Eighteen Lives in Social Science*. London: Routledge.
  A collection of articles by leading cross-cultural researchers who tell their personal stories of intercultural living and working.

Suggested movies to explore migrants' lives in media

  My Big Fat Greek Wedding
  Bend It Like Beckham
  Eat, Drink, Man Woman
  Wedding Banquet
  There are many television and radio comedy shows that feature migrants' lives. My favourite one is *Goodness Gracious Me*. Some clips are available on YouTube. Some stand-up comedians of migrant background reflect and make sharp and at the same time hilarious observations on their own cultures.

On intercultural families

Piller, I. (2002). *Bilingual Couples Talk: The Discursive Construction of Hybridity*. Amsterdam: John Benjamins.
  A must-read for anyone interested in a sociolinguistic account of the linguistic practices of bilingual couples.

Chapter 5

On study abroad

Jackson, J. (2010). *Intercultural Journeys: From Study to Residence Abroad.* New York: Palgrave Macmillan.
A research monograph documenting the experience of a group of university students during their 5-week study abroad programme in the UK.

Kinginger, C. (2009). *Language Learning and Study Abroad: A Critical Reading of Research.* Basingsoke: Palgrave.
A research monograph pulling together findings on the impact of study abroad on language learning. A must-read for anyone researching language learning and study abroad.

Vande Berg, M., Page, M. and Lou, K. (eds) (2012). *Student Learning Abroad: What Our Students Are Learning, What They're Not, And What We Can Do About It.* Sterling, VA: Stylus.
An edited volume questioning some claims about the benefits of study abroad.

On cultural adaptation

Kim, Y. Y. (2008). Intercultural personhood: Globalization and a way of being. *International Journal of Intercultural Relations*, 32(4), 301–304.
An article discussing cross-cultural adaptation and identity development.

On tourism

Jack, G. and Phipps, A. (2005). *Tourism and Intercultural Exchange: Why Tourism Matters.* Clevedon: Channel View.
A research monograph looking into where and how intercultural exchanges take place in tourism.

On language issues

Thurlow, C. and Jaworski, A. (2011). Tourism discourse: Languages and banal globalisation. *Applied Linguistics Review*, 2, 285–312.
A must-read on language matters in tourism.

Chapter 6

On high vs. low context

Hall, E. T. (1976). *Beyond Culture.* Garden City, NY: Doubleday.
An account of high vs. low context communication styles with examples from the author's observations.

On high involvement

Tannen, D. (1984). *Conversational Style: Analysing Talk among Friends.*
Norwood, NJ: Ablex.
   Providing an in-depth discussion of the features of high involvement with
plenty of examples.

On face and politeness

Scollon, R., Scollon, S. W. and Jones, R. (2012). *Intercultural Communication:*
A Discourse Approach (3rd edn). Chichester: John Wiley and Sons.
   A good overview of face and politeness.

On non-verbal communication in general

Andersen, P. A., Hecht, M. L., Hoobler, G. D. and Smallwood, M. (2002).
Nonverbal communication across cultures. In W. B. Gudykunst and B. Mody
(eds), *Handbook of International and Intercultural Communication* (pp.
89–106). Thousand Oaks, CA: Sage.
   An overview of non-verbal communication across cultures.

Chapter 7

Bremer, K., Roberts, C., Vasseur, M-T., Simonot, M. and Broeder, P. (eds)
(1996). *Achieving Understanding: Discourse in Intercultural Encounters.*
London: Longman.
   An excellent book on sources of misunderstanding in interactions concerning
minority workers and second language speakers with different degrees of
linguistic proficiency. Rich data and detailed information on methodology.

Bührig, K. and ten Thije, Jan D. (eds) (2006). *Beyond Misunderstanding.*
Amsterdam: John Benjamins.
   A collection of chapters on the issue of misunderstanding in intercultural
communication. A great variety of theoretical frameworks and analytical
approaches.

Chapter 8

On accommodation

Gallois, C., Ogay, T. and Giles, H. (2005). Communication accommodation
theory. In W. Gudykunst (ed.), *Theorizing about Intercultural Communication*
(pp. 121–148). London: Sage.

Ylänne-McEwen, V. and Coupland, N. (2000). Accommodation theory: A
conceptual resource for intercultural sociolinguistics. In H. Spencer-Oatey
(ed.), *Culturally Speaking: Managing Rapport through Talk across Cultures*
(pp. 191–216). London: Continuum.

These two articles give an overview of the key issues in communication accommodation theory. The first one is more theoretical and the second focuses more on intercultural communication.

On negotiating misunderstanding

Mauranen, A. (2006). Signaling and preventing misunderstanding in English as lingua franca communication. *International Journal of the Sociology of Language*, 177, 123–150. Reprinted in Zhu Hua (ed.) (2011) *The Language and Intercultural Communication Reader* (pp. 238–256). London: Routledge.

An overview of strategies in signalling and preventing misunderstanding in English as lingua franca communication.

On interpreting and mediating interactions

Davies, E. E. (2012). Translation and intercultural communication: Bridges and barriers. In C. B. Paulston, S. F. Kiesling and E. S. Rangel (eds), *The Handbook of Intercultural Discourse and Communication* (pp. 367–388). Malden, MA: Wiley-Blackwell.

A critical review of the role of translation and interpretation in intercultural communication.

On understanding professional and institutional discourse

Roberts, C., and Campbell, S. (2006). *Talk on Trial: Job Interviews, Language and Ethnicity*. Research report for the Department for Work and Pensions. Available at http://statistics.dwp.gov.uk/asd/asd5/rports2005-2006/rrep344.pdf

A highly accessible research report.

Chapter 9

On ICC in foreign language teaching and learning

Byram, M. (1997). *Teaching and Assessing Intercultural Communicative Competence*. Clevedon: Multilingual Matters.

A key publication by Michael Byram which outlines the theoretical framework and application of his influential ICC model.

On a multidisciplinary overview of ICC

Spencer-Oatey, H. and Franklin, P. (2009). *Intercultural Interaction: A Multidisciplinary Approach to Intercultural Communication*. New York: Palgrave.

Chapter 3 offers an overview of ICC models and chapter 8, ICC assessments with examples.

On intercultural learning through education and training

Spencer-Oatey, H. and Franklin, P. (2009). *Intercultural Interaction: A Multidisciplinary Approach to Intercultural Communication*. New York: Palgrave.

Chapter 9 provides an overview of development of ICC in professional contexts and school education contexts.

Cushner, K. and Brislin, R. W. (1997). *Improving Intercultural Interactions: Modules for Cross-Cultural Training Programmes* (vols 1 and 2). London: Sage.

These two volumes focus on the content and techniques of intercultural training in a variety of contexts including business, education, and social and health services. The array of exercises, activities and self-assessment tools in the books can be used by both trainers and learners themselves.

Landis, D., Bennett, J. and Bennett, M. (eds) (2004). *Handbook of Intercultural Training*. London: Sage.

An edited volume providing a comprehensive review of the history, concepts and methods underlying intercultural training.

On language socialisation

Ochs, E. and Schieffelin, B. (2012). The theory of language socialisation. In A. Duranti, E. Ochs and B. Schieffelin (eds), *The Handbook of Language Socialisation* (pp. 1–22). Oxford: Blackwell.

The chapter provides an up-to-date and authoritative review of language socialisation as a field.

Chapter 10

Sapir, E. (1933). Language. In *Encyclopaedia of the Social Sciences* (9, pp. 155–169). New York: Macmillan. Reprinted in D. Mandelbaum (ed.) (1949/1985) *Selected Writings of Edward Sapir in Language, Culture and Personality* (pp. 7–32). Berkeley: University of California Press.

Whorf, B. (1956). The relation of habitual thought and behaviour to language. In J. B. Carroll (ed.), *Language, Thought and Reality: Selected Writings of Benjamin Lee Whorf* (pp. 134–159). Cambridge: Cambridge University Press.

It is important to read Sapir and Whorf's arguments in their original presentation and entirety, since their views have been interpreted in many different ways.

Kramsch, C. J. (2004). Language, thought and culture. In A. Davies and C. Elder (eds), *The Handbook of Applied Linguistics* (pp. 235–261). Malden, MA: Blackwell.

The chapter provides an overview of the debate on language, thought and culture, and discusses its application and implications for the field of applied linguistics.

Pavlenko, A. (2005). Bilingualism and thought. In J. F. Kroll and A. M. B. De Groot (eds), *Handbook of Bilingualism: Psycholinguistic Approaches* (pp. 433–453). Oxford: Oxford University Press.

The chapter discusses implications of the debate on language, culture and thought for bilingualism, and insights from bilingual studies that inform the debate.

Chapter 11

Holliday, A., Hyde, M. and Kullman, J. (2010). *Intercultural Communication: An Advanced Resource Book for Students*. London: Routledge.

Section B contains a good selection of reading on definitions and perspectives of culture within the fields of anthropology, ethnography of speaking, language education, migration studies and communication.

Spencer-Oatey, H. and Franklin, P. (2009). *Intercultural Interaction: A Multidisciplinary Approach to Intercultural Communication*. New York: Palgrave.

Chapter 2 provides a multidisciplinary summary about definitions of culture and approaches in studying culture.

Nakayama, T. K. and Halualani, R. T. (eds) (2010). *The Handbook of Critical Intercultural Communication*. Malden, MA: Wiley-Blackwell.

Part 1 provides a review of conceptualisation issues in emerging critical studies of intercultural communication.

Chapter 12

On identity

Antaki, C. and Widdicombe, S. (eds) (1998). *Identities in Talk*. London: Sage.

A well-cited collection of chapters exploring how identities are constructed in talk.

On ethnic identity

Fought, C. (2006). *Language and Ethnicity*. Cambridge: Cambridge University Press.

A review of the relationship between language and ethnic identity. Very well written and easy to follow.

On interculturality

Zhu Hua (2011). *The Language and Intercultural Communication Reader*. London: Routledge.

Part V is relevant.

References

AIE (2009). *Autobiography of Intercultural Encounters: Context, Concepts and Theories*. Published on-line by the Council of Europe. Retrieved on 30 July 2012 at www.coe.int/t/dg4/autobiography/source/aie_en/aie_context_concepts_and_theories_en.pdf

Aitken, T. (1973). *The Multinational Man: The Role of the Manager Abroad*. New York: Halstead Press.

Allport, G. W. (1954). *The Nature of Prejudice*. Cambridge, MA: Perseus Books.

Ang, I. (2001). *On Not Speaking Chinese: Living Between Asia and the West*. London: Routledge.

Angouri, J. and Marra, M. (2010). Corporate meetings as genre: A study of the role of the chair in corporate meeting talk. *Text and Talk*, 30(6), 615–636.

——(2011). 'OK one last thing for today then': Constructing identities in corporate meeting talk. In J. Angouri and M. Marra (eds), *Constructing Identities at Work* (pp. 85–102). London: Palgrave.

Anisfeld, M., Bogo, N. and Lambert, W. (1962). Evaluational reactions to accented English speech. *Journal of Abnormal and Social Psychology*, 65, 223–231.

Antaki, C. and Widdicombe, S. (eds) (1998). *Identities in Talk*. London: Sage.

Arthur, N. (2001). Using critical incidents to investigate cross-cultural transitions. *International Journal of Intercultural Relations*, 25(1), 41–53.

Atkinson, D. (1999). TESOL and culture. *TESOL Quarterly*, 33(4), 625–654.

Austin, J. L. (1962). *How to do Things with Words*. Oxford: Oxford University Press.

Axtell, R. E. (1991). *Gestures: The Do's and Taboos of Body Language Around the World*. Chichester: John Wiley and Sons.

Bailey, B. (1997). Communication of respect in interethnic service encounters. *Language in Society*, 26(3), 327–56. Reprinted in A. Duranti (ed.) (2001), *Linguistic Anthropology: A Reader*. Malden, MA: Blackwell.

Bailey, K. M. and Nunan, D. (eds) (1996). *Voices from the Language Classroom: Qualitative Research in Second Language Education*. New York: Cambridge University Press.

Baker, W. (2009). The cultures of English as a lingua franca. *TESOL Quarterly*, 43(4), 567–592.

Baquedano-López, P. and Figueroa, A. M. (2012). Language socialization and immigration. In A. Duranti, E. Ochs and B. Schieffelin (eds), *The Handbook of Language Socialisation* (pp. 536–563). Oxford: Blackwell.

Baquedano-López, P. and Kattan, S. (2007). Growing up in a multilingual community: Insights from language socialization. In P. Auer and Li Wei (eds), *Handbook of Multilingualism and Multilingual Communication* (pp. 69–100). Berlin: Mouton de Gruyter.

Baraldi, C. (2012). Participation, facilitation and mediation in educational interactions. In C. Baraldi and V. Iervese (eds), *Participation, Facilitation and Mediation: Children and Young People in their Social Contexts* (pp. 66–86). New York: Routledge.

Baraldi, C. and Gavioli, L. (2010). Interpreter-mediated interaction as a way to promote multilingualism. In B. Meyer and B. Apfelbaum (eds), *Multilingualism at Work: From Policies to Practices in Public, Medical and Business Settings* (pp. 141–162). Amsterdam: John Benjamins.

Bargiela-Chiappini, F. and Harris, S. (1996). Interruptive strategies in British and Italian Management meetings. *Text*, 16(3), 269–297. Also available in Zhu Hua (ed), *The Language and Intercultural Communication Reader* (pp. 346–366). London: Routledge

——(1997). *Managing Language: The Discourse of Corporate Meetings.* Amsterdam: John Benjamins.

Bargiela-Chiappini, F., Nickerson, C. and Planken, B. (2007). *Business Discourse.* Basingstoke: Palgrave.

Barro, A., Jordan, S. and Roberts, C. (1998). Cultural Practice in everyday life: The language learner as ethnographer. In M. Byram and M. Fleming (eds), *Language Learning in Intercultural Perspectives: Approaches through Drama and Ethnography* (pp. 76–97). Cambridge: Cambridge University Press.

Basso, K. (1990). *To Give Up on Words: Silence in Western Apache. Western Apache Language and Culture.* Tuscon: University of Arizona Press.

Baugh, J. (1999). *Out of the Mouths of Slaves: African American Language and Educational Malpractice.* Austin: University of Texas Press.

Bell, A. (1984). Language style as audience design. *Language in Society*, 13, 145–204.

——(2001). Back in style: Reworking audience design. In P. Eckert and J. Rickford (eds), *Style and Sociolinguistic Variation* (pp. 139–169). Cambridge: Cambridge University Press

Bell, N. and Attardo, S. (2010). Failed humor: Issues in non-native speakers' appreciation and understanding of humor. *Intercultural Pragmatics*, 7(3), 423–447.

Bennett, J. M. (1977). Transition shock: Putting culture shock in perspective. In N. Jain (ed.), *International Intercultural Communication Annual* (vol. 4, pp. 45–52). Falls Church, VA: Speech Communication Association.

——(1998). Transition shock: Putting culture shock in perspective. In M. J. Bennett (ed.), *Basic Concepts of Intercultural Communication: Selected Readings* (pp. 215–224). Yarmouth, ME: Intercultural Press.

Bennett, M. J. (1986). A developmental approach to training for intercultural sensitivity. *International Journal of Intercultural Relations*, 10, 179–196.

Bennett, T. (2005). Culture. In T. Bennett, L. Grossberg and M. Morris (eds), *New Keywords: A Revised Vocabulary of Culture and Society* (pp. 63–69). Malden, MA: Blackwell.

Bennett, T., Grossberg, L. and Morris, M. (2005). *New Keywords: A Revised Vocabulary of Culture and Society*. Malden, MA: Blackwell.

Benwell, B. and Stokoe, E. (2006). *Discourse and Identity*. Edinburgh: Edinburgh University Press.

Berlin, B. and Kay, P. (1969). *Basic Colour Terms: Their Universality and Evaluation*. Berkeley: University of California Press.

Berry, J., Phinney, J. S., Sam, D. and Vedder, P. (eds) (2006). *Immigrant Youth in Cultural Transition: Acculturation, Identity and Adaptation across National Contexts*. Mahwah, NJ: Lawrence Erlbaum.

Berwick, R. F. and Whalley, T. R. (2000). The experiential bases of culture learning: A case study of Canadian high schools in Japan. *International Journal of Intercultural Relations*, 24, 325–340.

Bhabha, H. K. (1994). *The Location of Culture*. London: Routledge.

Bhandari, R. and Blumenthal, P. (2011). *International Students and Global Mobility in Higher Education: National Trends and New Directions*. London: Palgrave.

Bhawuk, D. P. S. and Brislin, R. (1992). The measurement of intercultural sensitivity using the concepts of individualism and collectivism. *International Journal of Intercultural Relations*, 16, 413–436.

Biesenbach-Lucas, S. (2007). Students writing emails to faculty: An examination of e-politeness among native and non-native speakers of English. *Language Learning and Technology*, 11(2), 59–81.

Block, D. (2006). Identity in applied linguistics. In T. Omoniyi and G. White (eds), *Sociolinguistics of Identity* (pp. 34–49). London: Continuum.

Blum-Kulka, S. (1997). *Dinner Talk: Cultural Patterns of Sociability and Socialization in Family Discourse*. London: Lawrence Erlbaum.

Blum-Kulka, S. and Olshtain, E. (1984). Requests and apologies: A cross-cultural study of speech act realisation patterns. *Applied Linguistics*, 5(3), 196–213. Reprinted in Zhu Hua (ed.) (2011), *The Language and Intercultural Communication Reader*. London: Routledge.

Bond, M. H. and Cheung, T. S. (1983). College students' spontaneous self-concept: The effect of culture among respondents in Hong Kong, Japan and the United States. *Journal of Cross-Cultural Psychology*, 14, 153–171.

Boud, D., Keough, R. and Walker, D. (1985). *Reflection: Turning Experience into Learning*. London: Kogan Page.

Boxer, D. (2002). *Applying Sociolinguistics: Domains and Face-to-face Interaction*. Amsterdam: John Benjamins.

Brein, M. and David, K. (1971). Intercultural communication and the adjustment of the sojourner. *Psychological Bulletin*, 76, 215–230.

Bremer, K. (1996). Causes of understanding problems. In K. Bremer, C. Roberts, M-T. Vasseur, M. Simonot and P. Broeder (eds), *Achieving Understanding: Discourse in Intercultural Encounters* (pp. 37–64). London: Longman.

Bremer, K. and Simonot, M. (1996). Preventing problems of understanding. In K. Bremer, C. Roberts, M-T. Vasseur, M. Simonot and P. Broeder (eds),

Achieving Understanding: Discourse in Intercultural Encounters (pp. 159–180). London: Longman.

Brooks, N. (1960). *Language and Language Learning*. New York: Harcourt Brace Jovanovich.

Brown, D. E. (1991). *Human Universals*. New York: McGraw-Hill.

Brown, P. and Levinson, S. (1978). Universals in language usage: Politeness phenomena. In E. Goody (ed.), *Questions and Politeness* (pp. 56–289). Cambridge: Cambridge University Press.

Brown, R. (1958). *Words and Things*. Glencoe, IL: The Free Press.

Brown, R. W. and Lenneberg, E. H. (1954). A study in language and cognition. *The Journal of Abnormal and Social Psychology*, 49(3), 454–462.

Bucholtz, M. (1995). From Mulatta to Mestiza: Language and the reshaping of ethnic identity. In K. Hall and M. Bucholtz (eds), *Gender Articulated: Language the Socially Constructed Self* (pp. 351–374). New York: Routledge.

Bunderson, J. S. and Barton, M. A. (2011). Status cues and expertise assessment in groups: How group members size one another up ... and why it matters. In J. L. Pearce (ed.), *Status in Management and Organizations* (pp. 215–237). Cambridge: Cambridge University Press.

Burgett, B. and Hendler, G. (eds) (2007). *Keywords for American Cultural Studies*. New York: New York University Press.

Byram, M. (1989). *Cultural Studies in Foreign Language Education*. Clevedon: Multilingual Matters.

——(1997). *Teaching and Assessing Intercultural Communicative Competence*. Clevedon: Multilingual Matters.

Byram, M., Estarte-Sarries, V. and Taylor, S. (1991). *Cultural Studies and Language Learning: A Research Report*. Clevedon: Multilingual Matters.

Byrne, D. (1971). *The Attraction Paradigm*. New York: Academic Press.

Campbell, S. and Roberts, C. (2007). Migration, ethnicity and competing discourses in the job interview: Synthesising the institutional and personal. *Discourse and Society*, 18(3), 243–271.

Canagarajah, A. S. (1993). Critical ethnography of a Sri Lankan classroom: Ambiguities in student opposition to reproduction through ESOL. *TESOL Quarterly*, 27(4), 601–626.

Canale, M. (1983). From communicative competence to language pedagogy. In J. Richards and J. Schmidt (eds), *Language and Communication* (pp. 2–27). London: Longman.

Canale, M. and Swain, M. (1980). Theoretical bases of communicative approaches to second language teaching and testing. *Applied Linguistics*, 1(1), 1–47.

Carbaugh, D. (2005). *Cultures in Conversation*. Mahwah, NJ: Lawrence Erlbaum.

Castles, S. (2000). International migration at the beginning of the twenty-first century: Global trends and issues. *International Social Science Journal*, 165, 269–81.

Chalak, A., Rasekh, Z. E. and Rasekh, A. E. (2010). Communication strategies and topics in e-mail interactions between Iranian EFL students and their instructors. *International Journal of Language Studies*, 4(4), 373–391.

Chamberlain, M. (2006). *Family Love in the Diaspora: Migration and the Anglo-Caribbean Experience.* New Brunswick, NJ: Transaction.

Charalambous, C. and Rampton, B. (2012). Other-language learning, identity and intercultural communication in contexts of conflict. In J. Jackson (ed.), *The Routledge Handbook of Language and Intercultural Communication* (pp. 195–210). London: Routledge.

Charles, M. and Marschan-Piekkari, R. (2002). Language training for enhanced horizontal communication: A challenge for MNCS. *Business Communication Quarterly*, 65(2), 9–29.

Chavez, M. (2002). We say 'culture' and students ask 'what?': University students' definitions of foreign language culture. *Die Unterrichtspraxis/ Teaching German*, 35(2), 129–140.

Chen, G-M. and Starosta, W. J. (1998). *Foundations of Intercultural Communications.* Needham Heights, MA: Allyn and Bacon.

Chiaro, D. (1992). *The Language of Jokes: Analyzing Verbal Play.* London: Routledge.

Chiu, L.-H. (1972). A cross-cultural comparison of cognitive styles in Chinese and American children. *International Journal of Psychology*, 7, 235–242.

Chomsky, N. (1965). *Aspects of the Theory of Syntax.* Cambridge, MA: MIT Press.

Chua, A. (2011). *Battle Hymn of the Tiger Mother.* London: Penguin Press.

Churchman, A. and Mitrani, M. (1997). The role of the physical environment in culture shock. *Environment and Behaviour*, 29, 64–87.

Coates, J. (1994). No gap, lots of overlap. In D. Graddol, J. Maybin and B. Stierer (eds), *Researching Language and Literacy in Social Context* (pp. 177–192). Clevedon: Multilingual Matters.

Cohen, E. (1972). Toward a sociology of international tourism. *Social Research*, 39(1), 164–182.

——(1985). The tourist guide: The origins, structure and dynamics of a role. *Annals of Tourism Research*, 12(1), 5–29.

Collins, S., Peters, S. and Watt, I. (2011). Medical communication. In J. Simpson (ed.), *The Routledge Handbook of Applied Linguistics* (pp. 96–110). London: Routledge.

Cook, G. (2000). *Language Play, Language Learning.* Oxford: Oxford University Press.

——(2001). *The Discourse of Advertising.* London: Routledge.

Corbett, J. (2003). *An Intercultural Approach to English Language Teaching.* Clevedon: Multilingual Matters.

Correll, J., Park, B., Judd, C. M. and Wittenbrink, B. (2002). The police officer's dilemma: Using ethnicity to disambiguate potentially threatening individuals. *Journal of Personality and Social Psychology*, 83(6), 1314–1329.

Cortazzi, M. and Shen, W. W. (2001). Cross-linguistic awareness of cultural keywords: A study of Chinese and English speakers. *Language Awareness*, 10(2 and 3), 125–142.

Coupland, J. (2000). Introduction: Sociolinguistic perspectives on small talk. In J. Coupland (ed.), *Small Talk* (pp. 1–26). Harlow: Longman.

Coupland, N., Coupland, J., Giles, H. and Henwood, K. (1988). Accommodating the elderly: Invoking and extending a theory. *Language in Society*, 17, 1–41.

Crawford-Lange, L. and Lange, D. L. (1984). Doing the unthinkable in the second language classroom: A process for the integration of language and culture. In T. V. Higgs (ed.), *Teaching for Proficiency, the Organising Principle* (pp. 139–177). Lincolnwood, IL: National Textbook Company.

Crozet, C. and Liddicoat, A. J. (1997). Teaching culture as an integrated part of language teaching: An introduction. *Australian Review of Applied Linguistics*, 14, 1–22.

Cutler, C. (2007). The co-construction of whiteness in an MC battle. *Pragmatics*, 17(1), 9–22.

Day, D. (1998). Being ascribed and resisting: Membership of an ethnic group. In C. Antaki and S. Widdicombe (eds), *Identities in Talk* (pp. 151–170). London: Sage.

Deardorff, D. K. (2004). *The Identification and Assessment of Intercultural Competence as a Student Outcome of Internationalization*. Raleigh: North Carolina State University Press.

——(2006). Identification and assessment of intercultural competence as a student outcome of internationalization. *Journal of Studies in Intercultural Education*, 10, 241–266.

de Bot, K. and Lintsen, T. (1989). Perception of own language proficiency by elderly adults. *ITL-Review*, 83/84, 51–61.

de Kadt, E. (1998). The concept of face and its applicability to the Zulu language. *Journal of Pragmatics*, 29, 173–191.

de Mooij, M. (1998). *Global Marketing and Advertisement: Understanding Cultural Stereotypes*. Thousand Oaks, CA.: Sage.

Dervin, F. (2012). Cultural identity, representation and othering. In J. Jackson (ed.), *The Routledge Handbook of Language and Intercultural Communication* (pp. 181–194). Cambridge: Cambridge University Press.

Dewaele, J-M. (2004). The emotional force of swearwords and taboo words in the speech of multilinguals. *Journal of Multilingual and Multicultural Development*, 25 (2 and 3), 204–222.

——(2010). *Emotions in Multiple Languages*. Basingstoke: Palgrave.

Dewey, D. (2006). Reading comprehension and vocabulary development in orthographically complex languages during study abroad. In S. Wilkinson (ed.), *Insights from Study Abroad for Language Programmes* (pp. 72–84). Boston: Thomson Higher Education.

Dioko, L., Harrill, R. and Cardon, P. (2010). Brand China: Tour guide perceptions and implications for destination branding and marketing. *Tourism Analysis*, 15(3), 345–355.

Dodd, C. and Baldwin, J. R. (2002). The role of family and macrocultures in intercultural relationships. In J. Martin, T. K. Nakayama and L. Flores (eds), *Readings in Intercultural Communication: Experiences and Contexts* (pp. 277–288). Boston: McGraw Hill.

Duff, P. A. (2002). The discursive co-construction of knowledge, identity and difference: An ethnography of communication in the high school mainstream. *Applied Linguistics*, 23(3), 289–322.

——(2010). Language socialization into academic discourse communities. *Annual Review of Applied Linguistics*, 30, 169–192.

——(2012). Second language acquisition. In A. Duranti, E. Ochs and B. Schieffelin (eds), *The Handbook of Language Socialisation* (pp. 564–586). Oxford: Blackwell.

Eades, D. (2000). I don't think it's an answer to the question: Silencing Aboriginal witnesses in court. *Language in Society*, 29(2), 161–195.

Eckert, P. and McConnell-Ginet, S. (1999). New generalisations and explanations in language and gender research. *Language in Society*, 28(2), 185–201.

Econonmidou-Kogetsidis, M. (2011). 'Please answer me as soon as possible': Pragmatic failure in non-native speakers' email requests to faculty. *Journal of Pragmatics*, 43, 3193–3215.

Ehlich, K. (1992). On the historicity of politeness. In R. Watts, S. Ide and K. Ehlich (eds), *Politeness in Language: Studies in Its History, Theory and Practice* (pp. 71–107). Berlin: Mouton de Gruyter.

Ehrenreich, S. (2010). English as a business lingua franca in a German multinational corporation: Meeting the challenge. *Journal of Business Communication*, 47(4), 408–431.

Ekman, P. and Friesen, W. V. (1975). *Unmasking the Face: A Guide to Recognizing Emotions from Facial Clues*. Englewood Cliffs, NJ: Prentice-Hall.

Elfenbein, H. A., Mandal, M. K., Ambady, N., Harizuka, S. and Kuma, S. (2002). Cross-cultural patterns in emotion recognition: Highlighting design and analytical techniques. *Emotion*, 2(1), 75–84.

Endrass, B., Rehm, M. and André, E. (2011). Planning small talk behaviour with cultural influences for multiagent systems. *Computer Speech and Language*, 25, 158–174.

Engle, L. and Engle, J. (2003) Study abroad levels: Toward a classification of program types. In Vande Berg, M. (guest ed.), *Frontiers: The Interdisciplinary Journal of Study Abroad*, 9, 1–20.

Enninger, W. (1987). What interactants do with non-talk across cultures. In K. W. Knapp, W. Enninger and A. Knapp-Potthoff (eds), *Analysing Intercultural Communication* (pp. 269–302). Berlin: Mouton de Gruyter.

Everett, D. L. (2008). *Don't Sleep, There Are Snakes: Life and Language in the Amazonian Jungle*. New York: Pantheon Books.

——(2012). *Language: The Cultural Tool*. London: Profile Books.

Faerch, K. and Kasper, G. (1986). The role of comprehension in second language learning. *Applied Linguistics*, 7, 257–274.

Fay, B. (1996). *Contemporary Philosophy of Social Science: A Multicultural Approach*. Oxford: Blackwell.

Fayer, J. M. and Krasinski, E. K. (1987). Native and nonnative judgments of intelligibility and irritation. *Language Learning*, 37, 313–326.

Ferguson, C. (1975). Towards a characterization of English foreigner talk. *Anthropological Linguistics*, 17, 1–14.

Firth, A. (1996). The discursive accomplishment of normality: On 'lingua franca' English and conversation analysis. *Journal of Pragmatics*, 26, 237–259.

Fought, C. (2006). *Language and Ethnicity*. Cambridge: Cambridge University Press.

Fox, K. (2004). *Watching the English: The Hidden Rules of English Behaviour*. London: Hodder.

Fredriksson, R., Barner-Rasmussen, W. and Piekkari, R. (2006). The multinational corporation as a multilingual organisation: The notion of a common corporate language. *Corporate Communications: An International Journal*, 11(4), 406–423.

Gallois, C., Franklyn-Stokes, A., Giles, H. and Coupland, N. (1988). Communication accommodation in intercultural encounters. In Y. Y. Kim (ed.), *Theories in Intercultural Communication* (pp. 157–185). Newbury Park, CA: Sage.

Gallois, C., Ogay, T. and Giles, H. (2005). Communication accommodation theory. In W. Gudykunst (ed.), *Theorizing about Intercultural Communication* (pp. 121–148). London: Sage.

Garcez, P. D. M. (1993). Point-making styles in cross-cultural business negotiation: A microethnographic study. *English for Specific Purposes*, 12, 103–120.

Gass, S. and Varonis, E. (1991). Miscommunication in non-native speaker discourse. In N. Coupland, H. Giles and J. Wiemann (eds), *Miscommunication and Problematic Talk* (pp. 121–145). Newbury Park, CA: Sage.

Geertz, C. (1973). *The Interpretation of Cultures*. New York: Basic Books.

Gentner, D. and Boroditsky, L. (2001). Individuation, relativity and early word learning. In M. Bowerman and S. Levinson (eds), *Language Acquisition and Conceptual Development* (pp. 215–256). Cambridge: Cambridge University Press.

Gibson, J. J. (1979). *The Ecological Approach of Visual Perception*. Hillsdale, NJ: Lawrence Erlbaum Associates.

Gidoomal, R., Mahtani, D. and Porter, D. (2001). *The British and How to Deal with Them*. London: Middlesex University Press.

Giles, H. (1973). Accent mobility: A model and some data. *Anthropological Linguistics*, 15, 87–105.

Giles, H., Coupland, J. and Coupland, N. (eds) (1991). *Contexts of Accommodation: Developments in Applied Sociolinguistics*. Cambridge: Cambridge University Press.

Giltrow, J. and Calhoun, E. (1992). The culture of power, ESL traditions, Mayan resistance. In B. Burnaby and A. Cumming (eds), *Socio-political Aspects of ESL in Canada* (pp. 50–66). Toronto: OISE Press.

Gimenez, J. C. (2001). Ethnographic observations in cross-cultural business negotiations between non-native speakers of English: An exploratory study. *English for Specific Purposes*, 20, 169–193.

Goddard, A. (1998). *The Language of Advertising*. London: Routledge.

Gordon, P. (2004). Numerical cognition without words: Evidence from Amazonia. *Science*, 306, 496–99.

Grindsted, A. (1997). Joking as a strategy in Spanish and Danish negotiations. In F. Bargiela-Chiappini and S. Harris (eds), *The Languages of Business* (pp. 159–182). Edinburgh: Edinburgh University Press.

Gu, Yueguo (1990). Politeness phenomena in modern Chinese. *Journal of Pragmatics*, 14, 237–257.

Gu, Yueguo and Zhu, Weifang (2002). Chinese officialdom (*guan*) at work in discourse. In C. Barron, N. Bruce and D. Nunan (eds), *Knowledge and Discourse: Towards an Ecology of Language* (pp. 97–115). Harlow: Pearson.

Gudykunst, W. and Hammer, M. R. (1983). Basic training design: Approaches to intercultural training. In D. Landis and R. W. Brislin (eds), *Handbook of Intercultural Training, Volume 1: Issues in Theory and Design* (pp. 118–154). New York: Pergamon Press.

Gumperz, J. (1982). *Discourse Strategies*. Cambridge: Cambridge University Press. A selection is reprinted in S. Kiesling and C. Paulston (eds) (2005), *Intercultural Discourse and Communication: The Essential Readings* (pp. 33–44). Malden, MA: Blackwell.

——(1992). Contextualization and understanding. In A. Duranti and C. Goodwin (eds), *Rethinking Context: Language as an Interactive Phenomenon* (pp. 229–252). Cambridge: Cambridge University Press.

——(1999). On interactional sociolinguistic method. In S. Sarangi and C. Roberts (eds), *Talk, Work and Institutional Order: Discourse in Medical, Mediation and Management Settings* (pp. 453–471). Berlin: Mouton.

Gumperz, J. and Levinson, S. C. (1996). Introduction: Linguistic relativity re-examined. In J. Gumperz and S. C. Levinson (eds), *Rethinking Linguistic Relativity* (pp. 1–20). Cambridge: Cambridge University Press.

Gutiérrez, K. D. and Rogoff, B. (2003). Cultural ways of learning: Individual traits or repertoires of practice. *Educational Researcher*, 32(5), 19–25.

Haghirian, P. and Madlberger, M. (2004). A cross cultural analysis of perceptions of mobile advertising. A survey among Austrian and Japanese students. *Vienna University of Economics and Business Administration* (pp. 3–8). Vienna University.

Hall, E. T. (1959/1973). *The Silent Language*. Garden City, NY: Doubleday.

——(1966). *The Hidden Dimension*. Garden City, NY: Doubleday.

——(1976). *Beyond Culture*. Garden City, NY: Doubleday.

Hall, E. T. and Hall, M. R. (1990). *Understanding Cultural Differences: Germans, French and Americans*. Yarmouth, ME: Intercultural Press.

Halualani, R. T. and Nakayama, T. K. (2010). Critical intercultural communication studies: At a crossroads. In T. K. Nakayama and R. T. Halualani (eds), *The Handbook of Critical Intercultural Communication* (pp. 1–16). Malden, MA: Wiley-Blackwell.

Hampden-Turner, C. (2003). The dilemmas of facilitation. *Interspective*, 19, 8–11. An electronic version of the article is available on CISV website at http://resources.cisv.org/docs/main?action=document.viewandid=141.

Hampden-Turner, C. and Trompenaars, F. (2000). *Building Cross-cultural Competence: How to Create Wealth from Conflicting Values*. Chichester: John Wiley and Sons.

Handford, M. (2010). *The Language of Business Meetings*. Cambridge: Cambridge University Press.

Hartford, B. and Bardovi-Harlig, K. (1996). 'At your earliest convenience': A study of written student requests to faculty. In L. F. Bouton (ed.), *Pragmatics and Language Learning*, vol. 3 (pp. 33–52). Urbana, IL: DEIL.

Hartog, J. (2006). Beyond 'misunderstandings' and 'cultural stereotypes'. In K. Bührig and Jan D. ten Thije (eds), *Beyond Misunderstanding* (pp. 175–188). Amsterdam: John Benjamins.

Hassan, R. (1975). International tourism and intercultural communication: The case of Japanese tourists in Singapore. *Southeast Asian Journal of Social Sciences*, 3(2), 25–38.

Hay, J. (2001). The pragmatics of humor support. *HUMOR: International Journal of Humor Research*, 14, 55–82.

He, A. W. (2012). Heritage language socialisation. In A. Duranti, E. Ochs and B. Schieffelin (eds), *The Handbook of Language Socialisation* (pp. 586–609). Oxford: Blackwell.

Hegel, G. W. F. (1807/1977). *Phenomenology of Spirit*, trans. A. V. Miller. Oxford: Clarendon Press.

Held, D. (1980). *Introduction to Critical Theory*. Berkeley: University of California Press.

Hendriks, B. (2010). An experimental study of native speaker perceptions of non-native request modification in e-mails in English. *Intercultural Pragmatics*, 7(2), 221–255.

Hewitt, R. (1982). White adolescent Creole users and the politics of friendship. *Journal of Multilingual and Multicultural Development*, 3, 217–232.

Higgins, C. (2007). A closer look at cultural difference: 'Interculturality' in talk-in-interaction. *Pragmatics*, 17(1), 1–8.

Hinkel, E. (2002). *Second Language Writers' Text: Linguistic and Rhetorical Features*. Mahwah, NJ: Lawrence Erlbaum Associates.

Hoeken, H., Brandt, van, C., Crijins, R., Dominguez, N., Hendriks, B., Planken, N. and Starren, M. (2003). International advertising in Western Europe: Should differences in uncertainty avoidance be considered when advertising in Belgium, France, the Netherlands and Spain? *The Journal of Business Communication*, 40(3), 195–218.

Hoffman, E. (1989). *Lost in Translation: A Life in a New Language*. New York: Penguin Books.

Hofstede, G. (2001) [1984]. *Culture's Consequences: Comparing Values, Behaviours, Institutions and Organizations across Nations*. London: Sage.

Holliday, A. (2003). Social autonomy: Addressing the dangers of culturism in TESOL. In D. Palfreyman and R. C. Smith (eds), *Learner Autonomy across Cultures* (pp. 110–128). Basingstoke: Palgrave.

——(2005). *The Struggle to Teach English as an International Language*. Oxford: Oxford University Press.

——(2011) [1999]. *Intercultural Communication and Ideology*. London: Sage.

Holmes, J. (2000a). Doing collegiality and keeping control at work: Small talk in government departments. In J. Coupland (ed.), *Small Talk* (pp. 32–61). Harlow: Longman.

——(2000b). Politeness, power and provocation: How humor functions in the workplace. *Discourse Studies*, 2, 159–185.

——(2007). Making humour work: Creativity on the job. *Applied Linguistics*, 28(4), 518–537.

Holmes, J. and Marra, M. (2002). Having a laugh at work: How humour contributes to workplace culture. *Journal of Pragmatics*, 34, 1683–1710.

Holmes, J. and Stubbe, M. (2003). *Power and Politeness in the Workplace.* London: Pearson Education.

Holmes, J., Vine, B., Marra, M. and Stubbe, M. (2009) *Research Summary for the Language in the Workplace Project.* accessed at www.victoria.ac.nz/lals/lwp/research/humour.aspx on 5 February 2013.

Hornberger, N. H. (2007). Biliteracy, transnationalism, multimodality and identity: Trajectories across time and space. *Linguistics and Education*, 8, 325–334.

House, J. (2000). Understanding misunderstanding: A pragmatic-discourse approach to analysing mismanaged rapport in talk across cultures. In H. Spencer-Oatey (ed.), *Culturally Speaking: Managing Rapport through Talk across Cultures* (pp. 145–164). London: Continuum.

Hughes, G. H. (1986). An argument for culture analysis in the second language classroom. In J. M. Valdes (ed.), *Culture Bound* (pp. 162–169). Cambridge: Cambridge University Press. A full version of the article was published in 1984, *American Language Journal*, 2(1), 31–51.

Humboldt, W. von (1963). *Humanist without Portfolio: An Anthology of the Writings of Wilhelm von Humboldt.* Detroit, MI: Wayne State University Press.

Hunter, B., White, G. P. and Godbey, G. (2006). What does it mean to be globally competent? *Journal of Studies in International Education*, 10(3), 267–285.

Hymes, D. (1972). On communicative competence. In J. B. Pride and J. Holmes (eds), *Sociolinguistics Selected Readings* (pp. 269–293). Harmondsworth: Penguin.

Ide, S. (1989). Formal forms and discernment: Two neglected aspects of linguistic politeness. *Multilingua*, 8(2/3), 223–248.

——(1992). On the notion of Wakimae: Toward an integrated framework of linguistic politeness. *Mosaic of Language: Essays in Honour of Professor Natsuko Okuda.* Mejiro Linguistic Society, 298–305.

——(2005). How and why honorifics can signify dignity and elegance: The indexicality and reflexivity of linguistic rituals. In R. Lakoff and S. Ide (eds), *Broadening the Horizon of Linguistic Politeness* (pp. 45–64). Amsterdam: John Benjamins. Reprinted in Zhu Hua (ed.) (2011), *The Language and Intercultural Communication Reader.* London: Routledge.

Iervese, V. (2012). Conflict and mediation in international groups of children. In C. Baraldi and V. Iervese (eds), *Participation, Facilitation and Mediation: Children and Young People in their Social Contexts* (pp. 128–146). New York: Routledge.

Isaksson, M. and Jørgensen, P. E. F. (2010). Communicating corporate ethos on the web. *Journal of Business Communication*, 47(2), 119–140.

Jack, G. and Phipps, A. (2005). *Tourism and Intercultural Exchange: Why Tourism Matters.* Clevedon: Channel View.

Jackson, J. (2010). *Intercultural Journeys: From Study to Residence Abroad.* New York: Palgrave Macmillan.

Jandt, F. E. (2001). *Intercultural Communication: An Introduction* (3rd edn). London: Sage.

Jaworski, A. (2000). Silence and small talk. In J. Coupland (ed.), *Small Talk* (pp. 110–132). Harlow: Longman.

Jefferson, G. (1989). Preliminary notes on a possible metric which provides for a 'standard maximum' silence of approximately one second in conversation. In P. Bull and R. Derek (eds), *Conversation: An Interdisciplinary Approach* (pp. 166–196). Clevedon: Multilingual Matters.

Ji, L-J., Zhang, Z. and Nisbett, R. E. (2004). Is it culture or is it language? Examination of language effects in cross-cultural research on categorization. *Journal of Personality and Social Psychology*, 87(1), 57–65.

Jin, Lixian and Cortazzi, M. (1998). The culture the learner brings: A bridge or a barrier? In M. Byram and M. Fleming (eds), *Language Learning in Intercultural Perspectives: Approaches through Drama and Ethnography* (pp. 98–118). Cambridge: Cambridge University Press.

Kamwangamalu, N. (2008). Ubuntu in South Africa: A sociolinguistic perspective to a pan-African concept. In M. K. Asante, Y. Miike and J. Yin (eds), *The Global Intercultural Communication Reader* (pp. 113–122). London: Routledge.

Kaplan, R. B. (1966). Cultural thought patterns in intercultural education. *Language Learning*, 16, 1–20.

Katriel, T. (1986). *Talking Straight: Dugri Speech in Israeli Sabra Culture.* Cambridge: Cambridge University Press. A selection is reprinted in Zhu Hua (ed.) (2011), *The Language and Intercultural Communication Reader.* London: Routledge.

Kay, P. and Kempton, W. (1984). What is the Sapir-Whorf hypothesis? *Anthropologist*, 86, 65–79.

Kealey, D. J. (1989). A study of cross-cultural effectiveness: Theoretical issues, practical applications. *International Journal of Intercultural Relations*, 13, 387–428.

Kember, D. (2000). Misconceptions about the learning approaches, motivation and study practices of Asian students. *Higher Education*, 40, 99–121.

Keshtgary, M. and Khajehpour, S. (2011). Exploring and analysis of factors affecting mobile advertising adoption: An empirical investigation among Iranian users. *Canadian Journal on Computing in Mathematics, Natural Sciences, Engineering and Medicine*, 2(6), 144–151.

Kim, Y. Y. (2001). *Becoming Intercultural: An Integrative Theory of Communication and Cross-cultural Adaptation.* Thousand Oaks, CA: Sage.

——(2008). Intercultural personhood: Globalization and a way of being. *International Journal of Intercultural Relations*, 32(4), 301–304.

Klopf, D. (1998). *Intercultural Encounters: The Fundamentals of Intercultural Communication* (4th edn). Englewood, CO: Morton.

Knapp-Potthoff, A. and Knapp, K. (1987). The man (or woman) in the middle: Discoursal aspects of non-professional interpreting. In K. Knapp, E. Enninger and A. Knapp-Potthoff (eds), *Analyzing Intercultural Communication* (pp. 181–212). Berlin: Mouton.

Knight, W. A. (2002). Conceptualising transnational community formation: Migrants, sojourners and diasporas in a globalized era. Special Issue on Migration and Globalization, *Canadian Studies in Population*, 29(1), 1–30.

Kolb, D. A. (1984). *Experiential Learning: Experience as the Source of Learning and Development.* Englewood Cliffs, NJ: Prentice-Hall.

Korzay, M. and Alvarez, M. (2011). Satisfaction and dissatisfaction of Japanese tourists in Turkey. *Anatolia*, 16(2), 176–193.

Kramsch, C. (1991). Culture in language learning: A view from the States. In K. de Bot, R. B. Ginsberg and C. Kramsch (eds), *Foreign Language Research in Cross-Cultural Perspective* (pp. 217–240). Amsterdam: John Benjamins.

——(1993). *Context and Culture in Language Teaching*. Oxford: Oxford University Press.

——(1998a). *Language and Culture*. Oxford Introductions to Language Study. Oxford: Oxford University Press.

——(1998b). The privileges of the intercultural speaker. In M. Byram and M. Fleming (eds), *Language Learning in Intercultural Perspective: Approaches through Drama and Ethnography* (pp. 16–31). Cambridge: Cambridge University Press.

——(2004). Language, thought and culture. In A. Davies and C. Elder (eds), *The Handbook of Applied Linguistics* (pp. 235–261). Malden, MA: Blackwell.

——(2005). Post 9/11: Foreign languages between knowledge and power. *Applied Linguistics*, 26(4), 545–567.

——(2006). From communicative competence to symbolic competence. *Modern Language Journal*, 90(2), 249–251.

——(2009a). *The Multilingual Subject*. Oxford: Oxford University Press.

——(2009b). Third culture and language education. In Li Wei and V. Cook (eds), *Contemporary Applied Linguistics. Volume 1 Language Teaching and Learning* (pp. 233–254). London: Continuum.

Kramsch, C. and Whiteside, A. (2008). Language ecology in multilingual settings: Towards a theory of symbolic competence. *Applied Linguistics*, 29(4), 645–71. Reprinted in Li Wei (ed.), *The Routledge Applied Linguistics Reader* (pp. 295–315). London: Routledge.

Kroeber, A., Kluckhohn, C., Untereiner, W. and Meyer, A. G. (1952). *Culture: A Critical Review of Concepts and Definitions*. New York: Vintage Books.

Kubota, R. (1999). Japanese culture constructed by discourses: Implications for applied linguistics research and ELT. *TESOL Quarterly*, 33(1), 9–35.

Kuhn, M. H. and McPartland, T. A. (1954). An empirical investigation of self-attitudes. *American Sociological Review*, 19(1), 68–76.

Lakoff, R. (1973). The logic of politeness; or minding your p's and q's. *Chicago Linguistics Society*, 8, 292–305.

Lave, J. and Wenger, E. (1991). *Situated Learning: Legitimate Peripheral Participation*. Cambridge: Cambridge University Press.

Lehtonen, J. and Sajavaara, K. (1985). The silent Finn. In D. Tannen and M. Saville-Troike (eds), *Perspectives on Silence* (pp. 193–201). Norwood, NJ: Ablex.

Leonard, R. (2010). *Von Neumann, Morgenstern and the Creation of Game Theory: From Chess to Social Science, 1900–1960*. Cambridge: Cambridge University Press

Leung, C. (2005). Convival communication: Recontextualizing communicative competence. *International Journal of Applied Linguistics*, 15(2), 119–143. Reprinted in Li Wei (ed.), *The Routledge Applied Linguistics Reader* (pp. 275–294). London: Routledge.

Levinson, S. (2003). *Space in Language and Cognition*. Cambridge: Cambridge University Press.

Levinson, S. C. and Wilkins, D. P. (eds) (2006). *Grammars of Space: Explorations in Cognitive Diversity*. Cambridge: Cambridge University Press.

Lewis, R. (2006). *When Cultures Collide*. London: Nicholas Brealey International.

Li, D. (2000). The pragmatics of making requests in the L2 workplace: A case study of language socialization. *The Canadian Modern Language Review*, 57(1), 58–87.

Li, W. and Zhu, H. (in press). Language and literacy teaching, learning and socialization in the Chinese complementary school classroom. In X. Curdt-Christiansen and A. Hancock (eds), *Learning Chinese in Diasporic Communities*. AILA Applied Linguistics Series. Amsterdam: John Benjamins.

Li, W., Zhu, H. and Li, Y. (2001). Conversational management and involvement in Chinese–English business talk. *Language and Intercultural Communication*, 1(2), 135–150.

Lippi-Green, R. (1997/2012). *English with an Accent: Language, Ideology and Discrimination in the United States*. London: Routledge.

Litvin, S. W. (1999). Tourism and understanding: The case of Japanese tourists in Singapore – revisited. *Asia Pacific Journal of Tourism Research*, 4(1), 12–21.

Lo Bianco, J., Orton, J. and Gao, Y. H. (eds) (2009). *China and English: Globalisation and the Dilemmas of Identity*. Bristol: Multilingual Matters.

Lonner, W. (1986). Foreword. In A. Furnham and S. Bochner (eds), *Culture Shock, Psychological Reactions to Unfamiliar Environments* (pp. xv–xx). London: Methuen.

Louhiala-Salminen, L. and Kankaanranta, A. (2012). Language as an issue in international internal communication: English or local language? If English, what English? *Public Relations Review*, 38(2), 262–269.

Lucy, J. A. and Shweder, R. A. (1979). Whorf and his critics: Linguistic and non-linguistic influences on color memory. *American Anthropologist*, 81, 581–615.

——(1988). The effect of incidental conversation on memory for focal colours. *American Anthropologist*, 90, 923–931.

Luo, Y. and Shenkar, O. (2006). The multinational corporation as a multilingual community: Language and organisation in a global context. *Journal of International Business Studies*, 37, 321–339.

McSweeney, B. (2002). Hofstede's model of national cultural differences and their consequences: A triumph of faith – a failure of analysis. *Human Relations*, 55(1), 89–118.

Malinowski, B. (1923). The problem of meaning in primitive languages. In C. K. Ogden and I. A. Richards (eds), *The Meaning of Meaning* (pp. 296–336). London: Routledge and Kegan Paul. Reprinted in A. Jaworski and N. Coupland (eds) (1999), *The Discourse Reader* (pp. 302–305). London: Routledge.

Malotki, E. (1983). *Hopi Time: A Linguistic Analysis of the Temporal Categories in the Hopi Language*. Berlin: Mouton.

Mao, L. R. (1994). Beyond politeness theory: Face revisited and renewed. *Journal of Pragmatics*, 21(5), 451–486.

Markus, H. R. and Kitayama, S. (1994). The cultural construction of self and emotion: Implications for social behavior. In S. Kitayama and H. R. Markus (eds), *Emotion and Culture* (pp. 89–130). Baltimore, MD: United Book Press.

Marra, M. and Holmes, J. (2009). Humour across cultures: Joking in the multicultural workplace. In H. Kotthoff and H. Spencer-Oatey (eds), *Handbook of Intercultural Communication* (pp. 153–172). Berlin: Mouton.

Martin, J. N. and Nakayama, T. K. (2010). Intercultural communication and dialectics revisited. In T. K. Nakayama and R. T. Halualani (eds), *The Handbook of Critical Intercultural Communication* (pp. 59–83). Malden, MA: Wiley-Blackwell.

Martin, J., Nakayama, T. K. and Flores, L. A. (2002). A dialectal approach to intercultural communication. In J. Martin, T. K. Nakayama and L. A. Flores (eds), *Readings in Intercultural Communication. Experiences and Context* (pp. 3–12). Boston: McGraw Hill.

Martin, L. (1986). Eskimo words for snow: A case study in the genesis and decay of an anthropological example. *American Anthropologist*, 88(2), 418–423.

Masuda, T., Ellsworth, P. C., Mesquita, B., Leu, J., Tanida, S. and Van de Veerdonk, E. (2008). Placing the face in context: Cultural differences in the perception of facial emotion. *Journal of Personality and Social Psychology*, 94(3), 365–381.

Matsumoto, D. (1989). Cultural influences on the perception of emotion. *Journal of Cross-Cultural Psychology*, 20, 92–105.

——(1992). American-Japanese cultural differences in the recognition of universal facial expressions. *Journal of Cross-Cultural Psychology*, 23, 72–84.

Matsumoto, D. and Hwang, H-S. (2012). Nonverbal communication: The messages of emotion, action, space and silence. In J. Jackson (ed.), *The Routledge Handbook of Language and Intercultural Communication* (pp. 130–147). London: Routledge.

Matsumoto, Y. (1988). Re-examination of the universality of face: Politeness phenomena in Japanese. *Multilingua*, 8(2/3), 207–222.

——(1989). Politeness and conversational universals: Observations from Japanese. In P. Clancy (ed.), *Japanese/Korean Linguistics*, vol. II (pp. 55–67). Stanford, CA: Center for Study of Language and Information.

Matthews, G. (2000). *Global Culture/Individual Identity: Searching for a Home in the Cultural Supermarket*. London: Routledge.

Mauranen, A. (2006). Signaling and preventing misunderstanding in English as lingua franca communication. *International Journal of the Sociology of Language*, 177, 123–150. Reprinted in Zhu Hua (ed.) (2011), *The Language and Intercultural Communication Reader* (pp. 238–256). London: Routledge.

May, S. (2001). *Language and Minority Rights*. London: Longman.

Meierkord, C. (1998). Lingua franca English: Characteristics of successful non-native-/ non-native-speaker discourse. *Erfurt Electronic Studies in*

English (EESE). Retrieved 3 June 2008 from http://webdoc.sub.gwdg.de/edoc/ia/eese/eese.html

——(2000). Interpreting successful lingua franca interaction: An analysis of non-native-/non-native small talk conversations in English. *Erfurt Electronic Studies in English (EESE)*. Retrieved 10 March 2009 from www.linguistik-online.de/1_00/MEIERKOR.HTM

Menard-Warwick, J. (2008). The cultural and intercultural identities of transnational English teachers: Two case studies from the Americas. *TESOL Quarterly*, 42(4), 617–640.

Mercer, N. (2000). *Words and Minds*. London: Routledge.

Mezirow, J. (1996). Contemporary paradigms of learning. *Adult Education Quarterly*, 46, 158–172.

Moon, D. G. (2002). Thinking about 'culture' in intercultural communication. In J. Martin, T. K. Nakayama and L. A. Flores (eds), *Readings in Intercultural Communication. Experiences and Context* (pp. 13–20). Boston: McGraw Hill.

Moon, J. (1999). *Learning Journals: A Handbook for Academics, Students and Professional Development*. London: Kogan Page.

Mori, J. (2003). The construction of interculturality: A study of initial encounters between Japanese and American students. *Research on Language and Social Interaction*, 36(2), 143–184.

Morita, N. (2004). Negotiating participation and identity in second language academic communities. *TESOL Quarterly*, 38(4), 573–603.

Moss, B. and Roberts, C. (2005). Explanations, explanations, explanations: How do patients with limited English construct narrative accounts?. *Family Practices*, 22(4), 412–418.

Mushin, I. and Gardner, R. (2009). Silence is talk: Conversational silence in Australian Aboriginal talk-in-interaction. *Journal of Pragmatics*, 41, 2033–2052.

Myska, S. (2012) The consequences of having a 'foreign' name. *BBC News Magazine Online* (retrieved at www.bbc.co.uk/news/magazine-20228060, 9 November 2012).

Naidu, M. (2011a). Indigenous cultural bodies in tourism: An analysis of local 'audience' perception of global tourist consumers. *Journal of Social Science*, 26(1), 29–39.

——(2011b). 'Topless' tradition for tourists: Young Zulu girls in tourism. *Agenda*, 23(79), 38–48.

Nakane, I. (2012). Silence. In C. B. Paulston, S. Kiesling and E. S. Rangel (eds), *The Handbook of Intercultural Discourse and Communication* (pp. 158–179). Malden, MA: Wiley-Blackwell.

Nakayama, T. K. and Halualani, R. T. (eds) (2010). *The Handbook of Critical Intercultural Communication*. Malden, MA: Wiley-Blackwell.

Nazzal, A. (2005). The pragmatic functions of the recitation of Qur'anic verses by Muslims in their oral genre: The case of Insha'allah, 'God's willing'. *Pragmatics*, 15(2–3), 251–274. Reprinted in Zhu Hua (ed.) (2011), *The Language and Intercultural Communication Reader*. London: Routledge.

Neeley, T. B., Hinds, P. J. and Cramton, C. D. (2012). The (un)hidden turmoil of language in global collaboration. *Organizational Dynamics*, 41, 236–244.

Neuliep, J. W. (2006). *Intercultural Communication: A Contextual Approach.* Thousand Oaks, CA: Sage.

Nevo, O., Nevo, B. and Yin, J. L. (2001) Singaporean humor: A cross-cultural, cross-gender comparison. *The Journal of General Psychology,* 128(2), 143–156.

Nickerson, C. (1998). Corporate culture and the use of written English within British subsidiaries in the Netherlands. *English for Specific Purposes,* 17(3), 281–294.

Nisbett, R. (2003). *The Geography of Thought: How Asians and Westerners Think Differently ... and Why.* London: Nicholas Brealey.

Nishida, H. (2005). Cultural schema theory. In W. Gudykunst (ed.), *Theorizing about Intercultural Communication* (pp. 401–418). Thousand Oaks, CA: Sage.

Nishizaka, A. (1995). The interactive constitution of interculturality: How to be a Japanese with words. *Human Studies,* 18(2–3), 301–326. Reprinted in Zhu Hua (ed.), *The Language and Intercultural Communication Reader* (pp. 277–290). Oxford: Routledge.

Norenzayan, A., Smith, E. E., Kim, B. J. and Nisbett, R. E. (2002). Cultural preferences for formal versus intuitive reasoning. *Cognitive Science,* 26, 653–684.

Norrick, N. and Chiaro, D. (eds) (2009). *Humor in Interaction.* Amsterdam: John Benjamins.

Norton, B. (2001). Non-participation, imagined communities and the language classroom. In M. Breen (ed.), *Learner Contributions to Language Learning: New Directions in Research* (pp. 159–171). Harlow: Pearson.

Nostrand, H. L. (1974). Empathy for a second culture: Motivations and techniques. In G. A. Jarvis (ed.), *Responding to New Realities.* ACTFL Foreign Language Education Series, vol. 5 (pp. 263–327). Skokie, IL: National Textbook.

Nostrand, H. L. (ed.) (1967). *Background Data for the Teaching of French.* Seattle, WA: University of Washington Press.

Oberg, K. (1960). Culture shock: Adjustment to new cultural environments. *Practical Anthropology,* 7, 170–179.

Ochs, E. and Schieffelin, B. B. (1995). The impact of language socialization on grammatical development. In P. Fletcher and B. MacWhinney (eds), *Handbook of Child Language* (pp. 73–94). Oxford: Blackwell.

——(2008). Language socialisation: An historical overview. In P. A. Duff and N. H. Hornberger (eds), *Encyclopedia of Language and Education.* 2nd edn, vol. 8: Language Socialisation (pp. 3–15). New York: Springer.

Omi, M. and Winant, H. (1994). *Racial Formation in the United States: From the 1960s to 1990s.* New York: Routledge.

Omoniyi, T. (2006). Hierarchy of identities. In T. Omoniyi and G. White (eds), *Sociolinguistics of Identity* (pp. 11–33). London: Continuum.

Orbe, M. P. and Harris, T. M. (2001). *Interracial Communication. Theory into Practice.* Melbourne: Wadsworth.

Osland, J. S. and Bird, A. (2000). Beyond sophisticated stereotyping: Cultural sensemaking in context. *Academy of Management Executive,* 14(1), 65–77.

Pavlenko, A. (2003). 'Language of the enemy': Foreign language education and national identity. *International Journal of Bilingual Education and Bilingualism*, 6(5), 313–331.

——(2005a). *Emotions and Multilingualism*. Cambridge: Cambridge University Press.

——(2005b). Bilingualism and thought. In J. F. Kroll and A. M. B. De Groot (eds), *Handbook of Bilingualism: Psycholinguistic Approaches* (pp. 433–453). Oxford: Oxford University Press.

——(2011b). Thinking and speaking in two languages: Overview of the field. In A. Pavlenko, A. (ed.), *Thinking and Speaking in Two Languages* (pp. 237–257). Bristol: Multilingual Matters

Pavlenko, A. (ed.) (2011a). *Thinking and Speaking in Two Languages*. Bristol: Multilingual Matters.

Pavlenko, A. and Blackledge, A. (2003). Introduction: New theoretical approaches to the study of negotiation of identities in multilingual contexts. In A. Pavlenko and A. Blackledge (eds), *Negotiation of Identities in Multilingual Contexts* (pp. 1–33). Clevedon: Multilingual Matters.

Peirce, C. S. (1898/1955). *Philosophical Writings of Peirce* (ed. Justus Buchler). New York: Dover Publications.

Pennycook, A. (2007). *Global Englishes and Transcultural Flows*. London: Routledge.

Pettigrew, T. and Tropp, L. R. (2011). *When Groups Meet: The Dynamics of Intergroup Contact*. New York and Hove: Psychology Press.

Pica, P., Lemer, C., Izard, V. and Dehaene, S. (2004). Exact and approximate arithmetic in an Amazonian indigene group. *Science*, 306, 499–503.

Piller, I. (2001). Identity construction in multilingual advertising. *Language in Society*, 30(2), 153–186.

——(2002). *Bilingual Couples Talk: The Discursive Construction of Hybridity*. Amsterdam: John Benjamins.

——(2011). *Intercultural Communication: A Critical Introduction*. Edinburgh: Edinburgh University Press.

Pinker, S. (1994). *The Language Instinct*. New York: W. Morrow and Co.

——(2007). *The Stuff of Thought: Language as a Window into Human Nature*. London: Penguin.

Pitzl, M.-L. (2009). 'We should not wake up any dogs': Idiom and metaphor in ELF. In A. Mauranen and E. Ranta (eds), *English as a Lingua Franca: Studies and Findings* (pp. 298–322). Newcastle Upon Tyne: Cambridge Scholars Publishing.

Poncini, G. (2002). Investigating discourse at business meetings with multicultural participation. *IRAL*, 40, 345–373.

Pullum, G. (1991). *The Great Eskimo Vocabulary Hoax and Other Irreverent Essays on the Study of Language*. University of Chicago Press.

Purnell, T., William, I. and Baugh, J. (1999). Perceptual and phonetic experiments on American English dialect identification. *Journal of Language and Social Psychology*, 18, 10–30.

Quinn, N. and Holland, D. (1987). Culture and cognition. In D. Holland and N. Quinn (eds), *Cultural Models in Language and Thought* (pp. 3–42). Cambridge: Cambridge University Press.

Ragan, S. L. (2000). Sociable talk in women's health care contexts: Two forms of non-medical talk. In J. Coupland (ed.), *Small Talk* (pp. 269–287). Harlow: Longman.

Rampton, B. (1990). Displacing the 'native speaker': Expertise, affiliation and inheritance. *ELT*, 44(2), 97–101.

——(1995). *Crossing: Language and Ethnicity among Adolescents*. New York: Longman.

——(1999). Styling the other. Special issue, *Journal of Sociolinguistics*, 3(4), 421–556.

Remennick, L. (2009). Exploring intercultural relationships: A study of Russian immigrants married to native Israelis. *Journal of Comparative Family Studies*, 40(5), 719–739.

Riley, P. (2007). *Language, Culture and Identity*. London: Continuum.

Risager, K. (2006). *Language and Culture: Global Flows and Local Complexity*. Clevedon: Multilingual Matters.

——(2007). *Language and Culture Pedagogy: From a National to a Transnational Paradigm*. Clevedon: Mutilingual Matters.

Roberts, C. (1996). A social perspective on understanding: Some issues of theory and method. In K. Bremer, C. Roberts, M-T. Vasseur, M. Simonot and P. Broeder (eds), *Achieving Understanding: Discourse in Intercultural Encounters* (pp. 9–36). London: Longman.

——(2009). Intercultural communication in healthcare settings. In H. Kotthoff and H. Spencer-Oatey (eds), *Handbook of Intercultural Communication* (pp. 243–262). Berlin: Mouton.

——(2010). Language socialization in the workplace. *Annual Review of Applied Linguistics*, 30, 211–227.

——(2011). Institutional discourse. In J. Simpson (ed.), *The Routledge Handbook of Applied Linguistics* (pp. 81–95). London: Routledge.

Roberts, C. and Campbell, S. (2006). *Talk on Trial: Job Interviews, Language and Ethnicity*. Research report for Department for Work and Pensions. Available at http://statistics.dwp.gov.uk/asd/asd5/rports2005-2006/rrep344.pdf

Roberts, C., Byram, M., Barro, A., Jordan, S. and Street, B. (2001). *Language Learners as Ethnographers*. Clevedon: Multilingual Matters.

Roberts, C., Sarangi, S. and Moss, B. (2004). Presentation of self and symptoms in primary care consultations involving patients from non-English speaking backgrounds. *Communication and Medicine*, 1(2), 159–169.

Roberts, C., Campbell, S. and Robinson, Y. (2008). *Talking Like a Manager: Promotion Interviews, Language and Ethnicity*. Research report for Department of Work and Pensions. Available at http://statistics.dwp.gov.uk/asd/asd5/rports2007-2008/rrep510.pdf

Rogerson-Revell, P. (2007). Humour in business: A double-edged sword: A study of humour and style shifting in intercultural business meetings. *Journal of Pragmatics*, 39(1), 4–28.

——(2008). Participation and performance in international business meetings. *English for Specific Purposes*, 27, 338–360.

——(2010). 'Can you spell that for us non-native speakers?': Accommodation strategies in international business meetings. *Journal of Business Communication*, 47(4), 432–454.

Ruben, B. D. (1989). The study of cross-cultural competence: Traditions and contemporary issues. *International Journal of Intercultural Relations*, 13, 229–240.

Rubin, D. L. (1992). Nonlanguage factors affecting undergraduates' judgments of nonnative English-speaking teaching assistants. *Research in Higher Education*, 33(4), 511–531.

Ryoo, H.-K. (2007). Interculturality serving multiple interactional goals in African American and Korean service encounters. *Pragmatics*, 17(1), 23–47.

Sacks, H. (1972). On the analyzability of stories by children. In J. Gumperz and D. Hymes (eds), *Directions in Sociolinguistics* (pp. 325–345). New York: Holt, Rinehart and Winston.

Sacks, H., Schegloff, E. A. and Jefferson, G. (1974). A simplest systematics for the organization of turn-taking in conversations. *Language*, 50(4), 696–735.

Samovar, L., Porter, R. E. and Stefani, L. A. (1998). *Communication Between Cultures*. Belmont, CA: Wadsworth.

Sapir, E. (1929). The status of linguistics as a science. *Language*, 5, 207–214. Reprinted in D. Mandelbaum (ed.) (1949/1985), *Selected Writings of Edward Sapir in Language, Culture and Personality* (pp. 160–166). Berkeley: University of California Press.

——(1933). Language. In *Encyclopaedia of the Social Sciences* (9, pp. 155–169). New York: Macmillan. Reprinted in D. Mandelbaum (ed.) (1949/1985), *Selected Writings of Edward Sapir in Language, Culture and Personality* (pp. 7–32). Berkeley: University of California Press.

Sarangi, S. and Roberts, C. (2002). Discourse (mis)-alignments in professional gatekeeping encounters. In C. Kramsch (ed.), *Language Acquisition and Language Socialisation* (pp. 197–227). London: Continuum.

Sarangi, S. and Roberts, C. (eds) (1999). *Talk, Work and Institutional Order: Discourse in Medical, Mediation and Management Settings*. Berlin: Mouton.

Schegloff, E. A. (1992). In another context. In A. Duranti and C. Goodwin (eds), *Rethinking Context: Language as an Interactive Phenomenon* (pp. 191–228). Cambridge: Cambridge University Press.

Schegloff, E. A., Jefferson, G. and Sacks, H. (1977). The preference for self-correction in the organisation of repair in conversation. *Language*, 53(2), 361–382.

Schein, E. H. (2004). *Organizational Culture and Leadership* (3rd edn). San Francisco: Jossey-Bass.

Scherle, N. and Nonnenmann, A. (2008). Swimming in cultural flows: Conceptualising tour guides as intercultural mediators and cosmopolitans. *Journal of Tourism and Cultural Change*, 6(2), 120–137.

Schmidt, R., Shimura, A., Wang, Z. and Jeong, H. (1995). Suggestions to buy: Television commercials from the U.S., Japan, China and Korea. In S. Gass and J. Neu (eds), *Speech Acts Across Cultures: Challenges to Communication in a Second Language* (pp. 285–316). Berlin: Mouton de Gruyter. Also appeared in Zhu Hua (ed.) (2011), *The Language and Intercultural Communication Reader* (pp. 326–346). London: Routledge.

Schneider, K. P. (1988). *Small Talk: Analysing Phatic Discourse*. Hitzeroth, Germany: Marburg.

Schnurr, S. and Holmes, J. (2009). Using humor to do masculinity at work. In N. Norrick and D. Chiaro (eds), *Humor in Interaction* (pp. 101–124). Amsterdam: John Benjamins.

Schwartz, S. H. (1992). Universals in the content and structure of values: Theory and empirical tests in 20 countries. In M. Zanna (ed.), *Advances in Experimental Social Psychology* (vol. 25, pp. 1–65). New York: Academic Press.

——(1994). Are there universal aspects in the structure and contents of human values? *Journal of Social Issues*, 50(4), 19–45.

Scollon, R. and Scollon, S. (1981). *Narrative, Literacy and Face in Interethnic Communication*. Norwood, NJ: Ablex.

——(2001). *Intercultural Communication: A Discourse Approach* (2nd edn). Malden, MA: Blackwell.

Scollon, R., Scollon, S. W. and Jones, R. H. (2012). *Intercultural Communication: A Discourse Approach* (3rd edn). Chichester: John Wiley and Sons.

Scollon, S. (2000). Not to waste words or students: Confucian and Socratic discourse in the tertiary classroom. In E. Hinkel (ed.), *Culture in Second Language Teaching and Learning* (pp. 13–27). Cambridge: Cambridge University Press.

Searle, J. (1975). Indirect speech acts. In P. Cole and J. L. Morgan (eds), *Syntax and Semantics, Vol. 3: Speech Acts* (pp. 59–82). New York: Academic Press.

Sercombe, P. and Young, T. (2010). Communication, discourses and interculturality. Special issue of *Language and Intercultural Communication*, 11(3), 181–272.

Sharifian, F. (2005). The Persian cultural schema of *shekasteh-nafsi*. *Pragmatics and Cognition*, 13(2), 337–361.

Slobin, D. (1996). From 'thought and language' to 'thinking for speaking'. In J. Gumperz and S. C. Levinson (eds), *Rethinking Linguistic Relativity* (pp. 70–96). Cambridge: Cambridge University Press.

——(2000). Verbalised events: A dynamic approach to linguistic relativity and determinism. In S. Niemeier and R. Dirven (eds), *Evidence for Linguistic Relativity* (pp. 108–138). Amsterdam: John Benjamins.

Sobre-Denton, M. and Hart, D. (2008). Mind the gap: Application-based analysis of cultural adjustment models. *International Journal of Intercultural Relations*, 32, 538–552.

Sony (2013). Website accessed 29 May 2013 at http://www.sony.net/SonyInfo/CorporateInfo/History

Spencer-Oatey, H. (2002). Managing rapport in talk: Using rapport-sensitive incidents to explore the motivational concerns underlying the management of relations. *Journal of Pragmatics*, 34, 529–545.

——(2005a). *E-China–UK E-Learning programme*. Seminar at the University of Newcastle Upon Tyne, UK, May.

——(2005b). Rapport management theory and culture. *Intercultural Pragmatics*, 2/3, 335–346.

Spencer-Oatey, H. (ed.) (2008). *Culturally Speaking: Culture, Communication and Politeness Theory* (2nd edn). London: Continuum.

Spencer-Oatey, H. and Franklin, P. (2009). *Intercultural Interaction: A Multidisciplinary Approach to Intercultural Communication*. New York: Palgrave.

Spencer-Oatey, H. and Xing, J. (2009). The impact of culture on interpreter behaviour. In H. Kotthoff and H. Spencer-Oatey (eds), *Handbook of Intercultural Communication* (pp. 219–236). Berlin: Mouton.

Spitzberg, B. and Changnon, G. (2009). Conceptualising intercultural competence. In D. Deardorff (ed.), *The Sage Handbook of Intercultural Competence* (pp. 2–52). Thousand Oaks, CA: Sage.

Spitzberg, B. H. and Cupach, W. R. (1984). *Interpersonal Communication Competence*. Beverly Hills, CA: Sage.

Stan Turton Solicitors (2012) E-bulletin accessed 8 March 2012 at www.swanturton.com/ebulletins/archive/CTSLegalrestrict.aspx

Stivers, T., Enfield, N. J., Brown, P., Englert, C., Hayshi, M., Heinemann, T., Hoymann, G., Rossano, F., de Ruiter, J. P., Yoon, K-E. and Levinson, S. C. (2009). Universals and cultural variation in turn-taking in conversation. *PNAS*, 106(26), 10587–10592.

Street, B. (1993). Culture is a verb: Anthropological aspects of language and cultural process. In D. Graddol, L. Thompson and M. Byram (eds), *Language and Culture* (pp. 23–43). Clevedon: Multilingual Matters.

Street, R. L. and Giles, H. (1982). Speech accommodation theory: A social cognitive approach to language and speech behaviour. In M. E. Roloff and C. R. Berger (eds), *Social Cognition and Communication* (pp. 193–226). Beverly Hills, CA: Sage.

Sultanoff, S. (1993). *Taking Humor Seriously in the Workplace*. Retrieved 2nd March 2012 at www.humormatters.com/articles/workplac.htm

Sweeney, E. and Zhu, Hua (2010). Accommodating toward your audience: Do native speakers of English know how to accommodate their communication strategies toward non-native speakers of English? *Journal of Business Communication*, 47(4), 477–504.

Taft, R. (1977). Coping with unfamiliar cultures. In N. Warren (ed.), *Studies in Cross-cultural Psychology Volume 1* (pp. 121–153). London: Academic Press.

Takaya, K. (2011). Organization of topics in intercultural and intracultural small talk. *Cross-cultural Communication*, 7(4), 17–24.

Takigawa, Y. (2010). *Dispute and Language Expertise: Analysis of Bilingual Couple Talk in Japanese*. Saarbrücken, Germany: Lap Lambert Academic Publishing.

Tannen, D. (1984). *Conversational Style: Analysing Talk among Friends*. Norwood, NJ: Ablex.

——(1986). *That Is Not What I Meant! How Conversational Style Makes or Breaks Relationship*. New York: Ballantine Books.

Thomas, J. (1983). Cross-cultural pragmatic failure. *Applied Linguistics*, 4(2), 91–112.

Thornton, R. (1988). Culture: A contemporary definition. In E. Boonzaier and J. Sharp (eds), *Keywords* (pp. 17–28). Cape Town, South Africa: David Philip.

Thurlow, C. and Jaworski, A. (2011). Tourism discourse: Languages and banal globalisation. *Applied Linguistics Review*, 2, 285–312.

Ting-Toomey, S. (1999). *Communicating across Cultures*. New York: Guilford Press.

——(2005). The matrix of face: An updated face-negotiation theory. In W. Gudykunst (ed.), *Theorizing about Intercultural Communication* (pp. 71–92). Thousand Oaks, CA: Sage.

Townsend, P. and Cairns, L. (2003). Developing the global manager using a capability Framework. *Management Learning*, 34(3), 313–327.

Tracy, K. (2002). *Everyday Talk: Building and Reflecting Identities*. New York and London: Guilford Press.

Tylor, E. B. (1871). *Primitive Culture*. London: John Murray.

Unsworth, S., Sears, C. R. and Pexman, P. M. (2005). Cultural influences on categorization processes. *Journal of Cross-Cultural Psychology*, 36(6), 662–688.

UNWTO (2012) *Tourism Highlights: 2012 Edition*. Available at http://www2.unwto.org/en/publication/unwto-tourism-highlights-2012-edition

Urry, J. (2002). *The Tourist Gaze* (2nd edn). London: Sage.

Usunier, J-C. (2000). *Marketing Across Cultures*. Harlow: Prentice-Hall.

Usunier, J-C. and Roulin, N. (2010). The influence of high- and low-context communication styles on the design, content and language of business-to-business web sites. *Journal of Business Communication*, 47(2), 189–227.

van Ek, J. A. (1986). *Objectives for Foreign Language Learning, Vol. 1: Scope*. Strasbourg: Council of Europe.

Vande Berg, M. (2009). Intervening in student learning abroad: A research-based inquiry. *Intercultural Education*, 20 (supplement S1–2), 15–27.

Vande Berg, M., Connor-Linton, J. and Paige, M. (2009). The Georgetown Consortium Project: Interventions for student learning abroad. *Frontiers: The Interdisciplinary Journal of Study Abroad*, 18, 1–75.

Vande Berg, M., Page, M. and Lou, K. (eds) (2012). *Student Learning Abroad: What Our Students Are Learning, What They're Not and What We Can Do About It*. Sterling, VA: Stylus.

Vasseur, M-T., Bremer, K., Broeder, P. and Simonot, M. (1996a). Case studies: The making of understanding in extended interactions. In K. Bremer, C. Roberts, M-T. Vasseur, M. Simonot and P. Broeder (eds), *Achieving Understanding: Discourse in Intercultural Encounters* (pp. 109–158). London: Longman.

Vasseur, M-T., Broeder, P. and Roberts, C. (1996b). Managing understanding from a minority perspective. In K. Bremer, C. Roberts, M-T. Vasseur, M. Simonot and P. Broeder (eds), *Achieving Understanding: Discourse in Intercultural Encounters* (pp. 65–108). London: Longman.

Vickers, C. (2010). Language competencies and the construction of expert-novice in NS–NNS interaction. *Journal of Pragmatics*, 42, 116–138.

Vignovic, J. A. (2010). Computer-mediated cross-cultural collaborations: Attributing communication errors to the person versus the situation. *Journal of Applied Psychology*. 95(2), 265–276.

Walters, K. (1996). Gender, identity and the political economy of language: Anglophone wives in Tunisia. *Language in Society*, 25, 515–555.

Watkins, D. A. and Biggs, J. B. (eds) (1996). *The Chinese Learner: Cultural, Psychological and Contextual Influences*. Hong Kong: Comparative Education Research Centre, University of Hong Kong/Australian Council of Educational Research.

Watson-Gegeo, K. (2004). Mind, language and epistemology: Toward a language socialization paradigm for SLA. *The Modern Language Journal*, 88, 331–350.

Watts, R. (2003). *Politeness: Key Topics in Sociolinguistics*. Cambridge: Cambridge University Press.

Wenger, E. (2006). *Communities of Practice: A Brief Introduction*. Accessed at www.ewenger.com/theory/, 23 September 2012.

Whitten, J. (2012). *Intercultural Communication, Humour and Workplace*. Essay submitted as part of assignment for the module of language, culture and communication, Birkbeck College, University of London.

Whorf, B. (1956). *Language, Thought and Reality: Selected Writings of Benjamin Lee Whorf*, ed. J. B. Carroll. Cambridge, MA: MIT Press.

Wierzbicka, A. (1997a). The double life of a bilingual: A cross-cultural perspective. In M. Bond (ed.), *Working at the Interface of Cultures: Eighteen Lives in Social Science* (pp. 113–125). London: Routledge.

——(1997b). *Understanding Cultures Through Their Key Words*. New York: Oxford University Press.

Wilkinson, S. (ed.) (2006). *Insights from Study Abroad for Language Programmes*. Boston: Thomson Higher Education.

Williams, F. (1983). Some research notes on dialect attitudes and stereotypes. In R. Fasold (ed.), *Variation in the Form and Use of Language: A Sociolinguistic Reader* (pp. 354–369). Washington, DC: Georgetown University Press.

Williams, R. (1979). *Politics and Letters: Interviews with 'New Left Review'*. London: New Left Books.

——(1983). *Keywords: A Vocabulary of Culture and Society*. New York: Oxford University Press.

Wittgenstein, L. (1922). *Tractatus Logico-Philosophicus* (Logical-Philosophical Treatise). New York: Harcourt, Brace.

Woodin, J. (2010). Cultural categorisation: What can we learn from practice? An example from tandem learning. *Language and Intercultural Communication*, 10(3), 225–242.

Wu, D. (2008). Patterns of global–local fusion in Chinese internet advertising. In D. Wu (ed.), *Discourses of Cultural China in the Globalising Age* (pp. 99–112). Hong Kong: Hong Kong University Press.

Yamamoto, M. (1995). Bilingualism in international families. *Journal of Multilingual and Multicultural Development*, 16(1 and 2), 63–85.

Yim, Y. K. (2011). Second language students' discourse socialization in academic online communities. *The Canadian Modern Language Review*, 67(1), 1–27.

Ylänne-McEwen, V. and Coupland, N. (2000). Accommodation theory: A conceptual resource for intercultural sociolinguistics. In H. Spencer-Oatey (ed.), *Culturally Speaking: Managing Rapport through Talk across Cultures* (pp. 191–216). London: Continuum.

Yli-Jokipii, H. (2010). Pragmatics and research into corporate communication. In A. Trosborg (ed.), *Pragmatics across Languages and Cultures* (pp. 489–512). Berlin: Mouton De Gruyter.

Zandpour, F., Chang, C. and Catalano, J. (1992). Stories, symbols and straight talk: A comparative analysis of French, Taiwanese and U.S. TV commercials. *Journal of Advertising Research*, 32, 25–37.

Zhu, H. (2007). Presentation of self in application letters. In Zhu Hua, P. Seedhouse, Li Wei and V. Cook (eds), *Language Learning/Teaching as Social (Inter)Action* (pp. 126–147). Mahwah, NJ: Lawrence Erlbaum.

——(2008). Duelling languages, duelling values: Codeswitching in bilingual intergenerational conflict talk in diasporic families. *Journal of Pragmatics*, 40, 1799–1816.

——(2010). Language socialisation and interculturality: Address terms in intergenerational talk in Chinese diasporic families. *Language and Intercultural Communication*, 10(3), 189–205.

——(2011). *The Language and Intercultural Communication Reader*. London: Routledge.

Zhu, H., Li, Wei and Qian, Y. (2000). The sequential organisation of gift offering and acceptance in Chinese. *Journal of Pragmatics*, 32, 81–103.

Zhu, Y. (2005). *Written Communication Across Cultures: A Sociolinguistic Perspective on Business Genres*. Amsterdam: John Benjamins.

Zimmerman, Don H. (1998). Identity, context and interaction. In C. Antaki and S. Widdicombe (eds), *Identities in Talk* (pp. 87–106). London: Sage.

Zimmerman, E. (2007). Constructing Korean and Japanese interculturality in talk: Ethnic membership categorization among users of Japanese. *Pragmatics*, 17(1), 71–94.

Ziv, A. (ed.) (1988). *National Styles of Humor*. New York: Greenwood Press.

Index of subjects

Index of languages, cultures and geographical areas